Towns in the Viking Age

Towns in the Viking Age

*Helen Clarke and
Björn Ambrosiani*

St. Martin's Press
New York

First published in the United States of America
in 1991

All rights reserved. For information, write:
Scholarly and Reference Division,
St. Martin's Press, Inc., 175 Fifth Avenue, New York, NY 10010

ISBN 0-312-06086-6

Library of Congress Cataloging-in-Publication Number 90-063782
Complete CIP data for this book is available from the Library of Congress

Typeset by Florencetype Ltd, Kewstoke, Avon
Printed and bound in Great Britain by Biddles Ltd, Guildford amd Kings Lynn

Contents

List of illustrations

Acknowledgments

This venture in Anglo-Swedish archaeological collaboration is an outcome of more than fifteen years of discussions, arguments and generally amicable disagreements about the early medieval archaeology of Sweden and Britain. We are grateful to Leicester University Press for giving us the chance to convert some of these conversations into print.

In this book we have attempted to outline the growth and development of towns throughout that area of Europe which was touched by Scandinavian influence during the Viking age. Clearly, the geographical range covered by our survey is immense, stretching as it does from Russia in the east to Ireland in the west, and we would not have been able to attempt it without the help of many colleagues whose knowledge of their specific regions and individual sites is much more detailed than our own. All with whom we have discussed our project have been most generous in their responses; they have helped us by reading and commenting on the manuscript, giving us up-to-date information about excavations still in progress, and providing us with illustrations.

Unfortunately space does not permit us to acknowledge everyone who has helped us, but particular thanks must be expressed to Flemming Bau, Mogens Bencard, Ulf Bertilsson, Helge Brinch-Madsen, Johan Callmer, Dan Carlsson, Howard Clarke, Wladyslaw Duczko, Willem van Es, Richard Hall, Ingmar Jansson, Stig Jensen, Bengt Lundberg, Gustav Milne, Richard Reece, Susan Reynolds, Else Roesdahl, E.A. Ryabinin, Karl Inge Sandred, Erik Schia, Kurt Schietzel, Sten Tesch, Lena Thålin-Bergman, Frans Verhaeghe, Adriaan Verhulst, Patrick Wallace, Claire Walsh, Martin Welch, and Hayo Zimmermann. Any misunderstandings which may have crept into the text are of course entirely our own responsibility.

Special thanks also go to Annika Boklund of Riksantikvarieämbetet in Stockholm for drawing many of the figures, and for skilfully devising ways through which the topography of these sites could best be depicted. Jill Gustafsson, also of RAÄ, drew figures 7.9, 7.11a and 7.11b. Riksantikvarieämbetet's aerial photography team of Jan Norrman and Kjell Edvinger also conducted Björn Ambrosiani on a memorable flight around Sweden to take air photographs for use in this publication, and University College London's Faculty of Arts Study Leave Fund financed a visit to Stockholm by Helen Clarke.

We thank everyone who has enabled us to bring this work to a conclusion. We do not pretend to have written the definitive book on

Viking-age towns; we hope, rather, that this summary of current knowledge will stimulate debate and controversy, and thereby encourage further research.

Helen Clarke and Björn Ambrosiani
London and Stockholm, March 1990

Chapter 1

Introduction

The Vikings have always appealed to the popular imagination, and the past couple of decades has seen this catered for by the publication of innumerable books – some highly coloured accounts and others more sober scientific reports. Despite this, one aspect of the cultural life of the Viking age has been largely neglected: the Vikings as town dwellers and urban founders. Some individual towns have been described, but there have been virtually no general surveys and it is this that we shall attempt here.

The spectacular growth in the number of archaeological excavations during the past thirty years makes this a suitable moment for such a survey, and a glance at the bibliography will confirm this. It is now possible to trace some general patterns in early medieval urban growth and development during the Viking age (roughly the two hundred years from AD 800), and also to see that there are distinct regional variations between the towns of northern and western Europe. This book sets out to highlight some of these similarities and differences and to explain them at least in part; but it cannot be the last word on a complex subject which will provide food for thought and speculation for years to come.

Because recent archaeological excavations in the early towns and market-places of Scandinavia and the Baltic region have revolutionized the picture of early medieval urbanization in these areas, and because much of the present evidence may be unfamilar to readers from English-speaking countries, most of this book has a Scandinavian and Baltic bias. We shall also attempt to set the sites in these areas in context by summarizing current knowledge of urban development in western Europe where early medieval towns were influenced by the heritage of the Roman Empire. By doing this we hope to show how the people of early medieval Scandinavia assimilated aspects of urbanization from many different regions, how they eventually became converted to Christianity and subsequently began to play their part as members of a wider European society in the high middle ages.

The early medieval towns of the North were evidently extremely complex organisms, as evidenced by their location, topography, communications, industry, trade, and connections with their respective hinterlands. Pre-literate societies, such as those which founded and inhabited the settlements of Scandinavia and the Baltic region in the Viking age, are often regarded as primitive and undeveloped, with social differentiation and hierarchy coming into being only on their conversation to Christianity in the eleventh century or even later. Archaeological research into their urban settlements shows that this is far from the truth, and this book attempts to present a new picture of the highly structured nature of these communities. Although most of the information presented here comes from recent archaeological excavations, we also refer to written sources where appropriate.

Few peoples have been the subject of more, and more widely divergent, interpretations than have the Vikings of ninth- to eleventh-century Scandinavia. The popular, romantic, view held today is that they were wild and barbaric warriors, following a heroic creed, wearing horned helmets, brandishing terrible weapons, and skilfully navigating both coastal waters and the high seas. This picture is partly derived from the contemporary accounts of the Vikings and their devastating raids which were written by the literate clerics of an already Christian western Europe. In their eyes the Vikings were buccaneers and pirates, more frightful and threatening than any other people known to the 'peaceful' inhabitants of the Christian west. There is also the more moderate, but perhaps introverted, Scandinavian view of the Vikings as the founders of a new social order. They were the people who laid the basis for a high-medieval social structure in the Nordic lands which was in many ways different from that of European countries with a classical heritage.

In spite of all the recent archaeological and historical research, there is still a great deal more to learn about the Vikings; even the derivation of their name is obscure. On the few occasions when the word Viking is used in early medieval sources it refers to people who had left the normal framework of everyday society and had gone out 'a-viking', that is, had turned to piracy and plunder. For instance, the rune stone at Bro in Uppland, raised in memory of Assur son of Håkon Jarl (thus a man of high rank), records that he 'kept watch against the Vikings', and a newly discovered stone from Hablingbo on Gotland mentions a man who journeyed to England with the Vikings. Such instances are rare and the eleventh-century German ecclesiastic Adam of Bremen, whose writings are a valuable source for the later Viking age, tells us that the people of Scandinavia usually referred to themselves as 'ascomannos', and certainly never thought of the majority of their compatriots as 'Vikings'.

A number of derivations have been suggested for the term 'Viking'. One of them is that Vikings were pirates who lurked in coastal bays and inlets (*vik* in the Nordic languages) waiting to swoop down on peaceful and unsuspecting seafarers. Another explanation is that the home of the first Vikings was the long arm of the sea reaching up from the Skagerrak to modern Oslo; this fjord and its surrounding region go by the name of *Viken*. The term could also have been used of men coming from towns or market centres which incorporated *wic* or *wik* in their place–name (p. 16). This seems rather unlikely as these men would have been merchants, and so would hardly have aroused fear such as that indicated by the inscription on the Bro stone. Nevertheless, it is possible that the urban connotation of *wic* is significant here, for the term Viking could have been used by those that stayed at home to describe the pirates who took part in plundering forays against the towns of western Europe.

Whatever the derivation of the word, it is certainly unhistoric and inaccurate to lump all the Danes, Norwegians and Swedes together under the single name Viking or, as sometimes, Northmen. Although they undoubtedly had much in common, they also had individual characteristics. Both these aspects emerge from a study of their towns.

So the question of terminology remains unresolved. All we can say is that at the end of the eighth century a number of fast and highly seaworthy longships appeared on the coasts of north-east England, attacking and looting the monastery of Lindisfarne in 793. This terrible event soon became known throughout the Christian world and was regarded as the inauguration of the Viking age. The beginning of the period, therefore, has commonly been set at about 800. That this is an arbitrary date can now be seen, for the recently developed scientific technique of dendrochronology (tree-ring dating) seems to have pushed back the start of the Viking age to *c.* 760, a time when artifacts of what are considered to be fully-developed Viking-age type were already in use in Scandinavia and the Baltic.

The two hundred years from the end of the eighth century were years of intermittent but fierce warfare between Scandinavia and the west, culminating in Knut the Great's (King Canute) conquest of England in 1016. In the eleventh century Scandinavia was gradually converted to Christianity and absorbed into the Christian world of the south and west, but the events of the 1060s, particularly the extinction of the ancient Swedish royal family and the Norman conquest of England in 1066, really mark the end of the Viking age.

The eleventh century was a revolutionary period in Scandinavia as elsewhere. But by the beginning of that century many of the medieval towns of Denmark, Sweden and Norway were being founded, and the earliest phase of Scandinavian urban development was over. So the year 1000 has been taken as the finishing date for this book.

We have already illustrated some of the difficulties of terminology which we have had to contend with when approaching our subject. An even more contentious issue arises with the definition of a town itself. We have attempted to resolve this by following that proposed by Susan Reynolds in 1977 and modified slightly in her article of 1987, that is, a town is

A permanent human settlement . . . in which a significant proportion of its population lives off trade, industry, administration and other non–agricultural occupations . . . It forms a social unit more or less distinct from the surrounding countryside (1977).

A town . . . lives off the food of the surrounding countryside and supplies this countryside with other goods and services in return (1987).

These definitions conform well with what might be expected to be found from archaeological, rather than purely historical, research and the towns which will be discussed in the following chapters have been selected according to these guidelines. They are simpler definitions than those used by many historians for whom the town is a legal entity, distinguished from non-urban settlements by its possession of a charter and with a complex administration, often also with defences and a mint. Those urban criteria refer in the main to the towns of the twelfth century and later, particularly in Scandinavia, which are the culmination of the developments which are outlined in this book. Thus, we have found that the definitions quoted above are more appropriate to the study of the towns of the Viking age.

Chapter 2

North-west European towns up to the end of the seventh century

Many of the countries subjected to the Viking raids which devastated north-west Europe from the end of the eighth century had once been part of the Western Roman Empire and were heirs to a well-organized urban system which originated in the Mediterranean ideal of an administration based on towns. By the fourth century, Gaul (most of modern France and the Low Countries up to the Rhine) and Britain were dotted with Roman towns and criss-crossed by networks of roads serving them. At the fall of the Western Empire in the fifth century these Roman provinces had had an urban infrastructure for several centuries, but recent archaeological research has shown that the collapse of the Western Empire also saw the collapse of urbanization, at least in Britain where the fifth and sixth centuries appear to be years of a reversion to a rural society.

Despite this setback, the lands which were subjected to the Viking attacks were no strangers to town life; they possessed some form of urban communities at a time when the Scandinavian homelands of the Vikings were still occupied purely by rural populations, living in small nucleated villages or isolated farmsteads, a situation which was still essentially the same at the time when the Viking erupted on to the European scene.

Fifth and sixth centuries: the question of continuity

Although Britain in the years after the end of Roman occupation seems to have suffered from a virtually total urban decline, brought about or at least exacerbated by the settlement of England by pagan Anglo-Saxons in the mid-fifth century, many of the Roman towns of Gaul continued in occupation. Most of the bigger Gallic towns perpetuated their Roman administrative role by becoming centres of royal and ecclesiastical power, some of them may also have maintained, albeit in a much modified form, their former commercial functions.

Much of our knowledge of Gallic towns in the fifth and sixth centuries (figure 2.1) is culled from writers such as St Gregory of Tours.[1] His *History*

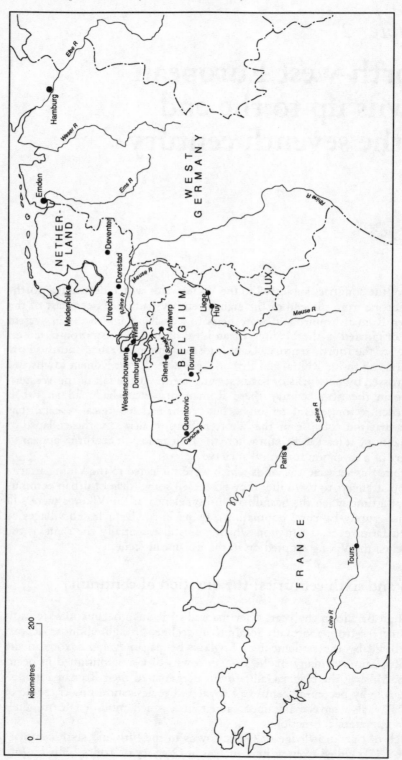

Fig. 2.1 Map of northern Gaul with the major places mentioned in the text

shows that the erstwhile Roman towns of Gaul may have served as the site of a royal court (*palatium*), as an episcopal seat, a monastic centre, or as all three, with the Roman walls still marking a defensible core. The often ruined Roman masonry buildings provided shelter for the royal or ecclesiastical authorities, or acted as quarries for newly constructed buildings. But there is little evidence from written sources to suggest that the Roman walls anywhere encircled a post-Roman commercial or industrial population which did anything but service the royal or ecclesiastical authorities. In many cases the population was probably limited to a small elite of clerics and royal retainers, served by a few artisans. The contacts between these centres and the surrounding countryside which must have furnished their basic needs are not illuminated by the documentary evidence, and it is here that archaeology could make a significant contribution.

Archaeology could show whether the fifth- and sixth-century towns of Gaul were manufacturing centres whose products were distributed locally or further afield, or whether they were merely consumption centres, living off the commodities provided by their hinterlands and giving nothing other than administrative services in return. If the former, then the Christian successors of the towns of Roman Gaul could truly be called towns in accordance with the definitions we are using here (p. 3). It seems more likely, however, that many of the old Roman towns served primarily as centres which were politically and ecclesiastically important but which, in urban terms, acted only as consumers, absorbing some of the produce of the countryside for their upkeep but giving nothing material back in return. One such town where recent excavations have helped to illuminate its early medieval history is Tours (Roman *Caesarodunum*) in the Loire valley, home of St Gregory from 573 to his death in 594. The excavations have shown that there was a continuity of administrative functions there from the Roman period, with monastic sites and fortifications being present in the seventh century and earlier. All the features so far discovered through the archaeological investigations of Henri Galinié were ecclesiastical in character and he describes Tours up to the tenth century as 'a town without urban life'.[2] Further afield, excavations in Geneva, Switzerland,[3] have shown a continuity of institutions between Roman and later periods, and it is becoming ever more obvious that the Western Roman towns of continental Europe preserved their administrative functions even after the collapse of the Western Empire.

Nevertheless, Galinié's vivid phrase 'a town without urban life' could probably be applied to most of the towns of Roman Gaul in their earliest medieval phases, but a few settlements of Roman origin have been shown by archaeological excavation to have been industrial and commercial centres in the fifth and sixth centuries. One of these is the small town of Huy in that area of Roman Gaul which today is Belgium, lying on a rocky outcrop at the confluence of the river Meuse and Hoyoux.[4] There was a settlement there from the first to fourth centuries AD, at the point where the Roman road from the Ardennes crossed the Meuse, and by the tenth century Huy consisted of a fortified centre, a residential area and two industrial quarters, one on the left bank of the Meuse and the other on the right bank of the Hoyoux. Its two industrial quarters seem to have been occupied as early as the fifth and sixth centuries, for excavation has revealed the remains of industrial production in both areas: objects of bone and horn, jewellery, and pottery were all made there. A mint had been established by the seventh century and the names of twelve moneyers are known. Huy may also have been a place where tolls were exacted as early as the seventh century, but there is no positive evidence of this until a document of 743. The settlement at Huy contrasts with other Roman sites in Belgium such as Liège, Tournai and Ghent which all continued as administrative and ecclesiastical centres after the Roman period but which did not develop any obvious sign of commercial life until the ninth century.[5]

Until there have been more excavations such as those at Huy the traditional view of continuity of urban occupation in northern Gaul from the late Roman period must still be one of a continuity of institutions. More investigations of fifth-, sixth- and seventh-century levels in the towns of Roman Gaul as a whole are needed before we can evaluate their position in the continuation of commercial and industrial activities in north–west Europe after the fall of the Western Roman Empire and before the rise of Charlemagne and the Holy Roman Empire at the end of the eighth century.

Although the lack of ecclesiastical organization in Britain in the fifth and sixth centuries means that documentary evidence for continuity between Roman towns and their successors in Britain is less helpful than that in Gaul, the archaeological evidence is fuller. Much research has gone into the question of continuity in recent years and the late Roman or sub-Roman levels of a number of towns have been investigated by excavation. Thus we probably have a better material picture of the situation in the centuries immediately following the breakdown of Roman rule in Britain than we have on the Continent. The general tenor of opinion is that, although the ruins of Roman towns were well known to the Anglo-Saxon immigrants in the fifth century, the lack of dwellings discovered through excavation indicates that the towns themselves were hardly used for general settlement, apparently being regarded more as status sites and perhaps as potential centres for the emergent Anglo-Saxon kingdoms.

As in other parts of Europe, on their arrival in Britain in the first century AD the Romans began to establish forts and towns in their newly-acquired colony. Both are well documented historically and archaeologically, but in recent years archaeologists have begun to question how thoroughly the towns of Roman Britain were urbanized and for how long they flourished as truly urban places. It has become axiomatic among those researching into Roman Britain that Roman civilization was spread over the country like a veneer, and that it never penetrated very deeply into, let alone replaced, native culture even though the upper echelons of society must have absorbed Roman culture to a considerable and noticeable extent. The villa farming system in Britain began to break down at the end of the fourth century, and some have argued that the towns themselves were already in decline early in that century and 'had gone by 350'.[6] This is an extreme view and evidence from sites such as St Albans, Hertfordshire (*Verulamium*), Cirencester, Gloucestershire (*Corinium Dobunnorum*), and Wroxeter, Shropshire (*Viroconium Cornoviorum*) (figure 2.2) shows that it cannot have been true over the whole country, but most archaeologists

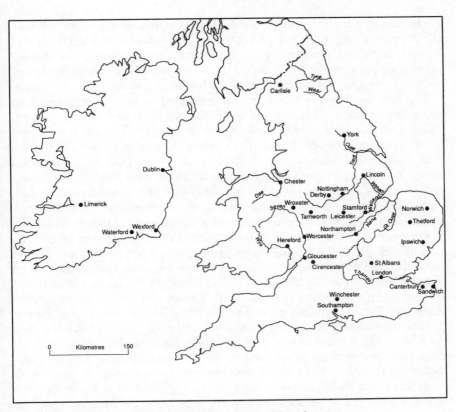

Fig. 2.2   Map of British Isles with places mentioned in the text

would agree that the towns of Roman Britain were in difficulties by 370 and unoccupied after the end of Roman administration, which cannot have lasted long into the fifth century. Excavations in many Roman towns in England have shown a distinct break in occupation of about 150 years from sometime in the early fifth century. This can be seen clearly from the layer of dark earth which has been found overlying late Roman levels in some towns; it is thought to originate from a time when most of the land inside the walls of the towns was either totally abandoned or was being used only for agricultural purposes, and when the towns' areas of occupation were strictly limited.

Excavations in Roman towns such as London (*Londinium Augusta*), Canterbury, Kent (*Durovernum Cantiacorum*), Gloucester, Gloucester-shire (*Glevum*), and Winchester, Hampshire (*Venta Belgarum*) have revealed this layer of dark humus overlying the latest Roman levels and sealing them from the Anglo-Saxon occupation above.[7] It is difficult to see how settlements where such a deep layer of soil was accumulating could have contained a population of any appreciable size, even though many Roman towns in England may have been used by the immigrant Anglo-Saxons as the administrative cores of their newly-established kingdoms. The presence of ancient defensive walls and the ruins (some perhaps not so ruinous) of grand masonry buildings obviously had a numinous effect on the minds of the Anglo-Saxons coming from countries where such structures were unknown, and these 'places built by giants' obviously lived on in the imagination as places where kings, if not giants, might rule. They cannot, however, have been regarded as potential areas for large-scale settlement.

The case for a Roman town being transformed without interruption into the administration centre of an Anglo-Saxon kingdom has been argued, using archaeological evidence alone, for Winchester.[8] There the Roman walls remain to form the boundaries of the early medieval town, but in the fifth and sixth centuries there is little evidence to indicate a continued urban presence within the walled area. Instead, we see a cluster of fifth- and sixth-century cemeteries outside the walls, representing contemporary rural settlements (as yet undiscovered). It has been argued that such a concentration of habitation sites around a walled enclave must indicate the pre-eminence of that enclave in the organization of settlement in general, and thus that Winchester must have maintained its importance as a central place during the formation of the West Saxon kingdom after the arrival of the Anglo-Saxon in the fifth and sixth centuries. The fact that Winchester subsequently emerged as the capital of Wessex can be taken as a confirmation of this opinion but it must be remembered that Winchester did not become the acknowledged and historically recorded capital of Wessex until long after the sixth century. Although Winchester and its environs have been the scene of many intensive campaigns of excavation in the past thirty years, the theory outlined above remains no more than a theory, as yet with insufficient material evidence to back it up. It will, therefore, be even more difficult to prove for other towns where excavation has been on a slighter scale, such as some of the Roman-founded towns which emerged as Anglo-Saxon urban centres by the ninth century.

For example, Canterbury, Kent and York, North Yorkshire (*Eburacum*) are equally good candidates for continuity of administrative importance in their respective kingdoms, but in these cases the theory has to be based on written sources, rather than archaeological evidence. Canterbury, for instance, was a royal centre for the kingdom of Kent by 597, and York is recorded as the capital of Northumbria in the 620s. It is obviously unsatisfactory to project this evidence back to the early fifth century, and as archaeological evidence either to confirm or disprove the theory is lacking they must be grouped together with Winchester in the category of 'continuity not proven'.

Several other Romano-British towns, however, show some sign of secular occupation, as opposed to administrative significance, in the years between the end of Roman rule and the seventh century. At Lincoln (*Lindum*), for instance, the situation of the church of St Paul-in-the-Bail in the forum of the Roman town may indicate the continued presence of a Christian community in Lincoln in the fifth and sixth centuries, although the date of foundation of the excavated church and the period of use of its associated Christian cemetery is not yet agreed by all.[9] Some authorities believe that this church could be the one described by Bede[10] as the 'stone church of fine workmanship' (*ecclesiam operis egregii de lapide*), founded by St Paulinus shortly after he had converted Blæcca, the Prefect of Lincoln, in

628, and thus not evidence for sub-Roman occupation of the town but rather the remains of one of our earliest Anglo-Saxon churches.

Even in the smaller Roman settlement of Worcester two probably sixth-century Christian graves under the medieval cathedral refectory[11] hint at some form of occupation after the end of the Roman period, and a number of other tantalizing signs of sub-Roman life in towns are beginning to emerge. But there are few indications of substantial permanent populations in Roman towns in Britain after the end of the Western Empire. Their sites may have been used as 'a useful ruin, as an enclave for an old or new aristocracy, spaciously arranged like a walled park',[12] but they were not towns in the sense of being significant centres of people engaged in commerce or other non-agricultural occupations. So even in Britain, where archaeological excavation has been more extensive and intensive than in Roman Gaul, it has been impossible to prove an indisputable continuity of function between the towns of the Romans and those of the later periods. The fifth and sixth centuries, then, have to be regarded as a largely non-urban episode in the history of north-western Europe and we must turn to the seventh century to look for signs of an urban renaissance.

Seventh century: the re-emergence of urban culture

In many respects the seventh century seems to have been the time when urban culture once again began to flourish throughout western Europe. There were various reasons for this: the discernible but patchy consolidation of royal power both in England and on the Continent, the new establishment of bishoprics and other ecclesiastical centres in England, and the general growth of industry and trade. As we shall see, some of the new settlements which began and prospered then were what might be called 'specialized' centres, with commerce and industry as their mainstay but with some sectors of their population also involved in support industries such as the provision of foodstuffs, clothing and so on for the governing elite. Other settlements were simply the continuation of the royal and ecclesiastical units which had already grown up in some of the former Roman towns in Gaul and which were to grow apace in England after the end of the sixth century. The two sets of functional criteria met and intermingled, but a certain bias towards either commerce/industry or administration/ecclesiastical organization can be discerned in most of the sites.

For England, the coming of St Augustine in 597 and the subsequent conversion of the country to Christianity served as a catalyst for the revival of some of the Roman towns. A hundred years later England had been divided into dioceses, the centre of each see often being situated in a former Roman town. Bede names the diocesan centres which had been established by the second half of the seventh century, in many cases mentioning the building of churches and associated missionary activities. In York, for instance, Bede[13] records that in 627 King Edwin of Northumbria was baptized by St Paulinus in a timber church which the King had caused to be built during the course of his religious instruction, and that St Paulinus became the first bishop of the see centred there. Unfortunately, this early wooden church and its masonry successor cannot now confidently be identified with any building still extant today, but there are sufficient standing remains of other stone churches mentioned by Bede, such as the monastic churches of Wearmouth and Jarrow, the crypt at Hexham (one of the early diocesan centres), and the church of St Martin in Canterbury built on Roman foundations, to give us a good idea of what the masonry church probably looked like. In addition, archaeological excavation in some of the diocesan centres such as York and Canterbury can give us some idea of their physical appearance and layout.

It seems quite certain that most of the centres chosen as bishops' seats in England still possessed considerable remains of their Roman past. Their town walls were still standing, for instance, very often to an imposing height, and their gateways were probably still in use. Many of the masonry buildings within the walled areas were preserved, often in a ruinous state but still sufficiently obvious to have influenced the planning of the seventh-century settlements. In York it is clear that the Roman military headquarters-building (*principia*) in the fortress was kept in a good state of repair even as late as the ninth century,[14] and Roman buildings were everywhere used as quarries for building stone for the newly-founded churches.

Canterbury, London, Winchester and York are some of the survivors from Roman Britain which became important centres in seventh-century England. They are all mentioned, however briefly, in written sources, and the excavations which have been carried out in them over the past couple of decades have helped to fill out their history. In all cases the excavators stress the importance of their discoveries for the administrative role of these towns; the archaeological evidence known up to now suggests that commerce and industry played a less prominent part in their seventh-century life.

Canterbury was already a royal centre for the kingdom of Kent when St Augustine met King Æthelbert there in 597. On his conversion to Christianity King Æthelbert gave Augustine some land immediately outside the walls of Canterbury for the foundation of the monastery of SS Peter and Paul (now known as St Augustine's Abbey), and soon afterwards the construction of the cathedral was begun in the north-east quarter of the walled area, perhaps using a Roman temple for its foundations. This sector of the city, now mainly occupied by the cathedral close and King's School, is thought to have been the royal base, surrounded by some form of fortification which enclosed the royal palace. Excavations in that area in 1985[15] unearthed traces of a small secular settlement probably founded shortly after 597 and in continuous occupation until sometime in the ninth century. This could have been the dwelling area for the servants of either cathedral or palace. In the south-east quarter of Canterbury, outside the royal fortified core but still within the Roman walls, there was a densely-packed settlement made up of so-called sunken-featured buildings (figure 7.9B), small rectangular structures with their floor dug down lower than the contemporary ground surface. The artifacts found in these buildings show that they made up another secular settlement contemporary with that near the cathedral, suggesting that people from the surrounding countryside were

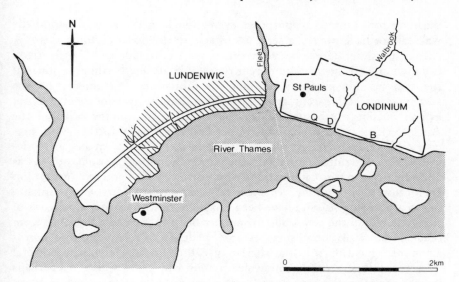

Fig. 2.3 Schematic plan showing the position of mid-Saxon LUNDENWIC in re-lation to Roman LONDINIUM. In the late ninth century harbours were established at Queenhithe (Q), Dowgate (D), and Billingsgate (B) (Milne 1989; copyright Museum of London)

beginning to move into Canterbury in the early years of the seventh century. There was, in addition, at least one street leading towards the cathedral, and perhaps a market. All were contained within the Roman walls whose continued existence is attested both historically and archaeologi-cally. Canterbury in the seventh century, then, comprised a royal and ecclesiastical presence with a small, but probably expanding, urban population.[16]

London also saw the foundation of a cathedral church at the beginning of the seventh century when Mellitus was consecrated as the first bishop of an initially transitory diocese. No remains of this early building have been found but the church is thought to have lain on or near the site of the present St Paul's cathedral, south of the walls of the Roman fort known since the middle ages as Cripplegate, also the traditional site of the slightly later Anglo-Saxon palace. London also seems to have had a mint by the end of the seventh century and a few sherds of Frankish pottery may indicate some international commerce.[17]

Nevertheless, there is no positive archaeological evidence for a contem-porary commercial settlement within the walls of Roman London even though a charter of the 670s mentions 'the port of London where the ships land', but recent archaeological work has indicated that by the middle of the seventh century a complementary settlement was beginning to grow up in the area now known as the Strand, outside the walls of the Roman town (figure 2.3). During the seventh and eighth centuries the Roman wall against the river may have formed a barrier between the settlement within the Roman town (the area known today as the City of London) and the river bank, so that waterborne traffic may not have been able to use that stretch of the river for commercial purposes even though in the Roman period the wall cannot have proved a serious obstacle to the boats berthing there. A change in water levels between the times of Roman and Anglo-Saxon occupation, and the use of different types of boats and berthing facilities at the two periods probably account for difficulties encountered by the seventh- and eighth-century sailors. The Roman riverside wall did not extend outside the boundaries of the walled town, so the boats of the Anglo-Saxons could probably have berthed more easily further west, precisely where archaeology suggests that the new settlement began to develop. Bede's eighth-century reference to the London (*Lundonia*) of 604 as a 'trading centre for many nations who visit it by land and sea' (*emporium populorum terra marique venientium*)[18] has, until recently, been tantalizing to archaeologists who have been unable to find any material remains of that date within the city walls to support Bede's statement. Evidence from outside the walls now suggests that Bede's *Lundonia* and the *portus Lundoniae* mentioned in the charter of 670 could have comprised several different sectors: a mainly administrative unit within the walls and a perhaps largely commercial centre to the west. Despite recent archaeological investigations, the physical remains of seventh-century London are still little known, and even in the eighth and ninth centuries no comprehensive plan of the settlement can be reconstructed.

York in the seventh century (known as *Eoforwic* or *Eoforwicceastre* to the Anglo-Saxons) is still best known from historical sources despite the excavations of recent years which have attempted to discover, and have finally found, some physical remains of so-called 'Anglian York', that is, York from the seventh to the ninth centuries.

The timber church founded by King Edwin in 627, and the well preserved Roman *principia* have already been mentioned, and there is further corroboration of the existence of the church in the 670s, by then transformed into stone, when Bishop Wilfrid ordered repairs to be carried out.[19] Sometime in the seventh century, too, a monastery with a school was founded, to become by the following century one of the most renowned in Europe for its scholarship and learning. The area of the Roman fort probably also contained the royal palace of the kings of Northumbria, but no remains have as yet been unearthed despite many excavations on potentially rewarding sites. As in London, there is little evidence for a commercial settlement within the Roman walls in the seventh century, but some signs suggest that there was habitation on the south bank of the Ouse (in the Roman *colonia*) at this time,[20] and further east, on the east bank of the river Foss, archaeological remains suggest that there was an incipient commercial core there also (figure 5.1).

The intensive campaign of excavation in Winchester over the past thirty years has produced much more, and the archaeological evidence for its physical layout in the seventh century is much fuller. Excavations on Cathedral Green, immediately north of the present cathedral, revealed the foundations of the Old Minster, the cathedral church until the construction, in the tenth century, of the New Minster which underlies the present post-Conquest structure. The Old Minister[21] was a complex building with many phases of extension and reconstruction from its establishment in the mid-seventh century until its abandonment in the tenth; at its core may lie the original church of SS Peter and Paul traditionally founded by King Cenwalh of Wessex in *c.* 648. A palace[22] of the royal house of Wessex may have stood to the west, in the south-west corner of the forum of the Roman town, a position in accord with the suggested sites of royal palaces at London and York, for instance. As in Canterbury, there is archaeological evidence for secular settlement in Winchester at this time, for excavations in Lower Brook Street[23] revealed four Christian burials, one containing a garnet necklace, which were subsequently, but still within the seventh century, overlain by timber buildings. These in their turn were replaced by a stone building *c.* 800. The excavator, Martin Biddle, has suggested that the Lower Brook Street discoveries represent the property of a high-ranking group of people associated with the royal court, thus a secular settlement but a rather special one. More recent excavations in St Martin's Close and Sussex Street[24] have unearthed remains suggestive of lower-status occupation a little further to the west; and the east end of High Street may have acted as a market. If this is so, then Winchester and Canterbury seem to have conformed to a very similar pattern in the seventh century.

All these four places show distinct parallels with each other: royal and ecclesiastical buildings within their Roman walls, supplemented by neighbouring small commercial settlements. This is also the pattern which emerges from equivalent contemporary continental sites. Less excavation has taken place in these and we have to rely mainly on historical records, but the message seems to be the same. The centres of dioceses were set up in Roman towns or forts where the walls were still standing and where there were masonry remains of Roman buildings. Cathedral churches, monastic houses, royal palaces and perhaps a few subsidiary secular habitations and service buildings were erected within the Roman walls. There is nowhere any archaeological evidence to suggest a density of occupation, and only seldom are there signs of industrial and commercial activities.

Recent excavations and research have led some archaeologists to suggest that at this period industrial and commercial activities may have been catered for by a specific settlement type which grew up on sites with no Roman antecedents. Such settlements were undefended and usually lay beside a river or on the coast and their names are often distinguished by having the suffix *wic.*

The importance of the so-called *wic* or *wik* sites has long been discussed by historians researching into the origins of medieval towns in Europe, and it has been suggested that they are synonymous with the *emporia* (trading centres) mentioned in early written sources such as Bede who also uses the Latin *portus* as the equivalent of the Old English *wic.* Names such as *Lundenwic* (London in the Anglo-Saxon Chronicle and the *Lundonia* of Bede), *Eoforwic* (York) and *Sliasvik* (Viking-age Hedeby and its medieval successor Schleswig), for instance, all bear the *wic* suffix and are early medieval towns well known historically and archaeologically with, as we shall see, commercial and industrial functions. This has led archaeologists to propose that in the early medieval period, and in the seventh and eighth centuries in particular, settlements of a specialized economic character grew up to supplement the mainly administratively-based towns on Roman sites, in other words that the *wic* sites were the commercial complements to the administrative centres in reoccupied Roman towns.

The archaeological view[25] is that the *wics* themselves were undefended, although associated with defensible sites and this has led to the term 'dual settlements' being used of pairs of towns (for example, Winchester and Hamwic, see below). Other, non-archaeological, evidence implies that this is much too simple an explanation, both for the *wics* and for their association with reoccupied Roman towns. Place-name evidence[26] for the interpretation of *wic* (the Germanic equivalent of the Latin *vicus* meaning a quarter or district of a town or, when applied to the countryside, a village, hamlet or estate or, alternatively, the equivalent of the Latin *portus* meaning port or harbour) shows that it was used for many different types of site. There is a single instance of its being used on its own to mean town (in a Kentish law of 673–85 which mentions *Lundenwic* and subsequently uses *wic* alone to refer to the town of London) and more numerous examples where it can be interpreted as port or harbour. For example, in addition to those mentioned above there are *Quentauic* in the Latin version of Bede and *Cwæntwic* in the Old English translation of his work; this is the site in the Canche valley in north-west France, deserted today but known to historians and archaeologists as Quentovic. In England there are *Gipeswic* (Ipswich, Suffolk), *Hamwic* (Saxon Southampton, Hampshire), *Duneuuic* (Dunwich, Suffolk), and many more.

But there was also a multitude of other usages of *wic*. In the west midlands of England it is applied to the salt-mining centres of Cheshire (Nantwich, for example, is mentioned as *Wich*, *Wicus* and *Nametwihc*) and Worcestershire (Droitwich is known as *Saltwich* in 716–17 and *Drihtwich* by 1347). Elsewhere it seems to have been applied to rural sites, particularly perhaps to specialized farms such as dairy farms or monastic granges, and even simple villages. The terminology, therefore, is too complex for the assumption that the suffix *wic* means purely a commercial centre and some recently published works on the archaeology of early medieval towns need to be treated with caution in this regard. An added complication is the derivation of the term 'Viking' from possible *vik* or *wic* place-names as mentioned in the Introduction (p. 2). There is no doubt that recent explanations of this term by archaeologists have been far too simple, although the occurrence of *wic* in a place-name must still be of great significance of our understanding of the development of early towns.

An illustration of the significance of *wic* in place-names can be seen from a number of early medieval settlements with names including the suffix *wic* which have recently been excavated and proved to have been undefended sites, with their livelihood in the seventh century and later being based largely on industry and trade. The archaeological evidence obtained from them points to their being mercantile centres, the *emporia* of Bede and other historical sources.

One of the best known (from written sources) of the emporia in north-west Europe at this time is Quentovic whose place-name means the *wic* (or *vicus*) on the River Canche. Its existence and commercial importance have long been known from early medieval written sources which name it as the seat of a *praefectus* (a royal official of the Frankish court) and a mint, the latter being confirmed by the discovery of coins bearing the name WICUS in the environs of Etaples, on the Channel coast of France near the mouth of the River Canche. Until recently Quentovic's site remained a matter of speculation but it was equated with St Josse, on the edge of the flood plain south of the River Canche a few kilometers south-east of the present port of Etaples, mainly because of the concentration of coins discovered there. Small-scale excavations directed by David Hill over the past years have suggested that a site a little further east but still in the flood plain south of the River Canche was the original Quentovic. It lies about 10km from the Channel coast, and in the early middle ages was easily accessible by river. Hill's excavations have unearthed artifacts which underline the site's international importance until the mid-ninth century or later, consisting as they do of very large quantities of pottery of types also found in English settlements such as *Hamwic* and *Eoforwic*, where they are considered to have been imported from north-western France.[27] Fragments of glass vessels have also been found in sufficient quantities to suggest that this site was not simply an agricultural settlement, and a few discoveries indicate the manufacture of small metal objects on the site.

The excavations which have been carried out so far have failed to reveal complete plans of buildings, but structural traces such as post-holes and slots into which sill beams for wall foundations were once sunk, plus other features such as wells and pits indicate where buildings once stood. The much larger-scale excavations which are planned for future seasons should expose part of the layout of what seems to have been an intensively occupied settlement some 53ha (about 130 acres) in extent.

Although the archaeological information for the precise date of occupation of the newly-excavated Quentovic site is still very slight, numismatic evidence suggests that it was in existence at least by 600. One of the thirty-seven Merovingian gold coins found in the ship-burial at Sutton Hoo in East Anglia whose deposition is dated *c.* 625 bears the name QUANTIA as the place of minting, and coins in a hoard found at Crondall, Hampshire,[28] and concealed before 640, carry the mint-place WICUS and the moneyer's name DVTTA. This is good evidence for both the early seventh-century minting of coins at Quentovic, and for the close connections between Quentovic and England at that date.

Close connections between Quentovic and England are also evidenced by the apparent Anglo-Saxon influence on the moneyers' names present on Quentovic coins in the seventh century and later, and Old English written sources mention Quentovic as the main port for the passage of pilgrims between England and the Continent, the so-called *via rectissima*. In 664, for instance, Theodore of Tarsus set sail from Quentovic to England, on his way to Canterbury after his consecration as archbishop,[29] and the route between the two countries is mentioned in the *Life of St Wilfrid* written in the 720s.[30]

The heyday of Quentovic continued throughout the eighth and ninth centuries, being mentioned as *Cwantawic* in the *Anglo-Saxon Chronicle* in 839 when the Vikings perpetrated 'great slaughter' there. Despite this, it survived the ninth-century Viking raids as the discovery at Fécamp, on the Channel coast just north of Le Havre, of a hoard of late tenth-century

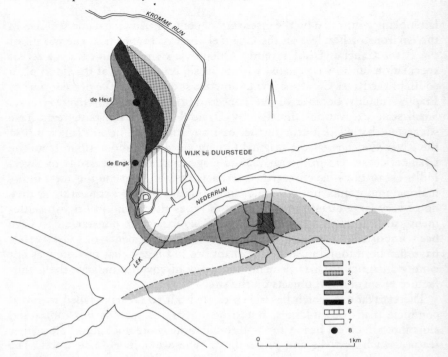

Fig. 2.4 Simplified plan of Dorestad showing
1   course of rivers Rhine and Lek during the lifetime of Dorestad
2   northern harbour
3   northern *vicus*
4   agragrian zone
5   probable site of Roman fort of *Levefanum*
6   medieval Wijk bij Dorestad
7   present course of rivers Rhine and Lek
8   Dorestad's cemeteries

Quentovic coins shows. The reason for the end of Quentovic is not known, but may become clearer as a result of future excavations.

Another notable continental emporium which began its life during the seventh century is that of *Dorestad* (modern Wijk bij Duurstede), The Netherlands, on the River Kromme Rijn (now an insignificant branch of the River Rhine). It also flourished mainly in the eighth century (as an important trading centre for north-west Europe in the Carolingian period) and the extremely large-scale excavations which were carried out in the 1970s have revealed an extensive and complex settlement with a wide range of industrial and commercial activities.[31] Its beginnings, though, are not well known, either archaeologically or from written sources, although its antecedent may have been the Roman fort of *Levefanum* whose site has now been swept away by the Rhine (figure 2.4). Levefanum was one of a string of forts along the Rhine which all seem to have been abandoned by the end of the third century, but were then resettled after a period of desertion early in the seventh century when the Merovingian kings of Francia were attempting to establish their rule in the area. This sequence of events can also be traced in places such as Ghent and Antwerp, but there must have been some differences in intention or in scale of the resettlement, because it is only at Dorestad that such a wealthy and influential emporium grew up. By the 630s gold coins were being struck at Dorestad, bearing the name MADELINUS, and thus it was already important enough to have a mint.

There is archaeological evidence for seventh-century occupation in the Trekweg area of Dorestad but it seems to have been a small and sparsely-populated settlement at that time, prehaps a rural manor of the Merovingian kings, and it is uncertain whether the site should be described as emporium proper until about 675 when tree-ring dating of some barrel-staves used to line wells belonging to dwellings a little way from the river bank, and thus not associated with the harbour, gives the earliest firm date. The development of the harbour area of Hoogstraat had not begun by then, and it was not until the eighth century that Dorestad reached its peak commercially and industrially. This development will be discussed in chapter 3.

Several other similiar commercial centres lay in the area of the modern Netherlands, at the mouth of the River Scheldt. Domburg[32] on the island of Walcheren and Westenschouwen[33] on the island of Schouwen in the Scheldt estuary both acted as centres for trade across the North Sea in the eighth and ninth centuries, and both may have been founded, like Dorestad, in the seventh century. Their sites are known today only from collections of artifacts picked up from the beaches and sand dunes by antiquarians over the years, and from a few minor excavations earlier this century. Even less is known about *Witla* at the mouth of the River Meuse whose site has now been totally lost.[34] It was another of the eighth- and ninth-century emporia in the Rhine delta, attested by written sources, and attacked by Vikings in 836. Its layout and economic organization cannot now be reconstructed by archaeological means and its seventh-century beginnings remain a matter of speculation.

All these sites were strategically placed to take advantage of waterborne traffic along the rivers of France, Germany and the Low Countries, and across the Channel and the North Sea to England where equivalent sites began to grow up at the same time, to become, like their continental counterparts, more flourishing in the eighth century. The earliest of these was probably Ipswich (Old English *Gipeswic*) at the mouth of the River Orwell in Suffolk (figure 2.5). It was ideally situated to cater for the traffic from the Rhine valley, and the imported pottery found by excavations in Ipswich confirms its close contacts with the Rhineland. Although not mentioned in documents until the tenth century, excavations[35] have shown that it was in existence by the early years of the seventh century when it became the first centre for the production of wheel-thrown and kiln-fired pottery in England since the end of Roman Britain some 200 years earlier. The development of the pottery industry in Ipswich is itself a reflection of contacts with the Rhineland where the Roman tradition of industrialized pottery manufacture had been maintained since the fall of the Roman Empire. Rhenish influence, perhaps carried by immigrant potters to Ipswich, is very evident in the innovatory Anglo-Saxon pottery which is known by archaeologists as Ipswich ware.[36] A number of pottery kilns have

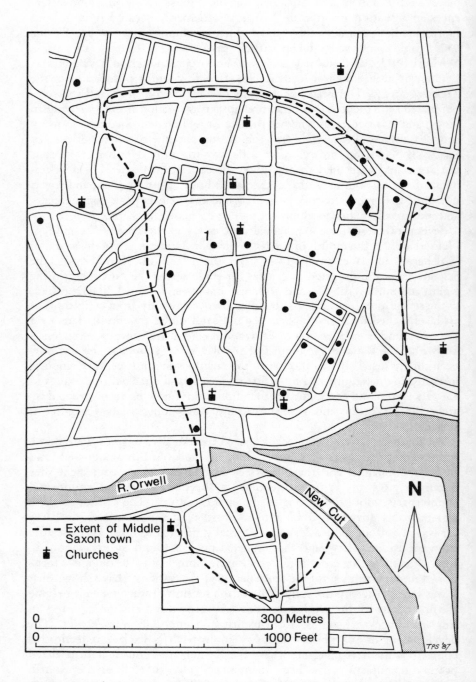

Fig. 2.5 Anglo-Saxon Ipswich (*Gipeswic*) showing sites of excavations (circles) and excavated kilns (diamonds). The site at Buttermarket is designated 1 (after Wade 1988)

been discovered and excavated both on the edges and in the centre of the early medieval and modern town. They date from the seventh to ninth centuries, and the vessels which were fired in them have been found in profusion in Ipswich itself and on rural settlements throughout East Anglia.

The occupation of Ipswich may have started even before the seventh century, for some local handmade pottery has been discovered together with Rhenish and Frankish wares and late sixth-century or early seventh-century Merovingian pottery (*blackware*) with parallels in what is now Belgium. The local handmade pottery must have been made before the wheel-thrown pottery industry began to dominate East Anglian production in the mid-seventh century, and thus a late sixth-century date for its production has been proposed. One focus of Ipswich's early occupation lay in present Lower Brook Street, on the north bank of the River Orwell, where several sunken-featured buildings have been found. Associated rubbish pits containing ironworking debris suggest that industries other than potting were already established in that part of Ipswich by the early seventh century, and traces of field boundaries on both the east and west edges of the settlement indicate agricultural activity at the same time. The excavator, Keith Wade, believes that Ipswich in this early period was occupied by an economically self-sufficient community which did not rely on produce from the countryside for its food, and, indeed that Ipswich may have remained fundamentally self-sufficient throughout its Anglo-Saxon lifetime. If this is so, Ipswich differs from most other early medieval towns in north-west Europe which seem to have acquired foodstuffs and other basic agricultural produce from their hinterlands (p. 129).

A cemetery of inhumation graves containing grave-goods has recently been discovered and excavated in Buttermarket, in the centre of the modern town of Ipswich. Eighty burials have so far been revealed, and the cemetery must originally have contained many more, for its boundaries extend beyond the excavated area. The mixture of burial rites (coffined and uncoffined burials, bodies on biers, chamber graves, some burials surrounded by ring-ditches and hence each probably once covered by a mound, and all orientations) indicates that the population which the cemetery served was either pagan or only recently converted to Christianity. No church is known in the vicinity of the cemetery, and this might be taken as support for the pagan interpretation, but such negative evidence is rather dangerous to argue from as the total area of the cemetery has not been uncovered and a church could yet be found.

The grave-goods show that the cemetery was in use from the beginning of the seventh to the end of the eighth century and that some of the population were very rich. One of the burials is a so-called 'warrior grave', containing a shield, a sword, spears and two glass vessels in addition to a body in a coffin. It is tempting to see this as the interment of one of the leaders of the community whose wealth may have been derived from contacts across the North Sea, for the grave-goods show close affinities with artifacts made and used in the Rhineland and Frankish areas. From this cemetery we can glimpse the make-up of Ipswich's first urban population, adding an extra dimension to other archaeological discoveries in the town which tell us about its economic basis and topography; these discoveries are mainly

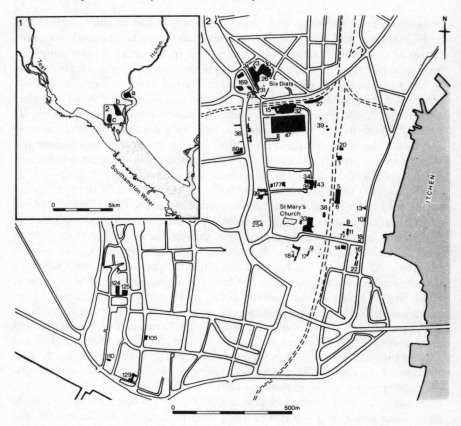

Fig. 2.6 Saxon Southampton (*Hamwic*) with excavated sites (Brisbane 1988; copyright Southampton City Council)

illustrative of Ipswich in the eighth and ninth centuries and so will be discussed further in chapter 3.

Another English trading centre on a previously unoccupied, and therefore non-Roman, site which is thought to have been founded in the seventh century, is Saxon Southampton (*Hamwic*, also called *Hamwih* by some authorities[37] after the first recorded mention of the place as *illud mercimonium quod dicitur Hamwih*, from which St Willibald set sail *c.* 720). The area of Hamwic lies south-east of modern Southampton and has been extensively excavated over the past twenty years (figure 2.6).[38] Archaeological evidence from excavated structures and artifacts at present points to occupation having begun there at the end of the seventh century, perhaps at the instigation of King Ine of Wessex (688–726). This date may have to be modified in the future because the most recent study of the coins discovered at Hamwic[39] suggest a slightly later date for its foundation, perhaps not before the beginning of the eighth century when Hamwic may have supplanted an earlier trading centre at the mouth of the Hamble or on the Isle of Wight. Whatever the exact date and circumstances of its foundation, Hamwic certainly flourished from the early eighth century onwards, both as an industrial and commercial centre and as a cross-channel port frequented by missionaries and pilgrims bound for Rome via Quentovic.

Some of the other sites in England which have the suffix *wic* have been mentioned above. *Lundenwic* (London) and *Eoforwic* (York) seem to have consisted of a walled Roman town with commercial sectors or suburbs. Other *wic* sites such as Gipeswic and Hamwic stand on previously unoccupied ground, as do others with no archaeological evidence to prove their medieval trading functions (such as Fordwich and Sandwich in Kent, thought to be outports for Canterbury[40]) but with their place-name to support the theory. As mentioned above, the simple distinction between administrative centres in Roman towns and commercial *wics* cannot be upheld on either archaeological or place-name grounds, nor can we assume the growth of trade without royal, or at least some other form of administrative support. Emporia and administrative centres were intimately associated, as can been seen for instance in the presence of royal officials at Quentovic, the possible association of King Ine with Hamwic, and the development of Dorestad from the suburb of a Roman fort and, perhaps, a sector of a Merovingian royal estate. Some emporia may have grown up on new sites, but they may equally have formed part of, or suburbs to, the walled towns which were the administrative centres themselves. The question is complex, and far from solution as yet. Nevertheless, what can be said is that even though we still know regrettably little about the seventh-century forerunners of later towns, it is becoming increasingly obvious that the origins of what were to become common and flourishing towns in the eighth century and later had their tentative beginnings in the hundred years from 600. Their development, and the many new foundations in the eighth and ninth centuries will be described in chapter 3.

Chapter 3

North-west European towns in the eighth and ninth centuries

When the Vikings began their attacks on Europe at the end of the eighth century they must soon have realized that the countries which were the objects of their raids were in many ways more complex than their Scandinavian homelands. By about 800 the west European states had developed elaborate forms of kingship, social hierarchies and economic systems, and one of the manifestations of this complex society was the presence of towns. These towns took on many forms; some were simple trading sites (emporia), some were highly specialized industrial units, others were more elaborate administrative and ecclesiastical centres, but whatever form they took they must have made a profound impression on Vikings coming as they did from countries where there were very few signs of urbanization in the ninth century.

The Viking raids on Britain began at the end of the eighth century with attacks on undefended monastic sites around the coast (for example when 'the harrying of the heathen miserably destroyed God's church in Lindisfarne by rapine and slaughter' in 793[1]), but it was not until some forty years later that the Vikings began to ravage the coastal ports. Hamwic was stormed in 837 and from then onwards the Anglo-Saxon Chronicle records ever more frequent attacks on English towns such as London in 839 and Canterbury and Sandwich in 851. During the same period Viking fleets had been ravaging the Low Countries and penetrating the rivers of western France, pillaging towns and monasteries wherever they went.[2] By the middle of the ninth century the Vikings must have seen many different types of towns in north-west Europe: defended and undefended, commercial and administrative, coastal and riverine. This experience was not wasted on them, for the ninth century also saw the beginning of towns in the Viking homelands. It is debatable whether the Vikings' west-European experience was the catalyst for the development of towns in Scandinavia, for the Vikings had already met the same phenomenon in the commercial settlements of the Baltic region in the eighth century (chapter 6), but some influences from west-European urbanization must have been carried back to their homelands by the returning warriors. The towns of north-west Europe may have been more complex in their organization, hierarchy, and social and commercial structure than their Baltic counterparts, and a combination of influences from both east and west was probably instrumental in the growth of Scandinavian towns which is discussed in chapter 4.

Chapter 2 has shown that towns were beginning to re-emerge in north-west Europe during the seventh century. This development continued during the following century at ever-increasing speed and when the Vikings began their westward expansion at the end of the eighth century urban settlements were already a well-established part of west-European life. Those which have been mentioned earlier continued to flourish and expand, and many new settlements came into being.

Continental Europe

Although the names of many eighth- and ninth-century urban settlements on the north-west Continent are known from documentary sources such as the Royal Frankish Annals and the Anglo-Saxon Chronicle, their physical appearance is still very largely a matter of speculation. Nevertheless, Wilson's statement[3] made in 1986, 'The whole problem of the physical structure of the towns of the North Sea littoral is still obscure' is rather too pessimistic; few such towns have been excavated thoroughly, but there are sufficient examples to give us some idea of their buildings and layout. The towns of this period seem originally to have been similar to those of the previous century, but as time went on different forms began to develop. The royal and ecclesiastical centres whose main function was administrative continued in existence and progressively acquired more and more commercial functions, and the trading centres mentioned in chapter 2 as a characteristic feature of the rebirth of towns in the seventh century flourished even more in the eighth and ninth centuries.

Of all the trading centres of north-west Europe, that of Dorestad has been most intensively investigated through excavation in recent years. Its origins can be traced in the early seventh century, but little is known about its physical appearance at that stage (p. 18). From the early eighth century to its decline and abandonment some time between 850 and 875, however, we now have a great deal of information, thanks to the intensive excavations carried out from 1967–77 by the Rijksdienst voor het Oudheidkundig Bodemonderzoek (State Service for Archaeology in the Netherlands), under the direction of W.A. van Es.[4]

The settlement stands on the west bank of the Kromme Rijn, close to the bifurcation of the rivers Rhine and Lek (figure 2.4). At the height of its prosperity it covered a strip of land about 3km long made up of several different areas, each with its specific settlement form. The northern settlement, extending as far as 1km west of the river bank, consisted of a group of about sixty buildings of a type more often associated with rural settlements than towns. They were long timber structures, their long walls slightly curved to give a bow-sided (sometimes called boat-shaped) plan, divided internally into dwelling quarters and animal stalls, probably roofed with turf

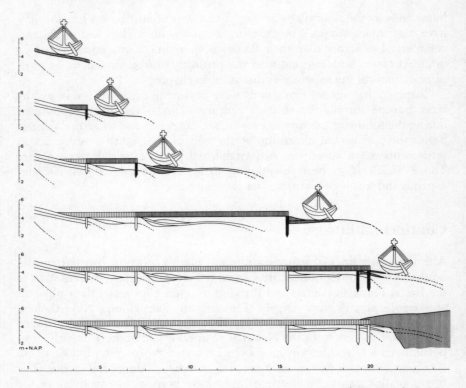

Fig. 3.1a   Reconstruction of the early medieval jetties at Dorestad (Copyright ROB)

or thatch, and each standing within a yard surrounded by a wooden fence. Associated with the buildings were features such as granaries and wells, together giving a distinctly agricultural feeling to the settlement which seems to have been made up of a group of farms standing in farmyards arranged along a network of wooden-paved streets.

At the same time a different form of settlement, devoted more to commercial than to agricultural activities, grew up along the bank of the River Kromme Rijn. Unfortunately the physical connection between these two areas could not be discovered through excavation because of the presence of modern housing along Hoogstraat (the road which still runs approximately parallel to what was the course of the river in the eighth century). But it seems probable that small, rectangular buildings occupied the land immediately to the west of the riverbank, and the bank itself was enlarged by a series of contiguous causeways serving as jetties. Each building, in its plot of land, probably faced on to a causeway leading to the west bank of the river. Gradually the river was displaced eastwards through natural forces, and as the bank receded the causeways were extended until by the middle of the ninth century they were some 200m long (figure 3.1). Excavations at Hoogstraat 1 have shown how the causeways were constructed. Rows of upright posts were sunk into the river bed and topped by horizontal timbers to form walkways. Gradually the space beneath the walkways silted up so that they finally rested on solid ground. As the river moved eastwards,

Fig. 3.1b Archaeological remains of the Dorestad jetties (Photo ROB)

access to the water was provided by extensions to the causeways until they reached their final length.

Dorestad has long been known from historical sources to have been one of the most important distribution centres for north-west European manufactures during the Carolingian period. The recent excavations have supplemented the written evidence by material remains: coins, glass and so on, but largely in the form of pottery. Because pottery is usually the best-preserved material found on excavated sites it is the type of evidence most commonly used by archaeologists to establish trading connections and even cultural traits. It has the advantage of being fairly easily traceable to its sources of origin, that is, the place from which the clay used in making the pottery was obtained can often be ascertained; in addition, pottery-making was essentially regional in its production in the early middle ages, and types of pottery foreign to the area in which they are found can be spotted by excavators today. Using pottery as a source of evidence for the trading connections of Dorestad, it has been possible to show that during the eighth and early ninth century Dorestad was the main distribution centre for goods assembled there from the middle reaches of the Rhine. These commodities were then sent out along the Rhine, the Lek and their tributaries to settlements in the north-west Netherlands, and overseas to England and southern Scandinavia.

It is, however, not always easy to specify through archaeological means what these commodities might have been. By their nature, goods made of organic material (grain, leather, furs, timber and so on) tend to decay in the ground and are only occasionally found in archaeological contexts. So although we can assume, using the written sources as evidence, that a multiplicity of commodities such as wine and textiles were exported through Dorestad to its environs and further afield, we cannot confidently list their variety. Nevertheless, some objects discovered during excavation can help to fill out the picture. Glass vessels found at Dorestad must have been brought in from near Cologne, still an industrial region in the Carolingian period as it had been during the Roman Empire, and then redistributed. Millstones for grinding grain were transported to Dorestad from the quarries of Niedermendig near modern Koblenz in Germany where they were then exported to other parts of Europe. For example, millstones of Niedermendig lava have been found on English sites occupied in the eighth and ninth centuries; they must have arrived there along Rhenish and North Sea routes. The famous correspondence[5] between Charlemagne and King Offa of Mercia in about 796 which mentions 'black stones' is thought to refer to lava millstones, perhaps even specifically to those found recently in the excavation of a watermill at Tamworth, Staffordshire (see below), and the same letter also refers to reciprocal trade in the form of woollen cloaks manufactured in England and exported to Charlemagne's kingdom. Dorestad may have been the assembly and transhipment point both for these 'black stones', and for the English cloaks. Millstones of Niedermendig lava have also been found on contemporary settlements in north Germany and Denmark, but they are conspicuously absent from excavated sites in Norway and Sweden. This suggests that the trade routes emanating from Dorestad in the eighth century did not reach the more northerly and easterly parts of the then known world, and raises the intriguing question of why the Vikings subsequently chose Dorestad as one of their prime targets of attack.

Wine was also an important trading or exchange commodity in this period, and numerous barrels found reused as the lining of wells at Dorestad must originally have contained Rhenish wine. Much of the pottery which was mentioned earlier must also have accompanied this Rhineland trade (the very distinctive Badorf ware, for example, was made in the central Rhineland and was probably distributed from its production centre as a concomitant to the wine trade).

Dorestad itself seems to have been not only a distribution centre but also a production centre in its own right, manufacturing goods which would both satisfy local needs and which could be exported to a wider market. Some of the inhabitants of Dorestad were industrial workers: shipbuilding, carpentry, basketmaking, leatherworking and smithing all went on there and other evidence shows that some of the population also worked with bone, antler, amber and textiles. But it is unlikely that the purely manufacturing output of Dorestad could have been of sufficient scale to enable the town to grow into the greatest emporium of north-west Europe during the eighth and ninth centuries. That side of life at Dorestad appears to have been secondary to trade and exchange.

Dorestad also differs from other contemporary sites by its sheer size. More than 30 hectares (about 75 acres) were uncovered during the 1967–77 seasons and this is known to represent less than half of the original settlement. The population of the site in the eighth and ninth centuries was also unusually large for a settlement at that time. The area occupied by buildings plus the size of the three cemeteries which encircle it suggest that there were between 1000 and 2000 inhabitants (minimum figures, see p. 157) at any one time during the Carolingian period. Even in later medieval terms this was a huge population (compare the populations of tenth-century Hedeby and Birka), and in itself helps to prove the pre-eminence of Dorestad over most other north–west European settlements in the early middle ages.

Second in importance to Dorestad as a Rhineland trading centre at this period was Domburg on Walcheren[6]. Although its site has been almost entirely eroded by incursions of the sea and engulfed by sand dunes, we can get some slight idea of its physical layout from observations made early this century and before. In the eighth and ninth centuries the settlement seems to have comprised a single street along the waterside, more than 1km long and with rectangular timber buildings of very variable size (from 3–4m square to 14m long) on each side. Because of the circumstances of discovery it is impossible to be sure whether all the buildings were contemporary, and the finer details of their construction cannot be established. They were, however, surrounded by middens and rubbish pits containing remains of shellfish and animal bones presumably from meals, and some few traces of jewellery-manufacture. Leather must also have been worked there as tanning pits were discovered through excavation, although no leather objects were found.

A number of cemeteries associated with the settlement are also known, now mostly beneath the sea. The grave-goods found in the graves and also represented by occasional finds washed up on the beach show that the *floruit* of Domburg was during the hundred years from the middle of the eighth century. Coins indicate contacts with England, the Carolingian empire and north Italy at this time. A sharp decline in the number of all types of finds after the middle of the ninth century suggests that Domburg was abandoned by the end of that century.

Because of the badly-preserved state of the site of Domburg it is difficult to be confident either about the physical aspect of the settlement or its economy, but the large number of chance discoveries of coins and jewellery suggests that it must have been a specialist trading centre rather than a purely agricultural focus. The same is probably true of its less well-known counterpart *Westenschouwen*, where similar conditions of erosion, blown sand, and shifting sand dunes have reduced the site to almost nothing.[7] A small-scale excavation in the 1920s, though, revealed remains of small timber buildings occupying a strip of land parallel to the coast. This evidence, plus the finds of pottery, metalwork and coins of Carolingian type, suggests that Westenschouwen was a trading centre comparable to Domburg.

While these sites were dominating the river traffic of the Netherlands and acting as transhipment ports for the goods produced by and exported from the Carolingian heartland of the Rhine, other subsidiary emporia were beginning to flourish elsewhere in the Low Countries. Deventer, for example, was in existence as a trading centre by the second half of the eighth century. Archaeological discoveries[8] indicate that it occupied a strip of land at least 600m long and 200m wide along the right bank of the River IJssel, with craftsmen's and merchants' quarters closest to the river, and agricultural zones on the edges of the settlement. Deventer seems to have been similar to Carolingian Dorestad, except in the vital point of size and volume of traffic, and the same is very probably true of Medemblik with its eighth-century commercial roots. The fairly limited amount of archaeological investigation which has taken place there has done little more than highlight the archaeological potential of the early medieval town.[9] The earliest settlement stood on the northern tip of a ridge only slightly above sea-level, on the south bank of a stream (Middenleek or Oude Haven) flowing into what is now the IJsselmeer, and on the water route between Dorestad and Scandinavia. Much evidence of early occupation must have been swept away by later medieval inundations and little can be said about the details of Medemblik's settlement pattern. The finds of pottery, glass and so on from the town, however, illustrate its commercial role in the eighth and ninth centuries, one probably closely comparable to that of Deventer.

Further north, the eighth century saw the foundation of Emden, on Germany's North Sea coast, as a trading settlement.[10] It stands on the north bank of the River Ems, in a good situation for both land and water communications, and its importance was probably based on the exchange of Frisian cattle and cloth for Westphalian grain. There is little evidence to suggest that it ever became a pre-eminent international point of exchange, its importance (which continued unbroken until the thirteenth century) being rather that of a regional market centre. Its layout, however, shows some similarities with the sites described above, with its axis being formed by a single street aligned parallel to the bank of the river and along which timber buildings stood. Their construction, of staves or wattle, and size (5–6m x 3–3.5m), have led to their being compared with the early buildings at Hedeby (see chapter 4) although, of course, Emden never grew to the same importance as the latter. Other similar sites such as Groothusen, Nesse and Langwarden lined this stretch of North Sea coast between the estuaries of the rivers Ems and Weser. Continuous occupation over many centuries has led to a build-up of occupation deposits so that these settlements now stand on elongated mounds, a distinctive settlement form known in German as *Langwurten*.[11]

Quentovic has already been mentioned (p. 17) as one of the greatest west European trading centres of the early middle ages. There is little more to be added to that brief summary of what was obviously an extremely important site. The excavations so far carried out promise much for the future when the large-scale investigations which are so desperately needed may help us to compare this site more confidently with its contemporaries such as Dorestad.

There is at least one further place in the area of modern France which should help us to understand the importance of early medieval emporia for the trade and contacts of Europe in the eighth and ninth centuries. This is the site of St Denis, outside the walled, and previously Roman, town of Paris. From the end of the seventh century St Denis was regarded by the English as the most important fair in all of north-west Europe and it was one of the main centres visited by Anglo-Saxon merchants, pilgrims and travellers.[12] Its situation close to but outside the walls of the fortified town of Paris is interesting as it seems to equate with the organization of some English towns with Roman origins which also display this combination of administrative centre and commercial site or suburb.

The emporia represent only one aspect of urbanism which expanded and flourished in north-west Europe in the eighth and ninth centuries. The administrative and ecclesiastical centres which were described in chapter 2 continued to grow, and were supplemented by numerous new settlements with church, monastery or palace as their core and sometimes now with markets and manufacturing functions. As with the towns of the previous centuries, most of our evidence for settlements comes from written rather than archaeological sources and, apart from some remains of church or monastery, the physical features of the towns remain largely unknown. Excavations in Antwerp, Belgium,[13] suggest the presence of wattle-walled dwelling houses and a wood-paved street in Mattestraat which may be as early as the ninth century, although doubts have recently been cast on the dating of this site. Some ninth-century features indicative of habitation have also been discovered in Hamburg, West Germany,[14] but much more archaeological work is needed in all the eighth- and ninth-century towns recorded in documents before an informative picture of their physical appearance can emerge. Some of these towns are shown in figure 2.1.

Anglo-Saxon England

The archaeological evidence for towns in the eighth and ninth centuries is rather fuller in England where excavations have expanded in both quantity and extent over the past twenty years, and the potential of archaeology for our understanding of early medieval towns has been increasingly appreciated. Archaeological excavations have produced abundant evidence to show that England supported some urban centres (using the definition in the Introduction) by the eighth century, even, as we have seen in chapter 2, a hundred years earlier in a few cases. The rest of this chapter will concentrate on what is now known of the types of urban settlements present in England before the Viking raids and colonization of the second half of the ninth century.

Chapter 2 has already shown that by about 700 there were in England a few settlements of urban character, some predominantly administrative and some with a commercial bias. During the next two centuries they continued to consolidate their urban status, either through the confirmation of their ecclesiastical and administrative role or by the expansion of their commercial and industrial base. At the same time these settlements were supplemented by new urban foundations which grew and flourished in response to increasing commerce and an expanding population.

Thus in England at the beginning of the eighth century urban settlements were in their infancy, but within the next hundred and fifty years or so they were to grow at a spectacular rate (as were their equivalents in northern France and the Low Countries). As we shall see, many of the new towns in England had their origins in non-urban sites: royal or monastic centres, for instance, which attracted concentrations of population and which by their nature 'lived off the food of the surrounding countryside and supplied the countryside with other goods and services in return'.[15] Thus, they eventually developed into towns serving larger or smaller hinterlands most, apart from erstwhile Roman towns with their ruinous but redefensible walls, being open and undefended settlements. The time of greatest growth of defended towns in England was in the early tenth century, perhaps as a response to the threat of Viking attack which, although present earlier, manifested itself most obviously then (chapter 5). Before that threat was responded to, though, new urban centres were beginning to grow up to supplement those already found in England in the seventh century.

Four such sites (London: *Lundonia* or *Lundenwic*; York: *Eoforwic*; Ipswich: *Gipeswic*; and Saxon Southampton: *Hamwic*) have already been mentioned as seventh-century settlements, but their period of true economic importance for the early medieval period was in the eighth and early ninth centuries. Excavations in all these places over the past twenty years have given us some idea of what they must have looked like and how their economy functioned in the early middle ages. They are representative of the west European towns visited by the Vikings in the ninth century and indicate what ideas of towns must have been taken home to Scandinavia after the Viking raids, perhaps to stimulate the urban growth which was already developing there at that time.

The physical remains of London and York of the eighth and ninth centuries are new discoveries, their locations only recently having been discovered through archaeological investigations. For London,[16] it now seems that the commercial centre was concentrated along the north bank of the River Thames, in the Strand region and stretching as far west as Westminster (figure 2.3). It must have been some form of ribbon development, looking towards the river as its mercantile lifeline and using the foreshore, probably suitably embanked, as its market place. Small-scale excavations in the Covent Garden and Strand areas have recently revealed tantalizingly fragmentary signs of occupation: a few post-holes are all that remain of rectangular timber buildings used probably as dwellings and warehouses, rubbish pits show where the inhabitants disposed of their refuse. Pottery and other artifacts found from these rubbish pits indicate the wide-ranging contacts of the population of London at that time: its merchants must have traded with the great emporia of north-west Europe and carried out their business in what was then, as now, one of the main entry-points to England.[17] Unfortunately it is impossible to be more specific about the layout of this commercial sector of London, and because of the intensive later occupation of the sites we shall probably never know precisely what this part of eighth- and ninth-century London looked like. It is also impossible to be certain of the type of settlement which was present within the Roman walls of London at this date. Apart from a few objects of Viking-age date, very little remains in the present City of its predecessor of a thousands years ago, but the early medieval cathedral probably stood on the site of its modern successor, there is documentary evidence for a royal palace and chapel (perhaps the church of St Alban's, Wood Street) in the Cripplegate area, and several other churches.[18]

In London we can probably never hope to acquire anything more than glimpses into its commercial and administrative past, but excavations in

York, the parallel to London in many ways, have produced a little more evidence, and a rather fuller picture.

Archaeological work on the Fishergate site,[19] on the east bank of the River Foss in York, has exposed some slightly more tangible remains of eighth-century occupation, sufficient to enable the excavator, Richard Kemp, to postulate that he had found the economic centre of *Eoforwic* (Anglian York), a kilometre or so outside the walls of the Roman fortress (figure 5.1). The remains of a few rectangular timber buildings arranged beside a gravelled street were discovered in his excavations. The site was occupied from sometime in the seventh century until the ninth century, but judging by the concentrations of finds, particularly coins, occupation was not equally intensive throughout the centuries.

The first half of the eighth century saw a great deal of economic activity, and this was followed by about fifty years of much less intensive occupation which was to pick up again at the beginning of the ninth century. The site was subsequently abandoned, perhaps to be replaced by the tenth-century settlement in the Coppergate area further west (chapter 5).

Elsewhere in York there are a few indications of some form of eighth- and ninth-century occupation. Excavations under the medieval minster church which stands on the site of the *principia* of the Roman fortress have revealed a Christian inhumation cemetery whose earliest burials have been dated by radiocarbon analysis to 790 ± 70.[20] Although no remains of a contemporary church were found, the cemetery is sufficient to show that the former Roman administrative centre maintained at least an ecclesiastical presence in the eighth century, perhaps a continuation of that begun by King Edwin and St Paulinus a hundred years before (p. 14). Close by, the so-called Anglian tower on the circuit of the Roman walls in the south-west of the fortress may have been built or refurbished in the eighth or early ninth century, when a short stretch of palisade was also erected along the line of the south-west wall of the Roman fortress, perhaps to repair a breach in the Roman defences.[21] If this is so, and the archaeological evidence strongly suggests it to be the case, we have here a rare example of Anglo-Saxon defensive activity before the Viking threat of the mid and late ninth century.

There are also some indications that the eighth century saw the development within the fortress of a new street pattern cutting across the regular Roman street grid, although excavations on several sites inside the walls, such as Blake Street and The Bedern,[22] indicate that much of the area was a deserted wasteland at least until the tenth century. In the *colonia*, however, there were churches, a monastery, and perhaps even a commercial centre near Skeldergate[23] at this period.

One of the most exciting discoveries (figure 3.2) to have been made in York in recent years was that of a magnificent helmet (dated on stylistic grounds to the early eighth century) found beneath the tenth-century levels at Coppergate.[24] The circumstances of its discovery unfortunately make it impossible to place it in a securely-dated context, but it seems to have been concealed and buried in a wood-lined pit. Interestingly, the site of this discovery lies between the Roman fortress and the Fishergate site further east; thus it comes from a place which corresponds neither to the supposed administrative and ecclesiastical centre in what had been the Roman

Fig. 3.2   The Coppergate helmet (Photo York Archaeological Trust)

principia, nor to the commercial *Eoforwic*. Of its very nature a helmet is what archaeologists call a 'status object', not something which would be in everyday use or in commonplace possession, and its presence at Coppergate suggests that in the eighth century this area of York was not of purely commercial importance.

Both London and York maintained their adminstrative roles during the eighth and ninth centuries: as capitals of kingdoms. Their contemporaries of Ipswich and Saxon Southampton grew to importance purely because of their commercial activities, and it is partly because of this that we now know more about their physical characteristics in the eighth and ninth centuries. Ipswich continued as a port of some significance throughout the medieval period and later; thus the opportunities for excavation on unoccupied sites are few. Saxon Southampton, however, was abandoned in the ninth century and not reoccupied until a thousand years later. The amount of destruction of the archaeological layers has been proportionately less in Saxon Southampton and it is, therefore, the eighth- and·ninth-century commercial centre about which we know most from recent archaeological work.

Ipswich (*Gipeswic*) was founded before the beginning of the seventh century and we have archaeological evidence for its earliest phases (p. 19ff. and figure 2.5). It subsequently grew into a port of considerable national and international importance with an economic strength which has continued right up to the present day. Excavations in the town centre,[25] carried out from 1972 onwards, have shown that early medieval Ipswich was an undefended settlement roughly 50 hectares (*c*. 125 acres) in extent with an economy based predominantly on the production of pottery, designed both for use in the town itself and for distribution to its hinterland. Other economic activities such as the production of metal objects, textiles, leather goods, and bone and antler combs, were carried on as cottage industries throughout the town, particularly in sunken-featured buildings in the back of plots in which there were post-built houses flanking gravelled streets. Agriculture continued to be practised on the periphery of the town. Some of the products from these manufactures must have been surplus to the requirements of the local population, for objects imported from the other side of the North Sea show some form of market trading was being carried on at this date. The discovery of coins, mostly from the middle of the eighth century, suggests the presence of a mint at *Gipeswic*, and the promotion of trade both within the town and beyond. The comparative scarcity of coins of the second half of the eighth century either discovered in excavations or from stray recovery is similar to the circumstances at Fishergate, York, at the same time, and seems to be a characteristic of towns of this period: perhaps an indication of decline in population (as suggested at York) or the result of changing economic practices. The trading settlement of *Hamwic* (Saxon Southampton) covered an area of *c.* 45 hectares in the early medieval period. From its foundation *c.* 700 until its decline and replacement by medieval Southampton sometime in the second half of the ninth century, it was a densely occupied town with a well-defined but non-defensible boundary, marked by a ditch, which was subsequently filled in and replaced by a fence. Within the enclosed area a grid of gravelled streets was flanked by rectangular wooden buildings constructed in a variety of techniques but none indicating any special status.

Some of the buildings discovered in the most recent excavations[26] in the Six Dials area (figure 3.3) had the dual function of dwelling and workshop, and virtually all the buildings were surrounded by yards riddled with rubbish pits in which have been found great quantities of industrial refuse. As at Ipswich, the whole area seems to have been devoted to manufacturing processes but, unlike Ipswich, pottery-making was of the most primitive form and industries such as iron-working, the production of small objects of bronze, lead and gold, textile manufacture, and glass bead-making were of much greater significance. Trade, both local and international, must have been of the highest economic importance at Hamwic, as the very great number of eighth- and ninth-century coins attests.[27] Mark Brisbane, former director of the archaeological project at Southampton, maintains that 'a sophisticated but controlled monied economy was the basis on which the production side of Hamwic functioned'.[28]

Some scholars have suggested that certain sectors of the town may have been inhabited almost exclusively by foreign merchants whose presence, or at any rate influence, is shown by the discovery of large quantities of imported pottery on most sites in the town. More recently, however, study of both coins and animal bones from archaeological excavations has shown there are concentrations neither of coins nor of bones in any part of the town.[29] So there is no discernible differentiation in wealth or standard of living throughout the settlement, and 'foreign enclaves' are now discounted. The discovery of a Christian graveyard, however, with a male:female ratio of 2:1 has been taken to mean that Hamwic was not a family-oriented settlement, but rather one where the economy was highly specialized in manufacturing and trade. This is probably another way in which Hamwic differed from its contemporary Ipswich which shows no such indications. At Ipswich, also, there was at least some marginal agriculture during its early

Fig. 3.3 Reconstruction of the Six Dials area, Saxon Southampton (Brisbane 1988; copyright Southampton City Council)

centuries; this cannot have been the case at Hamwic which was dependent on the surrounding countryside for its food. Thus, although these two trading centres of the eighth and ninth centuries are usually compared as if they were the same, they are appreciably different in several ways. Perhaps, then, there were a number of different types of English trading sites or emporia during the early middle ages, not a single basic form. Some of the other types of towns which were developing at the same time would certainly lead one to expect that, and these will be discussed in the next few pages.

Some other sites in England showed some form of incipient urban development by the middle of the eighth century. Settlements which began as royal estate centres, as temporarily (perhaps seasonally) reoccupied Roman towns, or as specialized industrial focuses, gradually evolved and became towns. At least one site with no Roman antecedents (Hereford; p. 45) seems to have been exceptional in combining administrative, ecclesiastical and commercial functions within a defensive circuit by the eighth or early ninth century and may be considered to have been the most sophisticated purely Anglo-Saxon urban settlement to have grown up in England by that time. Elsewhere, eighth-century defences were known only in Roman towns, and apart from rare exceptions such as York, those defences seem to have been put to little use.

Several royal estate centres which are known from either archaeological or written evidence, or both, grew from their eighth- or ninth-century beginnings to become towns by the tenth century. The example which can best be illustrated from archaeological sources is Northampton, mentioned in the Anglo-Saxon Chronicle in 916–17 when the invading Danes are recorded as having set out from there and from Leicester 'and broke the peace, slaying many men'; but neither has any earlier historical record. The Anglo-Saxon Chronicle entry implies that Northampton and Leicester were by then probably defensible centres which could have been used as strongpoints by the Danish army, but it gives us no information about their physical appearance. Excavations in Northampton since the early 1970s have been able to throw some light on this, although early medieval Leicester remains unknown.

The south-west quarter of modern Northampton, near to the present twelfth-century church of St Peter and not far from the now destroyed medieval castle, seems to have been the focus of a royal, ecclesiastical or aristocratic estate from at least the eighth century (figure 3.4). There is no positive evidence to support the excavator's (John Williams's) view that this was a royal estate centre, it could well have been monastic or otherwise ecclesiastical, but the grandeur of the eighth- and ninth-century buildings discovered east of St Peter's church implies that we are dealing with no ordinary settlement.[30] In the eighth century a massive timber hall was built there on a grand scale and with great precision and skill. The plan of this building, 8.6m wide and 29.7m long, consisting of a huge central hall with a rectangular annex at each end, is similiar to halls on other sites which have been excavated in recent years and interpreted as high-status estate centres. At Northampton a few smaller timber buildings flanked the eighth-century hall to its north-west, west and south-west sides but it seems to have been surrounded by no very well-defined street plan.[31]

In the early ninth century the timber hall at Northampton was rebuilt in stone. In early medieval England the use of masonry for buildings was confined almost entirely to churches, so the stone hall at Northampton must have been of extraordinary status to warrant such treatment. Another stone building was erected at the same time, a little to the west of the great hall and now lying partly under St Peter's church of which it could have been the predecessor. Several interesting structures were discovered associated with these two stone buildings, notably a group of mortar mixers which must have been used in their construction. Further to the east a cemetery of eighth- and ninth-century burials may mark the graveyard of the church of

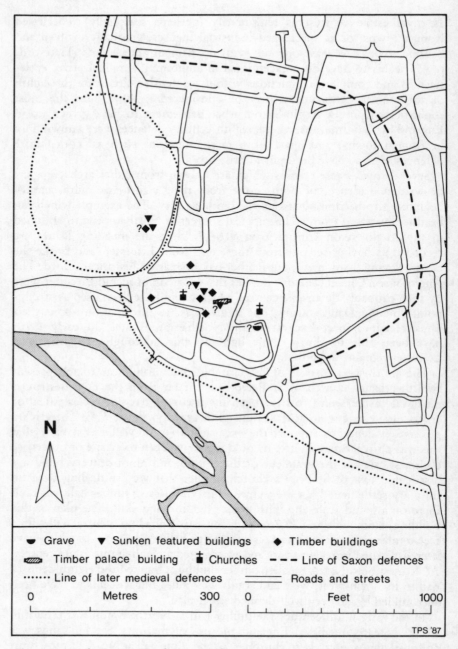

Fig. 3.4 Anglo-Saxon Northampton showing excavated features (after Williams 1979; Williams *et al.* 1985)

St Gregory, not recorded until the twelfth century but thought to have been in existence several centuries earlier.

Altogether, this concentration of features is most remarkable for its date, and justifies the excavator's interpretation of the site as one of more than usual importance. John Williams suggests that what is represented here is a 'palace' (the timber hall and its masonry successor), which was the centre of a royal estate, with a possible minster church (the later St Peter's), and at least one other church (St Gregory). Excavations within the vicinity showed that there had been some form of occupation around the central core over an area of about 8 hectares (20 acres) during the eighth and ninth centuries, but the buildings were flimsy and widely dispersed, and the dates of the phases of occupation are not easy to disentangle.

It was not until the tenth century that economic and commercial developments caused Northampton to grow into a town proper. At that time there was a spectacular increase in the number of buildings within the palace area and signs that they were arranged more formally around streets. Industrial activity, notably the production of pottery, began then and Northampton also had a tenth-century mint. That century also saw the first construction of defences – an earthen rampart and ditch – which were later replaced by a stone wall.

A town which may be compared with Northampton in its royal beginnings is Tamworth, considered to be one of the administrative centres of Offa, king of Mercia, in the late eighth century. A palace complex has been tentatively recognized archaeologically[32] although the remains are far less obvious than those at Northampton. A defensive circuit lying beneath the later, tenth-century, rampart seems to have surrounded the palace and to have enclosed a watermill of eighth-century date (see p. 28 for Offa's correspondence with Charlemagne about 'black stones'). In line with other royal centres one would expect Tamworth to have had some form of supporting settlement either within or immediately beside the palace boundary, but the archaeological evidence is insufficient to give us any idea of what this may have been like. It is unlikely, though, that Tamworth was anything more than a royal estate centre until the tenth century when it, like so many other sites, developed into a town.

Tamworth and Northampton must stand as examples of the development of possible royal estate centres into towns. There are, of course, many other places such as London, Winchester or York where the presence of royal centres in erstwhile Roman towns is well documented. The two sites described here differ from them in that they had no Roman roots, and grew up on previously unoccupied ground.

Several other early medieval sites with possible royal or other high-status connotations have been identified and excavated in recent years, but none grew into a town. The history of Yeavering, Northumberland, covers the sixth and seventh centuries. According to Bede[33] who calls it *Ad Gefrin*, it was abandoned shortly after the visit of King Edwin of Northumbria and St Paulinus in 627, to be replaced by *Maelmin* (probably modern Milfield some 5km away). Nothing now remains above ground to indicate Yeavering's former glory although excavations by Hope-Taylor in the 1950s revealed the remains of once magnificent buildings.[34]

Further south, a similar site (but without historical documentation) has recently been excavated at Foxley, near Malmesbury, Wiltshire.[35] This settlement was made up of buildings similar to those at Yeavering, dating from the sixth and seventh centuries, which also were subsequently abandoned and the site never reoccupied. The rather later Anglo-Saxon 'palace' at Cheddar, Somerset, has also been excavated.[36] Large timber halls and smaller outbuildings were occupied intermittently from the ninth to the thirteenth centuries, but the site was then abandoned without ever having developed into anything more than a rural, albeit royal, estate centre and hunting lodge.

Thus, not all Anglo-Saxon estate centres, either royal or aristocratic, developed into towns. Some, such as Yeavering and Foxley, were abandoned at a time when towns were very much in their infancy in England (the seventh century); others, such as Cheddar, continued into the high middle ages as royal manors or hunting lodges and nothing more; but some, such as Northampton and Tamworth, grew into towns in the tenth century and have continued as such until the present day. The reason for the failure of some estate centres to develop beyond their rural origins cannot be pursued here, but it is a subject which would repay further study in the context of Anglo-Saxon towns.

Some of the Roman towns of Britain which were reoccupied as administrative centres of early Anglo-Saxon kingdoms or chosen to be bishoprics on England's conversion to Christianity were discussed in chapter 2 and their continuing development in the eighth and ninth centuries has been described above. Some other Roman towns appear to have been almost totally deserted after the end of Roman administration at the beginning of the fifth century, only to come back into use some four hundred years later, and then as temporarily or seasonally occupied sites. Their true renaissance as towns cannot be dated before the tenth century when, in common with many other places both with and without Roman roots, they participated in the dramatic expansion of Anglo-Saxon urbanism which will be described in chapter 5.

Gloucester (*Glevum*), for example, can trace its urban origins back to Roman times, but after the middle of the fifth century it seems to have stood as a desolate place, an expanse of dark earth surrounded by decaying, but virtually intact, Roman walls. About 680 the abbey of St Peter was founded inside the circuit of the walls, but seems to have remained isolated, without surrounding secular occupation, until the ninth century when the area of what had been the Roman forum shows some signs of coming back into use (figure 3.5). At that time 2 metres of deposits of organic material (such as dung from cattle and decayed natural rubbish but lacking man-made artifacts) had accumulated, and rubbish pits were cut through the old Roman layers and filled with debris from leather-working and wood-working. Much of the organic accumulation was made up of dung, suggesting that animals were stabled there for considerable periods of time, and the industrial refuse from the pits indicates that some form of manufacturing activity was going on alongside this. But archaeology has been unable to show that there was any permanent occupation in Gloucester (apart from, presumably, inside the abbey precinct) during the ninth century and it was not until the

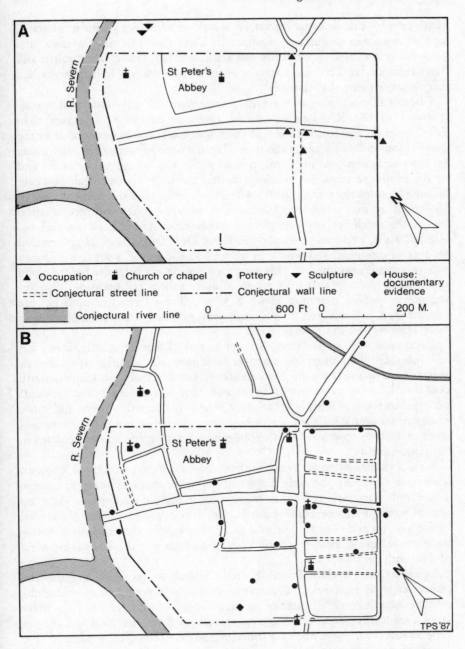

Fig. 3.5 Gloucester in (A) seventh and (B) tenth centuries (after Heighway 1984)

tenth century that an organized street system can be traced within the walls, and a permanent population postulated. Until then one must assume that Gloucester was used sporadically, perhaps seasonally, by agriculturalists and craftsmen, perhaps coming together every now and again to participate in a fair or some form of exchange.[37]

Chester (*Deva*), also was a highly important Roman settlement, head-quarters of the XX Legion and in many ways more important than Gloucester during Roman times. Like Gloucester, it was deserted after the end of Roman Britain, although its walls must have remained virtually intact (at least sufficiently so for them to have withstood a siege as late as the end of the ninth century) and buildings within the walled area stood, however ruinously, until the tenth century when they influenced the street system of the town at that period and later. The only evidence for reoccupation before the tenth century comes from excavations immediately outside the Roman walls, between them and the River Dee (figure 3.6). They revealed an area of ploughed soil which by about 850 supported a small and flimsy sub-rectangular building.[38] This structure had only a brief life before being demolished and replaced by a group of more substantial buildings display-ing some sort of planning along a street. These are attributed by the excavator, T.J. Strickland, to the tenth century when occupation also began once again within the Roman walls.

Excavations in some other Roman towns (Carlisle, *Luguvalium*, for example) are beginning to uncover evidence for similiar sporadic or seasonal occupation within or immediately outside their walls in the ninth century.[39] In no cases can it be shown that street plans or permanent occupation were present by that stage, but it is becoming more and more evident that some form of temporary use was being made of the walled areas of Roman towns before they began to serve again as urban centres in the tenth century.

Several other settlements (but without Roman roots) which we know to have been towns by the early tenth century were also beginning to emerge a hundred years earlier. Two of these were industrial sites which show no sign of having had a permanent population until some years after the arrival of the Vikings and their true origins must be sought in their industrial base – the manufacture of pottery – which began on a large scale about the middle of the ninth century.

By about 850 Thetford, Norfolk, seems already to have been an industrial centre some 60 hectares (150 acres) in extent, and recent finds of eighth-century *sceatta* coins[40] from the vicinity suggest commercial activity there at an even earlier date, although no structures from that period have yet been discovered. Nevertheless, most of the archaeological evidence[41] for Thetford dates from the late ninth century onwards, probably after the Danes wintered there in 869, when groups of kilns producing pottery known to archaeologists as Thetford ware attest the importance of this industry to the development of the town. Gravelled streets and timber buildings are also known from this period, and some primitive form of street planning seems to have been practised in the layout of the town.

At Stamford, Lincolnshire, another pottery-producing centre grew up in the middle of the ninth century before the arrival of the Vikings.[42] Neither

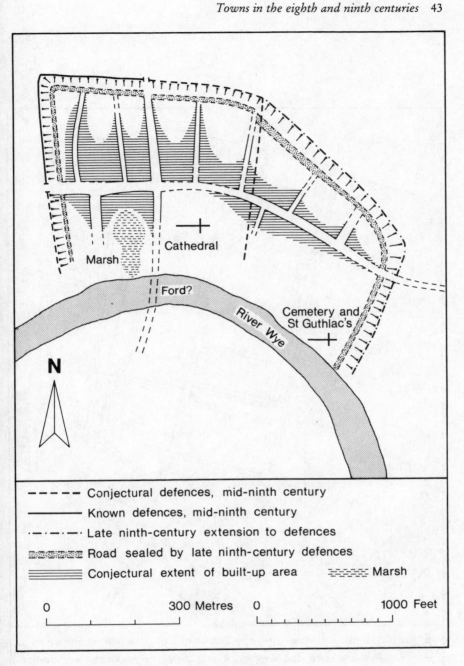

Fig. 3.6   Anglo-Saxon Chester (after Mason 1985)

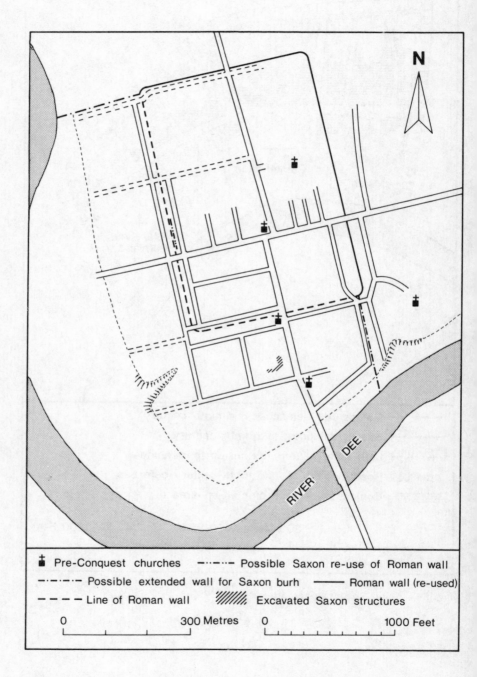

Fig. 3.7　Anglo-Saxon Hereford (after Shoesmith 1980, 1982)

here nor at Thetford is there any evidence for permanent occupation until they were adopted by the Danes as administrative centres some fifty years later, but both stand on navigable rivers, in ideal positions to act as local markets for their regions, and in the case of Stamford even farther afield.

Hereford stands at present as the one settlement in Anglo-Saxon England which has been shown by archaeological excavation and historical research to have had both newly-built, non-Roman, defences and a deliberately laid-out street pattern by the late eighth century or early ninth century.[43] Hereford was founded on a virgin site, beside a Roman road and a crossing of the River Wye, but some 8km east of the Roman town of Kenchester which, once abandoned about 400, was never reoccupied. Hereford (figure 3.7) was chosen as the site of a bishopric in 676 and at about the same time a monastic house (St Guthlac's) and cemetery were established. A simple timber building and burials have been discovered by excavation in the Castle Green area of the modern city and interpreted as the first wooden church or chapel of St Guthlac's monastery with its cemetery. Sometime in the eighth century a grid of streets was laid out to the north-west and by the middle of the ninth century they were surrounded by a defensive rampart which, however, excluded the monastery, leaving it in an exposed position to the south-east. Later in the ninth century the defences were extended eastwards to enclose St Guthlac's, and a regular grid of streets may have covered the whole intramural area apart from the cathedral and monastic precincts.

A number of rectangular timber buildings aligned with their gable ends to the street have been discovered in the north-west corner of the defended area, and evidence for industrial activities such as metal-working is well attested. It can be argued that Hereford is the earliest urban settlement in England without Roman antecedents to display administrative functions (primarily ecclesiastical through its cathedral and monastery; royal associations are with 'Offa's palace' at Sutton Walls, 6km north of Hereford), domestic and industrial activities, a recognizable street pattern, and defences. Hereford's defences and street pattern suggest that it may have been the prototype for the late ninth-century or early tenth-century urban developments which were to take place in the kingdom of Wessex through the stimulus of King Alfred and in response to the Viking threat, and which will be descibed in chapter 5.

Chapter 4

Towns in the Viking homelands

In this chapter we leave western Europe with its traditions inherited from the Roman world and look more closely at northern Europe whence the Vikings launched their piratical raids in the years just before 800. There is a tendency for both scholars and the general public to regard the Scandinavian homelands of the Vikings as barbaric and undeveloped, with ill-defined boundaries, where over-population and desire for adventure led to violent migration. This is a partial view which the following pages will try to modify, but the area certainly lacked direct contact with Roman civilization and this led to the indigenous development of towns which differed in many respects from their counterparts in north-west Europe.

The region which will be discussed in this chapter and in chapter 6 is an enormous one, centring on the Baltic but stretching to the shores of the Atlantic in the west and the Black Sea and Caspian Sea in the east. This vast area was the home of Nordic (Germanic) and Slavonic tribes, Fenno-Ugrian groups, and Balts.

This chapter will concentrate on the Nordic Scandinavian part of this widespread area, the real homeland of the Vikings; an area comprising such long distances and varied natural conditions that it cannot be considered as a single unit, either culturally or in its settlement pattern.

Geographical and historical background

The oldest geographical descriptions of this far northern edge of the world come from the works of Tacitus, Ptolemy (figure 4.1) and Jordanes who speak of 'the islands of the Baltic' inhabited by barbarian tribes. Even in the eleventh century Adam of Bremen had the same geographical concept.

We now know that these 'islands' included a number of large and small islands and also, in the north-east, a large stretch of land joined to the continental mainland: the Scandinavian peninsula. This largely consists of a

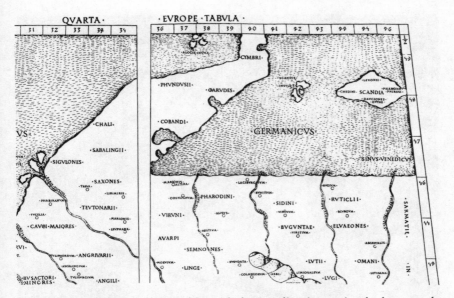

Fig. 4.1 Ptolemy's map of the Baltic, with the Scandinavian peninsula shown as the island of *Scandia* (after Nordenskiöld 1889)

plateau of pre-Cambrian granite covered, mainly on the Atlantic-facing west, by younger, stratified, heavily folded, and tilted rocks. In the south the granite is covered by limestone and chalk.

Today's landscape is the result of the ice ages having had one of their most important ice-generating points here. Time and again enormous glaciers of inland ice flattened the land, and on melting, they left behind them moraines and water-sorted deposits. The ensuing rock and moraine mean that large parts of Scandinavia have never been cultivable, supporting only forest and mountain heath.

The limestone region of the south (figure 4.2), covered by the ice-age glaciers only when they were at their greatest extent, is much more suited to agriculture. This makes up the whole of what was once the Danish area of south Scandinavia (Jutland, Fünen, Zealand, Scania and south Halland) and is the most northerly fringe of the great plain which stretches between the Baltic and the North Sea.

The glaciers of the ice age also forced the land down to several hundred metres below its natural level. When the ice melted and the pressure eased the earth's crust attempted to revert to its original level, and the consequent 'land elevation' is still noticeable in parts of Scandinavia, being at its most pronounced in the interior of the North where the land is still rising by *c.* 100cm per century. The land in the central parts of Sweden and Norway is today rising at the rate of *c.* 40–50cm per century, whereas Denmark lies on the line of equilibrium, with little movement.

Large parts of the flat eastern areas of Scandinavia are a brackish-water archipelago (figure 4.3) which was much more extensive a thousand years ago when arms of the sea penetrated much further inland than they do today and when water filled the deep fissure valleys. They formed the lines

Fig. 4.2   The south Scandinavian countryside typified by that of Fuglie parish, Scania (Photo Jan Norrman)

Fig. 4.3   Typical countryside of central Sweden: Tuna in Alsike, Mälaren valley (Photo Jan Norrman)

of communication in early periods. All heavy transports went by boat on open water and waterways, or by sledge over the ice in winter. There were few land routes, and overland communications between the areas of settlement were obstructed either by densely forested areas of moraine or by mountains.

The many small tribes mentioned by Jordanes in the sixth century occupied geographically limited areas bordered by forest and had hardly any overland contacts. When states began to crystallize in the early medieval period (known in Scandinavia as the late iron age, AD 500–1100) their component parts were linked together by water. Denmark came to encompass the islands and peninsulas of the limestone regions of the south; Norway the fjords and mountains of the North Sea and Atlantic coastland; and Sweden the large open expanse of land in the east and tracts of inland forests.

As early as the stone and bronze ages parts of Scandinavia supported an agricultural economic system which was continually expanding from the originally limited core areas into the marginal soils of predominantly hunting districts. The difficulties imposed upon agriculture by the climate in both the core and the marginal areas were outweighed by excellent and accessible pastures, opportunities for hunting and fishing, and, later, for mineral extraction.

There are numerous archaeological remains of the farming and hunting peoples of prehistoric Scandinavia. Well preserved in a landscape unsuited to ploughing, the features make Scandinavia an area where the study of settlement development is at its most rewarding. Settlement forms were well adapted to the physical geography. In the flat land of south Scandinavia the undulating hills and plains supported a settlement pattern made up of widely scattered long-houses. In the early iron age they tended to coalesce into villages, although the population was a mobile one, moving on when new, previously uncultivated, land was needed to replace fields impoverished by primitive farming methods. During the late iron age (early middle ages) this form of settlement was supplemented or replaced by scattered groups of sunken-featured buildings. It was not until the two centuries from 900 that the population established permanent villages which can still be seen today.[1]

There were no physical factors in south Scandinavia to prevent the development of a full-scale arable landscape, and the topography did not impose any limitations on the location of sites. But in the granite areas further north the situation was different. There, a settlement pattern of widely dispersed, isolated farmsteads was the norm until c. 1000. The earliest farmsteads were strung out along watersheds and beside inlets of the sea and only grew closer together when the population increased. It was not until the transition to the middle ages in the eleventh century that small villages began to develop,[2] and even then only in the eastern part of this area. At the same time new settlements began to grow up on marginal land in the forests, between and outside the areas of earlier occupation.

Over the whole of Scandinavia some type of social stratification is discernible in the agricultural communities. Demand for traded and manufactured products began to increase as indigenous raw materials such as furs, iron and certain agricultural products were becoming ever more sought after in other parts of Europe. It is in the light of this combination of local demand and foreign requirements that we must view the development of specialized sites and, eventually, towns.

Historians such as Pirenne, Bolin and Adolf Schück, and archaeologists such as Arbman[3] believed that the towns of Scandinavia were foreign introductions resulting from the long-distance trade, mainly in luxury goods, which followed new routes between east and west once Mediterranean-dominated trade declined in the early middle ages. Today we know more about local conditions in Scandinavia at that date and the accepted hypothesis now is that towns began to develop in response to their immediate hinterlands with which they were closely integrated.

Until recently only a few of these nucleated settlements were known: Hedeby, Birka, Staraya Ladoga and Kaupang, for instance; but now there are many more sites, newly discovered through archaeological excavations, mostly small markets and manufacturing centres. No doubt many more remain to be discovered.

Denmark and Scania

The land which stretches from the River Eider to the forests of Småland (Denmark before 1658) is the part of Scandinavia which has had the closest contacts with the trade routes of western Europe since the bronze age and iron age (figure 4.4). It is a lowland area and a direct continuation of the plateau north of the Alps.

The region was the core area of the Nordic bronze age, and then during the Roman iron age it contained sites which seem to have been the most important tribal centres in Scandinavia even though they were not permanently located on the same spot. Economic centres with craftmanship, trade and exchange gradually grew up, many of them situated in natural harbours on estuaries. Artifacts demonstrating wealth have been discovered at Dankirke immediately south of Ribe on the west coast of Jutland, and Gudme with its harbour at Lundeborg on the east coast of the island of Fünen. Their origins date from the earliest centuries AD, and they continued in occupation well into the seventh and eighth centuries.

At Dankirke Elise Thorvildsen[4] excavated the remains of a number of successively occupied buildings, situated on a ridge stretching out into the marshland of Jutland's west coast. They contained great quantities of glass sherds of migration-period (fifth- and sixth-century) date, most of which represent the fragmentary remains of green-glass drinking vessels (beakers) with applied trails. There are also other migration-period types and also some from the Roman iron age. This site is remarkable for the discovery of some seventh- and eighth-century sceattas; at the time of the excavations they were among the first to have been found in Scandinavia. The artifacts from Dankirke are of a completely different character from those discovered on more recently excavated contemporary villages in Jutland, such as Sædding and Vorbasse. Dankirke's role is still obscure, but it seems to

Fig. 4.4 Map of the Baltic region showing countries, provinces and peoples

have been a farm with unusually close contacts with western Europe, not a nucleated settlement.

The situation of Gudme is somewhat different, with Gudme itself lying a short distance from the coast and its harbour of Lundeborg at the mouth of a rivulet.[5] Large quantities of gold and silver of migration-period date have been found at both sites although Lundeborg alone shows signs of occupation. This area was important from the Roman iron age and earlier but it never developed into a Viking-age centre, and nothing is known of these two sites from written sources.

Roman historians and geographers name the tribes who lived in Scandinavia at the time when they were writing, but it is not until the eighth century that we have more definite information: the distorted names of Danish kings and descriptions of Christian missions such as that of St Willibrord. The Royal Frankish Annals of the beginning of the ninth century

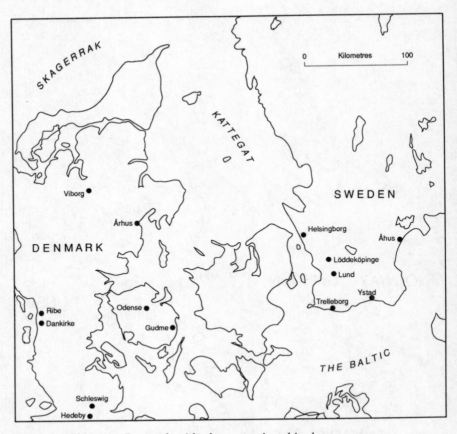

Fig. 4.5 Viking-age Denmark with places mentioned in the text

are more illuminating, telling us about the construction, in 808, of Dane-virke, the great defensive wall across the Jutland peninsula near Schleswig, by King Godfred of Denmark, and the settlement of Sliesthorp (Hedeby) in the same year. From then onwards there is a steady stream of information until the end of the ninth century, mainly from the annals but also in works such as the biography of St Ansgar (*Vita Ansgarii*) written by Rimbert, his successor as archbishop of Bremen.[6] This important and informative work was used as a source by Adam of Bremen[7] for his history of the church (*Gesta Hammaburgensis ecclesiae pontificum*), written *c.* 1070, in which he describes Ansgar's and Rimbert's visits to Hedeby and Ribe in the ninth century, and the establishment of the first bishoprics in Denmark at Hedeby, Ribe and Århus in 948 (figure 4.5).

This is the simple outline of events provided by the written sources. Archaeology has been able to show that the reality is much more complex, and excavations over the past few decades have provided sufficient evidence for us to build up a much more detailed picture of the early history of the area.

One of these excavated sites is Ribe in west Jutland,[8] by the marshland beside the Ribe river a little way from the coast (figure 4.6). In the high

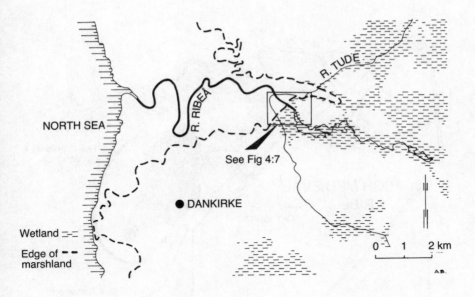

Fig. 4.6 The environs of Ribe (after Bencard 1981)

middle ages Ribe, with its castle and cathedral, was of prime importance for the Danish kingdom and a natural point of contact with western Europe. The high medieval town with all its institutional buildings such as the cathedral, monasteries and castle, lay on the south side of the river, but no traces of a Viking-age or earlier predecessor have ever been discovered there. When, therefore, Mogens Bencard, then director of Ribe Museum, discovered eighth-century occupation layers in a suburb of the high medieval town on the north side of the river during excavations in the 1960s it caused something of a sensation in archaeological circles.

Ribe stands in a river valley whose far-reaching flood plain is confined between slightly higher sandy hillocks. The high medieval town grew up at the point where the river ceased to be tidal and where mill dams were built to form large stretches of open water; it was bounded by a moat. Before the excavations of the 1960s a few Viking-age artifacts had been discovered on the low ridge along the river's north bank and the subsequent archaeological investigations revealed occupation debris with thin clay floors and manufacturing refuse, some sunken-featured buildings, and a rubbish layer of considerable thickness consisting very largely of cow dung, all lying above traces of ploughing. Further excavations in 1986 by Stig Jensen revealed more than six superimposed clay floors of the same type as those found earlier.

The clay floors have been shown to be the remains of workshops where combs, glass beads and bronze jewellery were made. The types of artifacts and a large number of sceattas date the beginning of the occupation to the early eighth century, and newly-reported dendrochronological analyses give a more precise starting date of *c.* 710. Earliest Ribe may have been

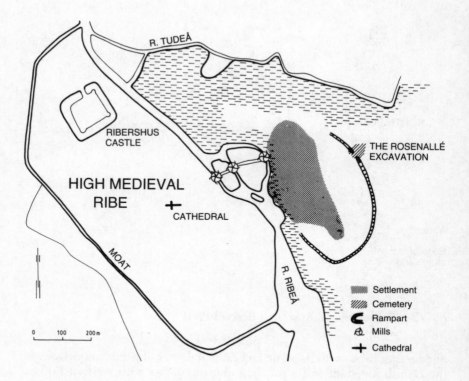

Fig. 4.7 Map of Ribe showing the pre-Viking and Viking-age settlement including the defences discovered in the 1989 excavations (after Feveile *et al.* 1990)

inhabited only seasonally, serving as a market centre, but the presence of ditches defining plots of land 8m wide at right angles to the river may indicate a more permanent population. Until excavations in 1989 there were few archaeological traces of settlement in Ribe after *c.* 800 and before *c.* 1000, and it was unclear whether there was any continuity between the settlement on the north bank and the Ribe of the high middle ages. Nevertheless, as Rimbert tells us that Ansgar visited Ribe in the ninth century and Adam of Bremen mentions a bishop there from 948, there must have been some type of nucleated settlement at Ribe throughout the Viking age. The 1989 excavations on a site in Rosenallé[9] showed that there was occupation to the north and north-east of this riverine settlement from at least the eighth century, as attested by a cemetery of cremation graves. A short stretch of a ninth-century boundary ditch and a tenth-century rampart and ditch were also discovered; their reconstructed line (as shown on figure 4.7) suggests that the Viking-age settlement of Ribe may have covered some 10 hectares of the sand spit which lies between two areas of wetlands.

Åhus (figures 4.8, 4.9), near the eastern border of Viking-age Denmark (in the present Swedish province of Scania), is similar to Ribe in that it was occupied as a market centre in the early eighth century. It was also inhabited during the Viking age and medieval period, although its location

Fig. 4.8 Early medieval Åhus and its hinterland (after Callmer 1986)

changed over time (see below). Unlike Ribe, however, it is not mentioned in written sources until *c.* 1200.

Åhus lies by the former mouth of the Helgeå river which flows from the highlands of Småland through Hammarsjön, a wide, flat area of lakeland near modern Kristianstad. The Helgeå's outflow from lake Hammarsjön bends sharply to the north parallel to the Baltic shoreline, and in the twelfth century a castle and a small town known as Åhus (from *aos* = the estuary) were founded by the archbishop of Lund. Recent excavations a little way upstream, directed by Johan Callmer,[10] have revealed some concentrations of occupation, the earliest of which dates from the first half of the eighth century. An area between this site and the medieval town was occupied at the end of the eighth century and into the ninth century.

There is, however, a structural difference between these two settlements. The earlier seems to have been a seasonally-occupied market centre whereas the later was a permanent settlement even though it seems also to have been a market centre. The finds from both are very rich, with about 70,000 fragments of glass and evidence of bead–making on the earlier site; the later settlement shows specialization in bronze and antler working rather than glass-bead production. The pottery (some of it of the *Feldberg* type, see figure 6.4) shows close contacts with the Slavonic region across the Baltic to the south, and there are also sherds of Tating ware jugs from the Rhineland.

Fig. 4.9   The medieval settlements of Åhus lie beside the River Helgeå, the oldest is upstream and the most recent at the mouth of the river (in the background here) (Photo Jan Norrman)

Sometime in the ninth century the site was deserted or moved to another site and nothing more is known of the occupation of the area until the foundation of the high medieval town.

On the former southern border of the Danish kingdom, where Jutland is almost cut off from continental Europe by fjords, rivers, and marshland, lies the settlement of *Hedeby*, also founded in the eighth century and in continuous occupation until the end of the Viking age.[11] The dry land between the Schlei fjord and the rivers to the west, which could be traversed with ease in the early middle ages, is only about 7km wide. Since the bronze age the trackway known as *Hærvejen* (Military Road) or *Oxevejen* (Ox Road) has run along the watershed of the Jutland peninsula, its route still being marked by numerous burial mounds. It crosses into modern Germany through this 7km-wide gap in the natural defences: the stretch of land which needed to be defended to protect Denmark from attack from the south. This is where Danevirke[12] was built (figure 4.10); its defensive capabilities have been appreciated from the pre-Viking age to the present day. The Royal Frankish Annals say that Danevirke was first built by King Godfred in 808 but archaeological excavations in the 1970s told a different story. Some sections cut through its ramparts revealed quantities of well-preserved timbers suitable for dating by dendrochronology and it is now known that the first phase of the Danevirke was constructed as early as 737. It was added to by later rebuildings and modifications in a complicated sequence whose chronology is not yet completely understood, but it is

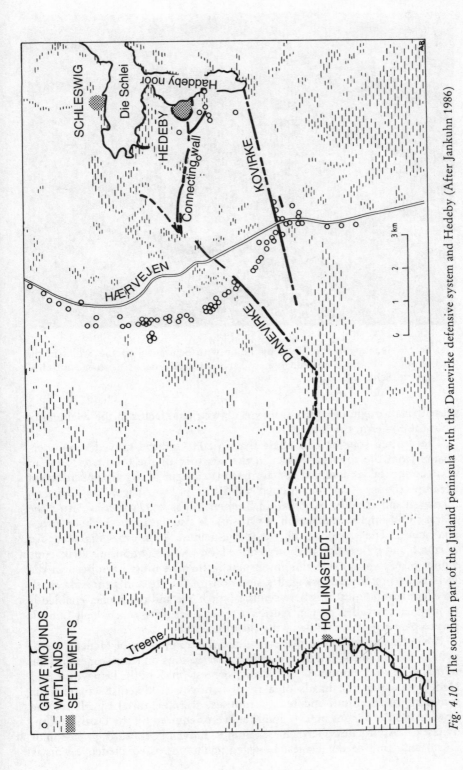

Fig. 4.10 The southern part of the Jutland peninsula with the Danevirke defensive system and Hedeby (After Jankuhn 1986)

Fig. 4.11 Hedeby on the Haddeby Noor with Schleswig on the Schlei in the background. (Photo Archäologisches Landesmuseum der Christian-Albrechts-Universität, Schloss Gottorf)

clear that throughout its life Danevirke was a vital factor in the wielding of political power in the area.

The written sources also relate that in 808 Godfred moved some merchants from the town of Reric, in the territory of the Obotrite Slavs, to *Sliasthorp*. This as assumed to have been the origin of the urban settlement *Hedeby* (figure 4.11) mentioned as *Sliaswig* by Ansgar, as *Sliaswig*, *Sliaswich* and *Heidiba* by Adam of Bremen and as *æt Hædum* in Alfred the Great's Old English translation of Orosius. It also figures in Arabian travellers' tales. The mingling of the place-names *Sliasthorp*, *Sliaswich*, *æt Hædum* and *Haithabu* (first mentioned on the neighbouring Erik rune stone, p. 62) shows that this important settlement must have been in the vicinity of present Schleswig. Its situation on the Jutland peninsula, with excellent communications between the North Sea and the Baltic, enabled it to play an unrivalled part in Baltic trade, equivalent to that which Lübeck was to play after the middle of the twelfth century.

The defensive system of Danevirke and the trading site of Hedeby were, as in all border areas, points of conflict. Inscriptions on rune stones and the writings of contemporary historians suggest that both Danevirke and Hedeby were in the hands of a royal family with Swedish connections sometime in the ninth and tenth centuries, were captured by Henry the Fowler and the Saxons in 934, and then were acquired by the Danish Gorm dynasty.[13] After a new German assault in 983, Sven Forkbeard, grandson of Gorm and king of the Danes, besieged and repossessed Hedeby. This is mentioned on two of the rune stones. The border zone remained in Danish hands for a long time thereafter, with Danevirke being rebuilt and extended throughout the centuries up to *c.* 1200, and even used as a defence as late as the wars between Denmark and Germany in the nineteenth century, and in the Second World War.

The location of Viking-age Hedeby was for a long time identified with modern Schleswig. In 1896 the Danish archaeologist Sophus Müller suggested that the site should be sought within the semi-circular rampart by Haddeby Noor, an inlet of the Schlei opposite Schleswig, where there were thick occupation deposits. The present parish church of Haddeby stands at the mouth of the Noor, but it has no physical connection with the rampart.

At Müller's instigation, the museum at Kiel began excavations inside the walled area in 1900. They quickly confirmed his theory about the site of the Viking-age settlement and in the following years there were excavations in the town directed first by F. Knorr and then, in the campaigns of 1930–9, by Herbert Jankuhn, later professor at Göttingen. Trial excavations at the beginning of the 1960s led to further excavations under the direction of Kurt Schietzel in which some 5 per cent of the area inside the ramparts were investigated, producing vast quantities of artifacts and other evidence.

In 1953 divers searched the bed of Haddeby Noor opposite the area enclosed by the semi-circular rampart and discovered a Viking-age ship which was raised at the end of the 1970s. A number of jetties were discovered between the ship and the shore. Spectacular objects such as a church bell, a collection of dies for the production of Viking-age gold and silver jewellery, and many other artifacts of great significance for our knowledge of trade, industry and communications during the Viking age were retrieved from their vicinity.

Hedeby stands to the west of Haddeby Noor on the banks of a former stream (figure 4.12). It covers an area of 24 hectares within the rampart. Excavations in the occupation deposit which is up to 2m thick have shown that while the site was inhabited the narrow stream was canalized by being lined with planks, and that it was crossed by several bridges. Because of the rise in the water table since Viking times the occupation deposit is waterlogged, thus preserving the remains of buildings which once stood on the site, and much other organic material.

As the buildings had no special foundations, the upright timbers used in their construction quickly became useless. They rotted at ground level and had to be replaced every ten to twenty years. A plot of land within which a house stood may, therefore, show a sequence of superimposed buildings whose archaeologically well-preserved timbers, mainly from below ground level, can be dated by dendrochronology. Unfortunately the occupation layers around them were so badly disturbed by contemporary digging that there is now hardly any discernible stratigraphy and most of the artifacts discovered cannot be assigned to specific levels. They therefore are no help in detailed chronology.

Most of the town today is surrounded by a rampart up to 10m high. It has only a few openings: one in both north and south, one in the west through which the stream flows, and a wide gap which may have resulted from the damage caused by Sven Forkbeard's documented attack at the end of the

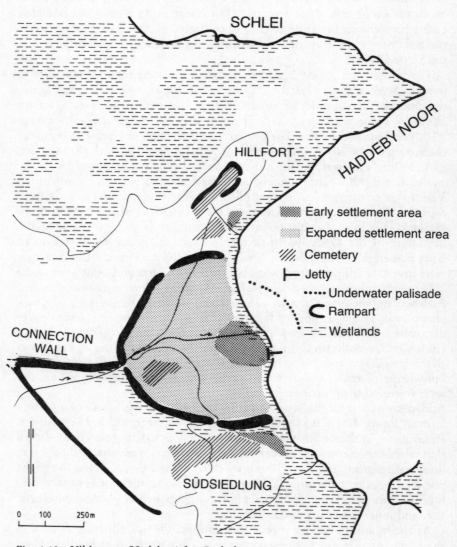

Fig. 4.12 Viking-age Hedeby (after Jankuhn 1986)

tenth century. The rampart extends down to the Noor where the shore is
sufficiently steep to prevent access between the ends of the rampart and the
water. It originated quite late in the history of the town with its core, an
earth bank 3m high, not being built until the tenth century. It soon
underwent rebuilding and alteration until it reached its present height.

The late date of its construction is shown by the early occupation debris
which lies near and beneath each end of the rampart and probably represents phases when Hedeby was an open, undefended, settlement.
Immediately to the north and outside the rampart, however, a fortress
(*Hochburg*) stands on an outcrop of diluvial clay, between the town and the

Schlei. This is earlier in date than the Viking age, but it probably acted as a refuge for the town population. A small cemetery lies within it.

The town rampart is joined to the main branch of Danevirke by the so-called 'connecting rampart' (*Forbindelsesvolden*) from which runs to the south another, lower, rampart concentric with that around Hedeby. It has a dry ditch outside it suggesting it was defensive, not just some sort of siegework. Hedeby's incorporation into the Danevirke system shows that the town was founded south of the earliest, eighth-century, Danevirke defences which were subsequently modified to include it.

Both within the defended area and, particularly, beyond it to the south-west lie extensive cemeteries whose graves are not visible above the ground surface. With the exception of a few graves in the bottom layer of the south-west cemetery and those in the fortress which are cremations under low mounds, all the graves in the cemeteries are inhumations: burials with or without wooden coffins and sometimes in wooden chambers. The grave-goods in those which are oriented east–west (often thought to indicate Christian practices) are usually few and undatable but the chamber graves are more richly furnished, most often with spear and shield and perhaps a wooden or bronze vessel. These include a very rich grave excavated in 1908 and thought to be an aristocratic or princely burial. It contained three heavily-armed men interred in a chamber which was surmounted by a boat covered by a low mound. H.H. Andersen has recently argued that this was the grave of one of the pre-Gorm rulers.

The chamber graves lie in an isolated group beside some form of 'funerary way', whereas the graves with simple coffins lie together as in churchyards. The largest group of coffin graves is west of the central occupation area within the rampart and comprises at least two thousand burials. There is another coffin-grave cemetery west of the South Settlement (*Südsiedlung*), immediately south of the walled area. It was made up of several distinct layers of graves: beneath the east–west oriented graves there were a number of north–south oriented examples which in their turn overlay simple cremations with pottery from the eighth century. These could be burials either of the population of a forerunner to the ninth- and tenth-century trading centre or of an agricultural settlement.

South and west of Hedeby, groups of larger mounds are associated with rune stones (figure 4.13). These mounds have been interpreted as graves of members of the royal family who ruled the region during the early tenth century, but one of them may date from Sven Forkbeard's conquest at the end of that century. Two of the four rune stones which have been discovered near Hedeby refer to this event and one of them stands near one of the mounds, so there may be a connection.

The extensive excavations at Hedeby have revealed immense quantities of artifacts, particularly of wood, antler and textiles. Many of them represent waste from industrial processes about which they provide a great deal of information (chapter 7).

Knorr and Jankuhn used a system of excavating trial trenches about $10m^2$ in extent over virtually the whole of the inhabited area. Jankuhn discovered that there were early centres of occupation both within the rampart and outside it to the north and south beside the mouths of streams flowing into

Fig. 4.13 The Erik rune stone, now in the Archäologisches Landesmuseum, Schloss Gottorf (Photo Archäologisches Landesmuseum)

the Noor from the west, and that their associated cemeteries lay a little further away from the shore. The central area gradually expanded into the large settlement which was finally surrounded by the rampart in the tenth century. In the early core of the central settlement a strip of land, about 80 × 30m in extent and running north–south, revealed a dense concentration of moulds and other refuse from workshops making metal objects, and also a furnace for melting glass to make beads. This area seems to have maintained the same industrial function throughout the lifetime of the settlement. Other industrial activities were carried on elsewhere; thus, many small buildings beside the rampart contained loom weights and other remains of textile manufacture, and another area shows signs of iron-working and smithing. There were also concentrations of refuse from the manufacture of combs, pins, and other objects of antler, bone and horn. The evidence shows that industrial activities were carried on throughout the whole settlement, and that there was no specialization into craftsmen's and merchants' quarters.

Although Kurt Schietzel now believes that Hedeby's contacts across the North Sea were negligible (reflected only in a tiny quantity of archaeological finds), Hedeby's location on the east side of the Jutland peninsula was of the utmost significance. Any cargoes from the North Sea to Hedeby would have had to be unloaded and carried overland along a route protected by the Danevirke. Hollingstedt has always been thought to have served as the harbour at the west end of this route but recent analyses have shown that it did not develop as a port until the eleventh century,[14] probably to serve as the westerly outport of Schleswig.

Hedeby seems to have started life sometime in the middle of the eighth century when the *Südsiedlung* was expanding, to have flourished particularly in the ninth and tenth centuries and then finally to have lost its importance, to be replaced by the new town of Schleswig which grew up during the eleventh century on the north bank of the Schlei. Dendrochronological analyses of timbers from buildings and wells in Hedeby give a series of dates from 811 to 1020, and the earliest date for Schleswig, obtained from timbers found during excavations in the medieval town, is 1071.[15]

Icelandic sagas describe the destruction of Hedeby, first through Harald Hardrada's burning of the town in 1050 and then by a Slavonic assault in 1066.[16] Some time after the abandonment of Hedeby, Schleswig grew to be the main trading centre in south Angeln, but in the thirteenth century it was supplanted by Lübeck which took over vital parts of the transit function of this region. Lübeck's trade depended on the rivers Elbe and Trave, and Schleswig then became merely an outpost of Danish power.

It was not until the tenth century that the Danish kingdom began to acquire other towns. *Århus*, for instance, named as the seat of a bishop as early as the middle of the tenth century, has been the scene of many excavations by H.H. Andersen and H.J. Madsen[17] which have shown that at that date a semi-circular rampart defined an area 4–5 hectares in extent, part of which was occupied by small sunken-featured buildings with daubed walls. Large numbers of tenth-century artifacts were found associated with the buildings. This area subsequently became the precinct of the medieval cathedral.

Near the north end of *Hærvejen*, where the river Nørreå cuts through the central Jutland plateau, the town of *Viborg* grew up in the eleventh century around the old site of the Jutland legal centre – the 'Thing'. The high medieval town with its cathedral (the bishopric is known from the eleventh century) lies at the edge of the river valley and has revealed no signs of Viking-age occupation, but waterlogged remains of eleventh-century date have been discovered down beside the lake through which the river flows. This late Viking-age town is unusual in Scandinavia for its inland situation with primarily land communications.

At Odense there is sixteenth-century pictorial evidence for one of the Danish late tenth-century ring-forts, Nonnebakken. This suggests some Viking-age presence in the area, and Odense's early importance is reflected by its being chosen as a bishop's seat in 988. But there is virtually no archaeological evidence for settlement until well after 1000.[18]

In eastern Denmark (Scania, now a part of Sweden) only two places are known from the earliest written sources: Lund and Helsingborg, both mentioned by Adam of Bremen in the 1070s.

The location of Helsingborg at the narrowest point of the Öresund suggests that it was where the straits were crossed in the Viking age, but the earliest known settlement stands on the cliff top high above the water, and is of twelfth-century date.[19] For *Lund*, however, there is archaeological evidence for settlement in the late tenth century. Excavations have been carried out in Lund since the beginning of this century by archaeologists such as Karlin, Blomqvist and Mårtensson.[20] Until recently, the town was thought to have originated no earlier than 1020 but new discoveries have changed this view, with dendrochronological analysis of wooden coffins in at least one of the excavated churchyards now giving a date of *c.* 990.

In its earliest phase Lund seems to have consisted only of an east–west main street, thus making it similar to other villages in the surrounding countryside but differing from them by having one or two churches. By the 1020s Knut the Great, king of Denmark, had established a mint there, and in *c.* 1050 five new churches were built. The bishopric was founded *c.* 1060. The later medieval town subsequently grew up around what was an important ecclesiastical centre with a cathedral, many churches and town walls.

Sites of Viking-age harbours, but without berthing facilities such as jetties, have been found in many of the estuaries around the coast of Scania. In Ystad, for example, small groups of sunken-featured buildings on the Litorina ridge, and finds indicative of fishing, craft-working and trade probably represent a non-agricultural settlement with its buildings irregularly arranged along the shoreline.[21] Some sunken-featured buildings on the Litorina ridge have also been found at Trelleborg. This settlement must have been vast, *c.* 800m long and defined at each end by a rivulet.[22] In 1989, excavation on the site of the former medieval castle of Trelleborg revealed remains of a ring–fort of the type which is thought to be typical of late tenth-century fortifications in Denmark. This new discovery has long been expected because the name of the present Swedish town is the same as Trelleborg in Zealand where one of the tenth-century Danish forts stands.

Scania also has many non-urban market centres (*köpingeorter*) which lie slightly inland from the coast. Their dating is uncertain, they are not mentioned in written sources until the later medieval period, and only a couple of them have been the scene of archaeological excavations.

Löddeköpinge lies about 4km from the coast, on the north bank of the Lödde river (figure 4.14), and has been excavated by Tom Ohlsson. A semicircular bank and ditch enclosing many sunken-featured buildings of early Viking-age date has been interpreted as the boundary of a non-urban market centre with no cemeteries to indicate permanent occupation.[23] If the buildings and rampart are contemporaneous then we have here a unique example of early Viking fortifications, but there is no firm evidence of this.

Three villages with *köpinge* names lie a couple of kilometres inland from Trelleborg. They may originally have been part of the area around a single early medieval market centre on the Litorina ridge where Trelleborg stands today. A further site, *Stora Köpinge* on the Nybro river, 4–5km from the sea and 10km east of Ystad, seems to have been occupied slightly later than the *köpingeorter* elsewhere in Scania, with its church being consecrated in the thirteenth century. It cannot have had any connection with the early medieval settlement at Ystad.

Fig. 4.14 Löddeköpinge and estuary of the River Löddeå from the east (Photo Jan Norrman)

Norway

Norway (figure 4.15) is not mentioned in *Vita Ansgarii*, and only one town in Norway is mentioned in Adam of Bremen's *Gesta*: Trondheim, 'the greatest settlement in Norway with many churches and visitors'. One Norwegian port is, however, referred to in another, ninth-century, source. An appendix to the Old English translation of Orosius's world history written at the court of King Alfred of Wessex in the late ninth century describes the journey of the Norwegian Ottar (Old English *Othere*) from his home in the far north of Norway to Hedeby in Denmark.[24] On the way there he visited a port called Skiringssal (Old English *Sciringesheal*) in southern Norway. This has been identified as Kaupang in Tjølling parish, Vestfold (figure 4.16).

The settlement of Kaupang stands in a narrow, sloping meadow between a high rocky ridge and the Viking-age sea whose water level was *c.* 3m above that of today. A small sample of the occupation deposit was excavated by Charlotte Blindheim[25] in the 1960s when she found the remains of six buildings irregularly arranged along the shore, and two stone jetties (figure 4.17).

Imported Rhenish and Slavonic pottery, objects from the British Isles, silver coins from East and West, and balance weights all show the trading activities of the site, and there are also traces of the manufacture of objects of iron, precious metals and glass. Ship building or ship repairing seem also to have been important in the economy of Kaupang. Most of the artifacts discovered in the settlement date from the ninth century, as do the grave-goods from the nearby boat-grave inhumation cemetery.

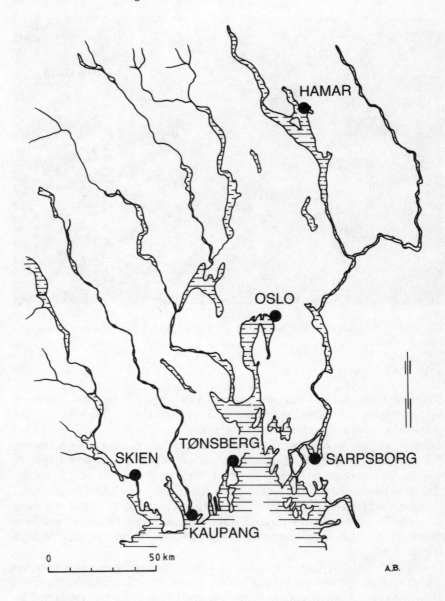

Fig. 4.15   Map of the Oslo fjord (Viken) with places mentioned in the text

Kaupang is ringed by cemeteries. The boat-grave inhumation cemetery of Bikjholberget lies on an islet on the east side of the inlet, and was excavated forty years ago. A very extensive cemetery of cremations under mounds at North Kaupang which lies to the north and north-west was excavated by Nicholaysen in the nineteenth century and there are also some cremation cemeteries south of the settlement and on the island of Lamøya further east.

Most of the finds from the inhumation graves and the settlement date from the ninth century. Many of the cremations, however, contain grave-

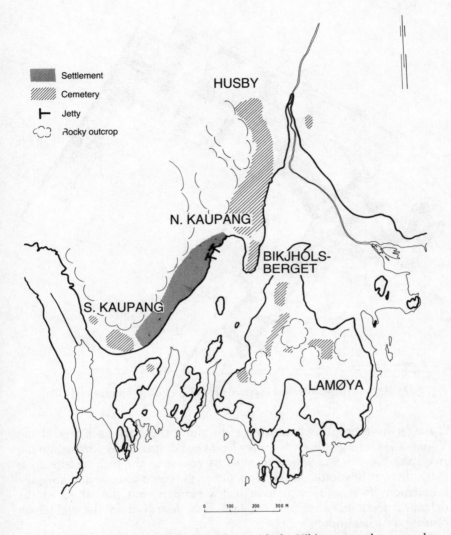

Fig. 4.16 Map of the environs of Kaupang with the Viking-age and present shore-lines (after Blindheim *et al.* 1981)

goods from the tenth century and the big cemetery of North Kaupang may have belonged to the royal estate, known as *Husby*, which lies further inland on the moraine ridge known as the Ra, rather than to the market settlement of Kaupang which seems to have been abandoned by about 900.

Skien, west of Kaupang, also shows traces of a late Viking-age settlement of nucleated character. It stands on a narrow isthmus between two lakes which can be reached by ship from a fjord and probably served as an export harbour for iron and hone stones brought downstream from the interior of Telemark. Recent excavations by Siri Myrvoll[26] have revealed small wattle buildings and artifacts of Viking-age date.

Kungahälla, now in Sweden, on the bank of the Göta älv, is thought to have been founded before 1000, but even though a few finds of Viking-age

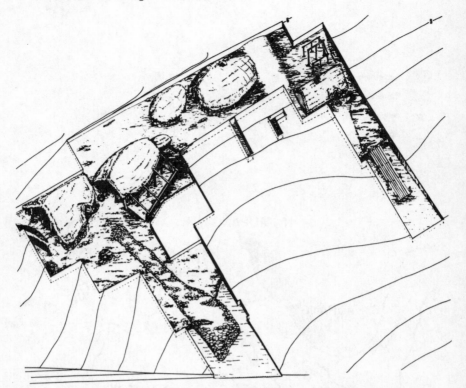

Fig. 4.17   Reconstruction of the excavated area of Kaupang (Blindheim 1987b)

character have been discovered near the shore there are no traces of the Viking-age settlement itself.[27] It may have been destroyed by a branch of the river, the Nordre älv, which changed its course in the high middle ages. *(Sarps)borg* in Østfold, on the river Glomma, could also be a Viking-age foundation. It is known to have had a rampart, but the whole of the defended area, including the rampart, was destroyed in the eighteenth century by a landslide.

There seem to have been no other urban settlements in Norway before the eleventh century. The Icelandic sagas, first written down in the thirteenth century, frequently mention Oslo, Bergen, Tønsberg, and Trondheim, but none of them have traces of occupation from before 1000.

Sweden

The Swedish kingdom began to grow up in the seventh century around the great lakes of central Sweden (Mälaren, Hjälmaren, Vättern and Vänern) where, according to tradition, the Svear and Geats lived, and the kingdom also included the Åland islands (figure 4.18). The land around Lake Mälaren forms the most northerly agricultural zone of Sweden. To the north-west lies Bergslagen, a region rich in iron ore and woodland, where hunting and fishing also add to the resource potential. Thus the Mälaren valley became

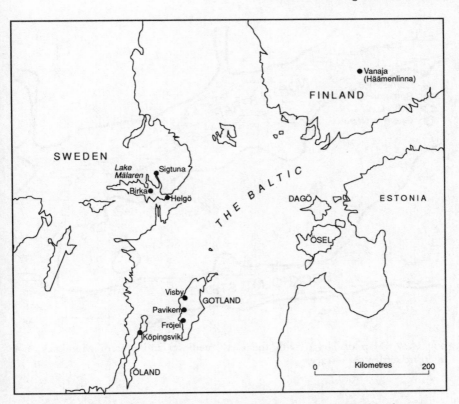

Fig. 4.18 Map of central Sweden and Finland with places mentioned in the text

the most densely populated area of Sweden in the iron age, capitalizing on the excellent conditions for subsistence and access to trading goods. This is reflected in the presence there of some of Sweden's most famous archaeological sites: the boat-grave cemeteries of Vendel and Valsgärde which were in use from 600 to 1000, and the royal and religious centre of Gamla Uppsala with its huge sixth-century burial mounds, all lie along a waterway leading from the Mälaren to Bergslagen.

By about 1100 the land around Lake Mälaren contained many thousands of farms, the result of a population explosion during the previous centuries.[28] The type of countryside and land use around Lake Mälaren have preserved remains of this cultural landscape with its early farms. The farms are often represented by one or more well-drained terraces on a moraine ridge on which stood long-houses, where the various activities of the farm were gathered together under the same roof. A cemetery lies adjacent to each settlement.

Many of these farm buildings have been investigated in recent decades. With a few exceptions they have been notably lacking in artifacts, only a few potsherds and occasional unidentifiable pieces of iron being discovered on them. The one outstanding exception is *Helgö* on the island of Lillön in Lake Mälaren. When it was first discovered it was described as an early market and trading centre, even as a 'proto-town'; more recently scholars have,

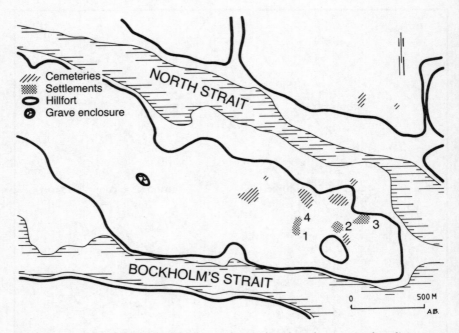

Fig. 4.19 Map of Helgö with the early medieval and present shorelines. 1–4 indicate settlement terraces

rightly or wrongly, played down its 'proto-urban' role but it still needs to be included briefly here as a possible counterpart to the Danish sites of Gudme and Dankirke.

Excavations began at Helgö in 1954 under the direction of Wilhelm Holmqvist.[29] The island of Lillön, which is now officially called once again by its medieval name of Helgö, is only 4 × 1km in area. Up to the early medieval period the western half was still under water, with the eastern half consisting of a clay-filled basin between rocky ridges. A prehistoric fortress dominates the southern ridge and groups of terraces supporting buildings lie several hundred metres apart along its north slope. A cemetery stands above the central group of terraces and there are others further north. About 200 stone settings for burials and mounds are still visible today (figure 4.19).

Excavations have shown that not all the groups of terraces were occupied simultaneously. The earliest settlement seems to have been concentrated in the eastern group where long-houses in use in the fifth and sixth centuries may have served as workshops for the production of jewellery and dress accessories. Some 90,000 fragments of moulds and c. 300kg of crucibles underline its industrial character.

In the seventh and eighth centuries the emphasis of the site seems to have moved to the central group of terraces and the character of the settlement may have changed. Many remarkable objects such as a figurine of Buddha, an enamelled Irish crozier-head, a Byzantine silver dish, a Coptic ladle, large quantities of glass from the Rhineland, and some pieces of gold foil with figural designs, were found on the middle terrace, associated with a frequently rebuilt long-house and some sunken-featured buildings. In addition, there were more mundane finds such as locks and keys and domestic refuse.

In the Viking age the western group of terraces took over the main role. Sunken-featured buildings were more common than before and industrial activity seems to have been limited to iron-working.

The cemeteries show the same wide chronological span, their small number of graves indicating that Helgö supported a population of no more than twenty individuals at any one time. Most of the graves have few and simple grave-goods and are of the same type as burials elsewhere in the rural settlements of the Mälaren valley, although the settlement itself displays most unusual character. No other site so far discovered in the Mälaren area has produced such an assemblage of imported objects nor so many bronze-casting moulds, all from the period before 800. It is clear that Helgö was a specialized settlement which had broken away from its agricultural background. This aspect of Helgö is illustrated by the discovery of a hoard of about 70 Byzantine gold coins (*solidi*) of sixth-century date. This is the largest known hoard of minted gold of that date from the Swedish mainland and indicates Helgö's economic importance in the migration period.

It is this that has led to Helgö having been called an independent unit, a 'proto-town', a royal centre, and the forerunner of Birka. The evidence from the cemeteries, however, indicates that Helgö was no different from other farm sites in the Mälaren valley in its size of population and social status. It differs only in its external contacts and manufacturing aspects. It could be that what we have on Helgö is a settlement of average size which at the same time was a part of a larger, perhaps royal or aristocratic, estate which fostered Helgö's non-agricultural activities.

One such estate[30] lies some kilometres east of Helgö and on the other side of the water: *Hundhamra* (figure 4.20), mentioned in many sources throughout the middle ages. Two great burial mounds stand on its land. The one which has been excavated produced high-status grave-goods from the eighth century, that is, contemporary with the main building on the central group of terraces at Helgö.

Although Helgö cannot be considered to have been a town, its specialized functions were taken over c. 800 by *Birka*, one of the earliest true urban centres of the North, mentioned by Rimbert in the ninth century as *portum regni ipsorum qui Birca dicitur* and by Adam of Bremen in the 1070s. Most scholars since the middle ages have been convinced that the *Birca* of Rimbert is a Latin form of the name Björkö, an island in Lake Mälaren about 30km from Stockholm, although some local historians have attempted to place it in their home areas elsewhere in Sweden.

The first excavations[31] on Björkö were carried out in the 1680s by Johan Hadorph, one of Sweden's first State Antiquaries, but it was Hjalmar Stolpe's excavations from 1871 to 1890 that produced the thousands of artifacts which are now stored in the Museum of National Antiquities in Stockholm. Several small trenches have been excavated more recently. Today the site is owned by the state and protected as an area of outstanding archaeological importance.

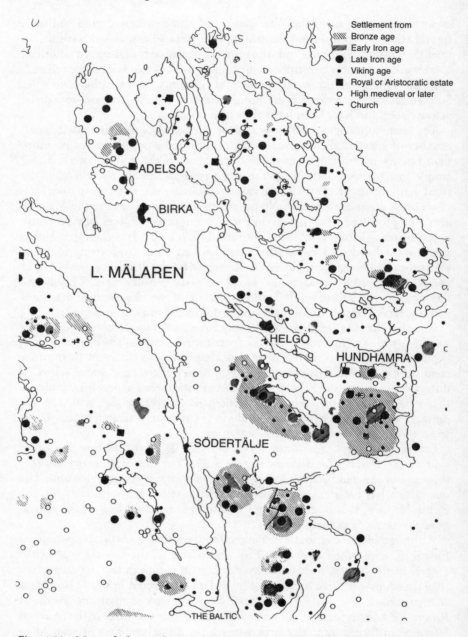

Settlement from
///// Bronze age
▨ Early Iron age
● Late Iron age
• Viking age
■ Royal or Aristocratic estate
○ High medieval or later
+ Church

ADELSÖ

BIRKA

L. MÄLAREN

HELGÖ

HUNDHAMRA

SÖDERTÄLJE

THE BALTIC

Fig. 4.20 Map of the settlements in the hinterland of Helgö and Birka. The shorelines shown on this map lie 5m higher than those of today and show the situation in the Viking age

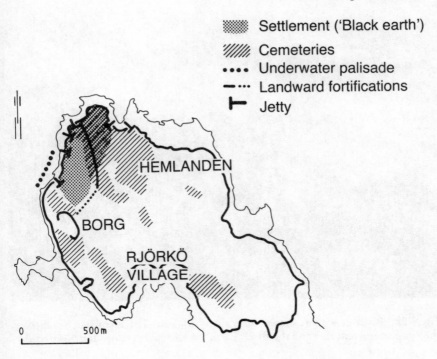

Settlement ('Black earth')
Cemeteries
Underwater palisade
Landward fortifications
Jetty

Fig. 4.21 Map of Birka on the island of Björkö with the Viking-age and present shorelines

Björkö preserves many remains of the Viking-age town of Birka (figure 4.21). The Viking-age town itself (the area known as *Svarta Jorden* = Black Earth) is situated on the slope down towards the west shore of the island and comprises *c.* 7 hectares of occupation deposit up to 2m thick. Detailed surveys using phosphate analysis of the soil have shown that the occupation deposit continues under the cemetery to the north, as far as the bay of Korshamn on the northern point of the island, and that the settlement must originally have been some 13 hectares in area.

Stolpe investigated only a small proportion of the Black Earth, *c.* 3000m^2 (0.25ha), and another 40m^2 were dug in the campaigns from 1969–71. Although the occupation deposit is about the same thickness as that at Hedeby it is not waterlogged and so does not contain the organic material which is present there and in many other Viking-age towns. The 'dry' occupation layers at Birka result from the desiccating effect of land elevation; the occupation deposit would be much thicker were it a waterlogged site.

Despite this, the soil of Birka is unusually productive of finds. Bones from household refuse dominate, making up about 10 per cent of the volume; Stolpe, for instance, discovered about 100,000 bird bones. Metal objects, combs, beads, pottery, slag and other manufacturing debris are also very abundant.

Fig. 4.22 Birka in winter, shown from the north-east. The Hemlanden cemetery, the rampart, the hill fort and the Black Earth are all visible (Photo Jan Norrman)

The Black Earth (the settlement area) is surrounded by a rampart in the north-east and overlooked by a hillfort in the south. Remarkably, there are no visible signs of the rampart along a length of *c.* 300m between its present south end and the hillfort. Either the town was abandoned before the rampart was finished, or it was built of wood along that stretch and has now disappeared completely. Until recently a semi-circle of piles was visible under the water opposite the Black Earth, but only a few submerged fragments remain today.

Cemeteries containing many different types of graves, the most noticeable consisting of mounds and occasional boat-shaped stone settings and triangular graves with concave sides, flank the Black Earth (figure 4.22). These cemeteries lie outside the rampart in what is known as Hemlanden, and south of the hillfort. There are about 1600 burial mounds in Hemlanden and 400 south of the hillfort, mainly cremations of a type characteristic of the early medieval farm cemeteries of central Sweden.

Beside the rampart and north of the hillfort next to the Black Earth, there are further large groups of chamber graves and coffin graves, usually covered originally by only a slight mound and identifiable today as depressions in the ground caused by subsidence of the decayed wooden structures beneath. The dead in these graves were inhumed not cremated.

Stolpe excavated almost 560 cremations and about 550 inhumations in coffins and chambers. The chamber graves were particularly rich, with weapons, jewellery and imported objects as grave-goods: they have subsequently been used to define the character of the Swedish Viking age even though the graves were probably of foreign merchants practising their own, non-Swedish burial customs (chapter 7).

The north coast of Björkö is indented with several bays, two of which are called harbours on seventeenth-century maps: for example, *Korshamn* or *Kornhamn*, and *Kugghamn*. Both have stone jetties, probably from the Viking age. It used to be assumed that these harbours lay outside the boundary of the Viking-age town, but we now know that the Black Earth (that is, the occupation deposit) originally extended under the graves of the Hemlanden cemetery as far as the coast where the harbours lie.

Another Viking-age stone jetty was found during the excavations of 1969–71, beside a broad inward curve in the 5m contour, on the western side of the island. It was probably the earth-fast foundation for a freestanding jetty on wooden piles which stretched out into the water. Stratified layers of debris containing many artifacts were found around the stones of this jetty.

Artifacts from the graves and the Black Earth can be used to date the lifetime of Birka, even though its beginning and end dates are both still a matter of debate. Most of the excavated graves seem to belong to the tenth century but quite a number must be of ninth-century origin. The datable grave-goods show that the site was continuously occupied throughout its lifetime although its population must have fluctuated, perhaps reaching its maximum in the tenth century (chapter 7).

The foundation of Birka has conventionally been attributed to *c*. 800 which has been used as the starting date for the beginning of the Viking age. The absolute chronology of the site is still unconfirmed and it is quite likely that Birka's origins should be pushed somewhat earlier, perhaps as much as 25–50 years. Some combs from Birka are identical with those found in levels at Staraya Ladoga (p. 120) securely dated by dendrochronology to *c*. 760,[32] and the other grave-goods in the earliest graves at Birka show pure Viking-age characteristics but were buried together with some few objects of late Vendel type.

Ever since Hjalmar Stolpe discovered (in the Black Earth) a hoard containing silver jewellery and *c*. 450 arabic coins (with the latest coin minted no earlier than 962) the end of Birka has been attributed to the 970s, a date supported by the absence of Anglo-Saxon coins at the site. This evidence suggests that Birka was in decline by the beginning of the 970s. The excavations in the Black Earth in 1969–71 revealed a few objects of later date, so there must have been some presence on the island after the 970s although Birka's economic importance cannot have been as great as it was earlier. The two Christian cemeteries of Grindsbacka and Lilla Kärrbacka on Björkö seem to belong to the later medieval village whose population farmed the island after the desertion of the Viking town.

On the island of Adelsö on the other side of the strait stand the remains of a royal manor, Adelsö Hovgården, now consisting only of the ruins of a high medieval brick-built palace on a man-made mound, surrounded by a small village, a church, a harbour whose entrance is marked by a rune stone referring to the king, and some great burial mounds.[33] A cemetery of cremations under smaller mounds lies *c*. 400m away. The palace and its surroundings acted as an important meeting place for the Swedish royal court and council during the thirteenth century, but the grave-goods excavated from the cemetery show that the site was occupied as early as the

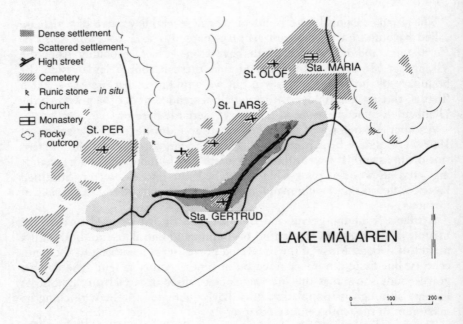

Fig. 4.23   Map of Sigtuna with the Viking-age and present shorelines (after Tesch 1989)

seventh century. When one of the great burial mounds, in themselves indicators of aristocratic, or more probably, royal status, was excavated a magnificent set of horse harness decorated in the art-style known as Borre (dated *c.* 900) was found. This suggests that Adelsö was already a royal manor or estate centre in the Viking age, with Birka forming a part of its lands.

According to *Vita Ansgarii*, Ansgar visited Birka twice as the leader of a Christian mission, in 829–30 and 851–52, when he is recorded as building a church there. At least one priest remained at Birka for some time after his visits and he was responsible for a Christian congregation. Nevertheless, the Christian clergy were driven out after a few years, leaving only a few Christians in the town. In the 930s Birka was visited by Archbishop Unne of Bremen, who died and was buried there (although his head was sent back for burial in the cathedral of Bremen). Even after its late tenth-century desertion Bremen continued to elect bishops for Birka, and the tradition of Birka lived on even longer in the realm of Swedish town law, for in the fourteenth century the first law governing towns in Sweden was known as *Bjärköarätt* (Birka law). The Danish and Norwegian town laws are known as *Bjerkerätt*.

Sigtuna (figure 4.23) is also mentioned by Adam of Bremen.[34] It was the only town in the Mälaren valley during the eleventh century and *c.* 1060 it was visited briefly by Adalvard the Younger, one of the missionary bishops from Bremen. Sigtuna became the centre of the first diocese of central Sweden but the see was moved to Gamla Uppsala by *c.* 1130 once paganism had finally been driven out of that royal and religious centre, and Sigtuna's economic functions were taken over by Stockholm c. 1250.

Sigtuna today is a small town. Medieval chronicles and seventeenth-century scholastic traditions attribute the great period of Sigtuna to the beginnings of the Christian period in Sweden, the two hundred years from 1000.

Archaeological excavations were begun there in the 1910s by the historian Olof Palme who lived in the town and founded its museum. He carried out excavations which were large-scale for the time, and showed that the occupation deposit around Stora gatan (High Street) was almost 4m deep. During the next decades all the commercially-dug trenches for water pipes and other services were examined superficially by archaeologists and some idea of the extent of the occupation deposit was gained, but it was not until 1988 that further large-scale excavations were carried out, once again along Stora gatan. They have shown that the origins of Sigtuna must be pushed back into the tenth century.

The ruined churches of Sigtuna have also attracted the attention of art historians and ecclesiastical historians whose dating has varied from 1050 to 1200. No one has as yet investigated Sigtuna as a unit but an interdisciplinary project designed to study the town as a whole has recently begun.

Sigtuna stretches along the southern shore of a rocky and wooded strip of land, on a large peninsula between bays leading up to Uppsala. The original shoreline, 4–5m higher above sea level than today's, now lies buried beneath thick occupation deposits. The first settlement stood on and to the north-west of a small headland protruding into the water near the centre of the present town, and it later expanded eastwards along Stora gatan. The only land suitable for occupation and building was a narrow strip about 100m wide between the shore and a steep rocky ridge to the north, and this confined area led to an urban expansion with a linear arrangement along the shore. The central area (with the deepest occupation deposit) was defined on east and west by two streams and recent research has shown that occupation also extended beyond both streams, but to a lesser extent.

The excavations of 1988–89 show that Sigtuna had a regular plan with parallel rows of small buildings running inland from the street and divided from each other by narrow lanes, narrow yards, or eavesdrips. The original plots on which these buildings stood were surrounded by shallow ditches. This arrangement can be seen in the earliest, late tenth-century, phase of occupation where it runs under the site of the present Stora gatan, suggesting that the street system must be later than the first buildings.

After c. 1100 the town was surrounded by a number of stone churches which have long been abandoned and now stand as ruins. The importance of Christianity in Sigtuna in the eleventh century is also shown by the thirty complete or fragmentary rune stones which have been found in the town. Most of them have been reused as building material in the churches but a couple still stand in their original positions, their cruciform decoration carved into massive boulders or slabs of stone. Two of the stones carry runic inscriptions commemorating members of the Frisian gild who died in Sigtuna in the eleventh century: either native-born Frisians, or Swedish merchants who had visited Frisia on their trading ventures.

Fig. 4.24   A Kiev ceramic Resurrection egg, glass finger-ring and spindle whorl of Volhynian schist found at Sigtuna. They illustrate the easterly connections of the town in the eleventh century (Photo Bengt A. Lundberg)

Like Birka, Sigtuna is surrounded by an almost continuous chain of cemeteries. Many of the churches stand in these cemeteries, some of which were probably Sigtuna's earliest Christian churchyards. Almost all the burials at Sigtuna are inhumations and only a few are still visible as mounds or stone-settings above ground level. The churches, the cemeteries and the rune stones indicate that Sigtuna was a Christian town virtually from its beginning even though it had its roots back in the pagan period before 1000.

In the town there was intensive production of antler, leather and metal objects, evidenced by the enormous quantity of debris which is still well preserved. Outside contacts seem to have been mainly directed across the Baltic to the east and south. Resurrection eggs made of glazed earthenware, and glass finger-rings (figure 4.24) must have been brought from Russia, and some of the pottery found in Sigtuna originated in the lands of the western Slavs.

It is difficult to say precisely when the occupation of Sigtuna began, although the excavations in 1988 and 1989 have given dendrochronological dates before 980. It has always been assumed that the town originally grew up on the early royal estates of *Fornsigtuna* (Early Sigtuna) which lies

+ OLAF REX SVEVORUM

+ GODWINE MO SIHT

Fig. 4.25 Coin of type 11/55 minted in Sigtuna at the end of the tenth century. About forty examples are known (Transcription after Malmer 1989; photo Antikvariskt Topografiska Arkivet, Stockholm)

across the water from the present town, but recent excavations[35] have shown that from the sixth to the eleventh centuries Fornsigtuna was an estate with no manufacturing or trading functions. Sigtuna must have been a deliberate royal foundation at the end of the tenth century on common land adjacent to the estate. Fornsigtuna was later granted to one of the first bishops of Sigtuna for his maintenance.

The artifacts which have been discovered in the latest levels at Birka and in the earliest levels at Sigtuna are so very similar that they could overlap in date, although the contemporaneity of the latest levels at Birka and the earliest levels at Sigtuna has not yet been proved by archaeology. The most important dating evidence for early Sigtuna is given by the 'Sigtuna coins' of Olof Skötkonung and his son and successor Anund Jakob; they reigned from 990 to 1050. The earliest coins[36] in the series carry the legend SIDEI (God's Sigtuna) (figure 4.25) and are copies of the Anglo-Saxon crux type which were minted in England from 991 to 997. The first minting period at Sigtuna probably lasted no more than about ten years; later, the legends on the coins copy the originals and become more or less illegible. The dies used at Sigtuna were probably not current after the validity of the English coins, thus the minting of the first coins at Sigtuna should be ascribed to sometime during the last decade of the tenth century, a little later than the date given by archaeology.

Södertälje is the only other town in the Mälaren valley of Viking-age significance.[37] It lies on a narrow isthmus which joined the peninsula of Tören to the mainland to the west. It is *c.* 15km due south of Birka and was an important point on the route between Birka and the Baltic Sea with a portage some 400m long where the boats could be transported overland to the Mälaren (figure 7.3). The centre of modern Södertälje with its medieval church lie near the Viking-age portage. Occupation layers containing pottery and other artifacts of late Viking-age date have been found immediately north of the church, suggesting that there was a small settlement beside the portage; this could well be the *Tälje* mentioned by Adam of Bremen in IV: 29 of his *History*.

Fig. 4.26   Aerial view of Köpingsvik from the south-west. The Viking-age site lay between the cliff and the shore but is now almost totally destroyed by modern development (Photo Björn Ambrosiani)

With this we must leave the problem of the Mälaren valley and turn to other areas where density of settlement in the Viking age led to the development of towns and markets with manufacture and trade as their main functions. One such place is Köpingsvik on Öland where large cemeteries, a church, rune stones, and a 'Thing' site indicate the presence of a nucleated settlement, now completely built over by modern development (figure 4.26). All the disparate features have been brought together into a whole through the work of Ulf Erik Hagberg[38] who has been able to trace the occupation deposit representing early Köpingsvik by investigating small trenches in the low-lying area which is the modern settlement. His excavations produced quantities of late Viking-age material, mostly of eleventh-century date. He associates this settlement with the early medieval export of polished limestone, a commodity which was much in demand when the great phase of church building began in northern Europe after 1000. The gently sloping beach below the limestone cliffs is characteristic of a simple lagoon harbour between raised beaches (figure 4.27). The site later developed into an important centre for trade and communications on the island before the foundation of the castle of Borgholm on a headland some kilometres to the west, and the subsequent growth of the town there, still the only town on Öland.

One other place in the Baltic must be attributed to Sweden here even though it was under Danish overlordship from 1361 to 1645. In the early middle ages it seems to have been its own free state: the island of Gotland. The archaeological conditions there are unique, and the island has its own

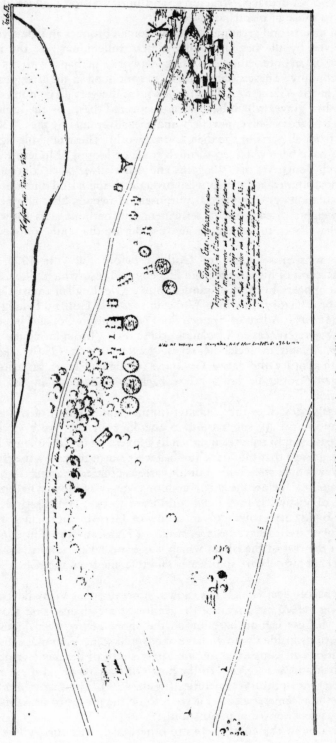

Fig. 4.27 The eighteenth-century drawing by Hilfeling showing the Viking-age cemeteries of Köpingsvik and Klinta (Royal Library, Stockholm)

particular types of artifacts, structures, and burial customs which do not correspond to those of mainland Sweden.

Hoards of *denarii* and great quantities of Roman bronzes and glass vessels show that even by the beginning of the first millennium AD the island formed part of an international trading network, perhaps with its own monetary economy. These external contacts continued in the later periods, particularly in the Viking age. This is shown by the very large numbers of richly-furnished graves which have been discovered there, by the hundreds of Viking-age hoards of silver jewellery and hacksilver, and by the *c.* 130,000 silver coins from all parts of the then known world. These tangible signs of wealth must have been obtained through trade or looting. Modern numismatic research[39] suggests that the coins and other silver were concealed as treasure almost immediately they were brought to the island and were not in open circulation for commercial purposes. However, the innumerable scales and weights discovered on settlement and harbour sites show that silver must have been in circulation and use during the tenth and eleventh centuries.

The only written reference to Gotland before the year 1000 is in Wulfstan's account of his voyage from Hedeby to Truso which, like Ottar's voyage, also appears in the late ninth-century Old English translation of Orosius's world history, in which Wulfstan says that Gotland belonged to the Swedes (*Sweon*). Adam of Bremen does not mention Gotland but there are many other references in Upplandic runic texts ('brought tribute from Gotland', etc.), and in Icelandic sagas, particularly St Olaf's saga. In the thirteenth century the native *Gutasaga* (Gotlandic saga), appendix to the *Gutalagen* (Gotlandic law), refers back to conditions in the early medieval period.[40]

The *Gutasaga* describes the *landnam* (initial 'land taking') of the island in remote antiquity, its submission to the king of the Svear (Swedes) through the payment of tribute, and then its conversion to Christianity by St Olaf in 1029. It says that the first churches were burnt down by the pagans almost as soon as they were built, but for various political reasons the one at *Vi under Klinten* (Vi below the cliff), modern Visby, was allowed to remain.

The town of Visby has long been considered to be a comparatively late foundation, owing its growth to an influx of German merchants in the twelfth century, and to have been primarily a Hanseatic town in constant conflict with the rest of the island which was a medieval 'peasant republic' (whose merchant farmers are sometimes said to come from the 'Gotlanders' coast').

Recent archaeological work[41] has shown, however, that Visby developed as a town long before the arrival of the Hanseatic merchants, first growing up round a shallow lagoon harbour on the shore below steep limestone cliffs. Excavations inside the town have uncovered some Viking-age graves, but investigations at Kopparsvik, immediately south of the medieval town, and Gustavsvik and Snäckgärdet to the north of it, have revealed extensive tenth- and eleventh-century cemeteries (figure 4.28). The many hundreds of burials in these cemeteries do not seem to be the graves of peasants and probably indicate a non-rural population.

Elsewhere around the coast there are other small harbours where rich

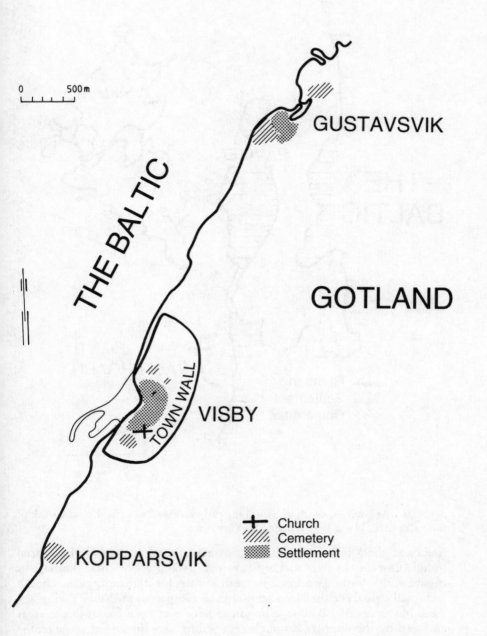

Fig. 4.28 At least three early medieval harbours lie along the shore near Visby, Gotland

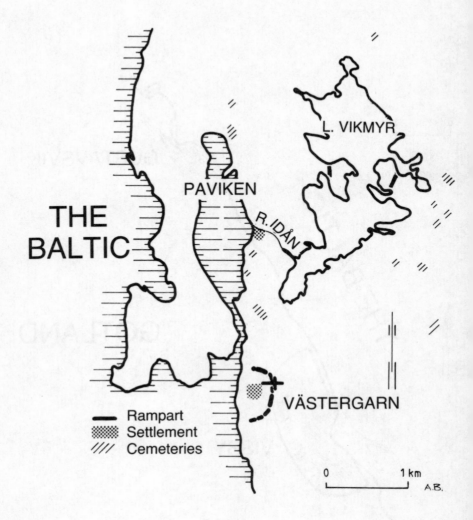

Fig. 4.29   At Paviken, south of Visby, the early medieval site stood on the bank of the River Idån. It was later replaced by Västergarn

finds and characteristic remains of non-agricultural settlements have been found. One of the first to be discovered[42] was *Paviken* near *Västergarn* (figure 4.29). Västergarn has long been known for its Romanesque church and small chapel enclosed by a semi-circular rampart of probably Viking-age date. No traces of Viking-age buildings have ever been found in the areas enclosed by the rampart although excavations have unearthed some tenth-century pottery. Its attribution relies mainly on topographical features, notably the position of the ends of the rampart in relation to the shoreline of *c.* 1000. Västergarn stands by the mouth of a narrow stream which in the Viking age was the entrance to the lagoon of Paviken. Over the years

Viking-age objects have occasionally been picked up on the headland on the east side of the lagoon, at the mouth of the Idån, and when the site was surveyed archaeologically, first by Hasse Hansson and then by Per Lundström, occupation deposits with a high phosphate content were discovered. Lundström's excavations revealed what appears to have been a market-place where boat-repairing, goldsmithing and other industries were practised. Imported objects from various parts of the outside world indicate long-distance trade. It cannot have been a permanent settlement, however, for there are virtually no graves in the vicinity.

Paviken dates from the eighth century to *c*. 1000. A few magnificently furnished graves from Valve, a farm at the northern end of the Paviken lagoon, also date from this period and this may be the cemetery of an estate which had special responsibility for the Paviken market-place. Paviken did not continue in occupation into the eleventh century, perhaps because waterborne access to the lagoon had silted up. The rampart at Västergarn may have been an unsuccessful attempt to develop a successor to Paviken, but it failed because by the eleventh century Visby was beginning to supplant all other coastal sites on Gotland.

The east coast of Gotland possesses several harbours of the same type as Paviken: *Bogeviken* in the north and *Bandlundeviken* in the south, the latter with numerous silver hoards, remains of buildings, coins, and weights, indicative of Viking-age occupation.[43]

Other similar sites around the coast of Gotland (figure 4.30) are represented by early medieval cemeteries beside what were once small lagoons.[44] Recent excavations of a high-phosphate area adjacent to a cemetery near *Fröjel* church have revealed a settlement consisting of a regular layout of plots containing buildings.[45] One of these buildings was much bigger than the others. Abundant industrial evidence including moulds for the manufacture of bronze jewellery of typical Gotlandic type, and raw material for making glass beads has been found throughout the settlement. Worked pieces of red deer antler indicate not only the manufacture of antler objects on the site, but also the existence of some trading activities, for red deer have never been native to Gotland and so the antler must have been brought over from the Swedish mainland.

Fröjel is like Paviken, Bandlundeviken, Bogeviken, Snäckgärdet and Visby in being a non-agricultural settlement. This can be seen from the nature of the artifacts found through archaeological excavation and confirms the environmental and ecological evidence which point to early medieval agricultural settlement on Gotland being confined to the interior.

Several Viking-age inhumation graves which were discovered within the inhabited area of Fröjel throw an interesting sidelight on what must have been troubled times. A woman and a child or young adolescent were buried in the midst of the settlement. Slash marks on their skeletons show that they had both been savagely slaughtered, perhaps during an attack on the settlement, and were then hurriedly buried on the spot where they met their deaths. One of the graves contained a spear, the weapon responsible for this murder.

During the middle ages the 'Gotlanders' coast', was in competition with the German Hanse and its base at Visby. The name seems to have had a long

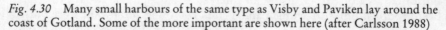

Fig. 4.30   Many small harbours of the same type as Visby and Paviken lay around the coast of Gotland. Some of the more important are shown here (after Carlsson 1988)

tradition and to have arisen from the presence of many small harbours with limited industrial and trading interests, and often with a cemetery. These features suggest that the harbours were not only used for the export of goods from the interior but that they were permanently inhabited, for it is unlikely that the graves are those of foreigners who happened to die there on their occasional visits.

Finland

The northern parts of Scandinavia extend into the Eurasian taiga region. The land between the Bothnian Sea and the great north Russian lakes of Ladoga and Onega forms part of the region which is still greatly affected by land uplift (p. 47). Its interior is riddled with extensive lake systems, formerly inlets of the sea, around the shores of which Finnish tribes such as Tavasts (Finnish = Hääme) and Savolaxians lived. This occupation was scattered, dependent on simple agriculture, hunting and fishing, and it has been assumed that nucleated settlement did not develop there before the high middle ages when the population was influenced by Sweden and the consequent conversion to Christianity.

In recent years, though, a small nucleated settlement has been discovered on the shore of Lake Vanajavesi, opposite the medieval Swedish castle of Tavastehus (Finnish: Häämenlinna). Occupation deposits *c.* 6 hectares in area lie on the Varikkoniemi headland which is now surrounded by a silted-up part of the lake.[46] Excavations and surveys undertaken by Museiverket (National Board of Antiquities) since 1986 have identified many buildings, a harbour basin, and a timber and stone rampart along the original shoreline. The artifacts discovered there include those which are commonly found in Viking-age towns: antler, slag, moulds, etc., and the evidence indicates substantial occupation from *c.* 800 to *c.* 1300. At the end of the nineteenth century a hoard of eleventh-century silver jewellery including chains and pendants was discovered on the same headland, then called Linnaniemi. All these features probably represent the Tavasts' town of Vanaja which, according to written sources, was destroyed by fire in 1311 when under siege by the people of Novgorod.

Summary

The centuries from 700 to 1000 made up a dynamic period in Scandinavia, with immense expansion both in non-agricultural and agricultural settlements. At the same time the old tribal units were beginning to amalgamate into states. Demand for specialized products emerged and craftsmen needed places where they could both acquire raw materials and dispose of their finished products. Dankirke, Helgö and Paviken are some of the earliest examples of these places, often without a large permanent population. They may be regarded as settlements with specialized functions and contacts. Ribe and Åhus represent a middle stage: early market-places, embryonic nucleated settlements with a permanent population. The larger towns such as Hedeby and Birka developed rather later, in the late eighth century or c. 800.

This is not to say that these developments occurred simultaneously over the whole area. The coastal sites and *köpingeorter* of Scania are most closely connected to the middle stage, that of market-places, but they continued in existence much longer and were still present when developed towns such as Lund flourished. Whatever the dates of these developments, the emergence of nucleated settlements depended on the level of economic prosperity of their hinterlands.

The choice of site is also interesting, for many market-places and early towns lay on the shoreline where they would have been in constant danger of flooding at high water and during storms. Shelter for ships must have been the primary consideration in their location. On the open coasts of Scania, Öland and Gotland the sites lay beside lagoons protected by spits of sand or gravel, and open shoreline sites without natural protection seem only to have developed on inland waters, as at Hedeby, Kaupang, Birka and Sigtuna.

Only a few of these towns, notably those of the latest phase of foundations such as Lund, Visby, and Sigtuna, are still in existence today. The reasons for the abandonment of the earlier sites are complex. It was not that one area suddenly lost all its nucleated settlements, rather their functions were transferred to a new site: hence the chains of settlements such as Helgö – Birka – Sigtuna, Hedeby – Schleswig, or the different phases of the market-places at Åhus. Each chain was composed of ever more complex, town-like, links (chapter 7).

The crucial factor in the siting of a settlement seems to have been its position in relation to routes of communication. A site may have been abandoned because factors such as land elevation or silting caused a route to change, or the means of transport to be modified. Land elevation was particularly influential in the Mälaren district and on Öland and Gotland, where the old sites fell out of use because they could no longer be reached by waterborne transport, particularly when ships of deeper draught became common in the tenth and eleventh centuries. For instance, when the Södertälje portage became impassable, boats sailed into Lake Mälaren ⁺hrough the straits where Stockholm now stands and no longer needed to call at Birka on their way to the political and religious centre of Gamla Uppsala.

Change of site can hardly have been a response to pressure on space, as both Sigtuna and Stockholm, the latter founded in the middle of the thirteenth century when it took over Sigtuna's economic functions, each had about the same surface area as Birka.

As far as the buildings in early medieval towns are concerned, there was no real reason why the site of a town should not be relocated and its inhabitants moved elsewhere. Their simple wooden houses must have been cheap to erect, and in any case were frequently destroyed by fire or decay during the lifetime of a town. It was only when stone churches and other buildings involving considerable capital outlay began to be erected that towns became permanently fixed in one place.

Royal authority was probably the prime mover in the foundation of both early and late medieval towns in Scandinavia, but noblemen and ecclesiastics closely related to the king might also have played their part. Erik Cinthio[47] has suggested that in Scania, with its complex structure of nucleated settlements, the inland *köpingeorter* were founded by local nobles and that only later, in a more advanced stage of state formation, did the kings and archbishops establish the coastal sites such as medieval Åhus, Ystad and Trelleborg. This is thought to be the reason why the *köpingeorter* never developed into true towns. Anders Andrén has used this theory to argue that the organization of early medieval Lund with its many urban parishes must have been connected with the adaptation of the nobility to the new system, whereby it was important for their status to settle near to the royal estate centre and the cathedral.

The connection between towns and market–places and royal or aristocratic estates is fairly clear. Helgö, Birka, Sigtuna, Lund, and Kaupang, for instance, are all directly associated with known properties of this type (Helgö with Hundhamra and Kaupang with Husby, for instance). The role of the kings can also be seen at other sites, at Hedeby for example (p. 58). The question remains as to where and when the Scandinavian Vikings acquired their idea of towns. Whether they travelled to the east, to the west, or to the south, towns were their first port of call.

Chapter 5

The Vikings in Britain

It was in the British Isles that the Vikings made their greatest impact on urban development in western Europe. On the Continent their influence, particularly in the ninth century, was one of destruction rather than renewal. Contemporary written sources record attacks of the Vikings on flourishing trading centres such as Quentovic and Dorestad, and also on administrative towns such as Paris. In many cases the sources imply that these attacks signalled the end of the settlements which were subjected to such devastation, although we can now see that some of them would inevitably have declined through natural forces such as the changes in the course of the rivers which were their lifeline (Dorestad and the changing course of the River Kromme Rijn is a good example of this) or other more intangible reasons. Some settlements obviously did decline after the Viking raids but others (Quentovic, for example, which continued to mint coins into the tenth century) obviously outlived the Viking devastation, and some such as Paris were hardly affected at all in the long run. Nevertheless, on continental Europe the visitations of the Vikings cannot be seen as stimuli to urban development, whereas the converse seems to be true in at least some parts of the British Isles.

Chapters 2 and 3 have shown that in the lowland areas of Britain towns were being established and were developing into commercial centres during the ninth century and earlier. The highland zones of the north and north-west of England, Wales and Scotland, and Ireland to the west, were still mainly without urban development at that time, and this situation very largely continued until well on into the high middle ages.

The tenth century, however, witnessed a change in at least some of these areas: lowland England acquired even more towns, and urban nuclei began to grow up in the previously non-urban country of Ireland where monastic settlements with their concentrations of population and manufacturing activities were the closest thing to towns known before the tenth century. Many of these developments can be ascribed to the influence of Scandinavians who attacked, settled, or colonized various parts of the British Isles. In this chapter we shall concentrate on the Viking penetration of England and Ireland, and the consequent development of towns in those two areas.

Urban development in England: Wessex

By the middle of the ninth century the Vikings' previously sporadic attacks on England were transformed into a concerted movement which seems to have been a deliberate colonizing venture. The 'Great Army', composed largely of Danes, arrived in south-east England in 851 and in the following years it marched throughout much of eastern England, overcoming the population and settling the land. This culminated in the establishment of the Danelaw through the Treaty of Wedmore in 878 whereby the lands north and east of Watling Street (roughly the line from London to Chester) were deemed to belong to, and be ruled by, the Danes, and thus subject to Danish law. As a result of this, some towns in that part of England began to develop through Scandinavian influence, the most notable example being York which acted as the Scandinavian capital of the Danelaw for the following century.

In southern England one example of the influence of the Viking Great Army can be seen in Wessex where the military threat of the mid-ninth century resulted in the construction of the 'burhs' (defended sites, some of which subsequently developed into towns) following the designs which were laid out for them in the document known as the Burghal Hidage, devised by King Alfred in the 880s but which only achieved its final form during the reign of his son and successor Edward the Elder.[1] The Burghal Hidage lists thirty settlements in Wessex which were to be defended against the Great Army, and which were distributed over the countryside in such a way that no area of the kingdom was further than c. 30km from a place of refuge. Some of these settlements were already towns, most of them with roots in the Roman period, and needed little more than a refurbishment of their defences to make them secure. Winchester exemplifies this type. Others (Pilton, Devon, for example) used already existing iron-age fortifications, modified as necessary, and yet others were founded on sites without previous occupation (Cricklade, Gloucestershire or Wallingford, Oxfordshire).

Although the strategic positioning of these defended places was of prime importance, some of them seem also to have been intended to act as fairly densely populated centres. Their populations must have been needed for constructing, refurbishing, and manning their defences, but must also have performed economic or administrative services for the surrounding rural sites. The area enclosed by the walls of some of the burhs was laid out with a system of streets defining plots of land on which dwellings, shops and other buildings could be built. Even in burhs with Roman antecedents, where traces of the Roman street pattern may still have been visible in the ninth and early tenth centuries, the streets laid out in Alfred's and his successor's reigns were quite new, following an alignment totally different from their Roman predecessors.[2] The organization of space within the walls of the burhs has been called the first attempt at Anglo-Saxon town planning, and can most easily be seen in Winchester. Martin Biddle's excavations in the 1960s and subsequent investigations revealed a street pattern within the walled area of Winchester whereby the land was apportioned into plots for settlement, but which also provided easy access to the walls when defence was necessary.[3] Other burghal hidage settlements show signs of a similar organization, emerging from the demands imposed on these sites by imminent attack by the Vikings and the need to accommodate a population of some size.

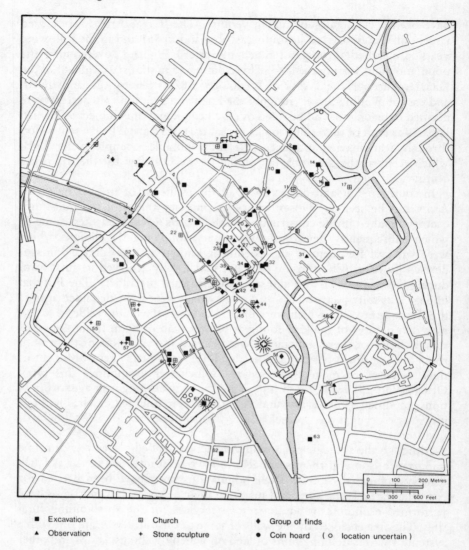

Fig. 5.1 Anglo-Scandinavian York with excavated sites. The numbers on the sites refer to figure 1 in Moulden and Tweddle 1986, but note particularly (3) Anglian Tower, (7) York Minster, (41) 5–7 Coppergate, (42) 2–6 Coppergate, (63) Fishergate (copyright York Archaeological Trust)

Urban development in England: the Danelaw

Those towns, however, represent the Anglo-Saxon reaction to the presence of Vikings on English soil. There are very few settlements in England which merit the title 'Viking towns', and they are to be found in the Danelaw. The most important of these is York (*Jorvic* to the Scandinavians). When the Great Army arrived in York in 867 it must have found a complex settlement, with high-status nuclei in the former Roman fortress and *colonia* areas on both banks of the River Ouse, and a commercial centre *c.* 25 hectares in extent on the east bank of the River Foss (figure 5.1). Written sources[4] such as the Anglo Saxon Chronicle record the early years of Scandinavian occupation of the town, but there is little archaeological evidence to back this up until the tenth century.

The initial occupation of York was brief, for the Great Army left in 868, to return in 869 when it seems to have been regrouping prior to its attack on Wessex. In 876 the army was disbanded and its members were given land in the surrounding countryside in which they were to settle and finally to become assimilated into the local population. Even by the early tenth century 'the Northumbrians (that is, the Anglo-Saxon population) . . . were already mingled with Danes into one race'.[5] This act of colonization and assimilation is recorded in the many Scandinavian place-names which are still attached to the villages of north-east England.[6] York remained the administrative, and probably commercial, centre of the north, and acted as the capital of the Danelaw after the Wedmore treaty of 878. From then until 954 York and its surroundings were ruled by a number of Scandinavian kings, both Danish and Norwegian, pagan and Christian, with a slight interruption of Anglo-Saxon rule c. 920. From the end of the ninth century there were close contacts between York and the Norwegian Viking dynasty of Dublin (p. 104) until the expulsion from York of Eric Bloodaxe in 954, the last Viking (Norwegian) king.[7] After that York was reincorporated into the English kingdom, but it was still under strong Scandinavian influence as its street names show.[8] The suffix gate which occurs so often in York is Scandinavian in origin (today gade (Danish), gate (Norwegian) and gata (Swedish) = street), not Old English (geat = opening or gate), and must indicate Scandinavian presence in the town over a considerable period of time. Scandinavian influence is also evidenced by personal names: at the end of the tenth century, for instance, about 70 per cent of the moneyers in York had names of Old Norse derivation.[9]

The archaeological evidence for the physical structure of what is usually called 'Anglo-Scandinavian York' (York from the late ninth to the mid-eleventh centuries) has increased enormously since the formation of the York Archaeological Trust in 1972, with Peter Addyman as its Director. The Trust is concerned with the archaeological investigation of and research into all periods of York's history (thus from the Roman period up to the present day), but much of its work has concentrated on the seventh to eleventh centuries for which there were, before its formation, written rather than archaeological sources. The relatively sparse archaeological evidence available before the formation of the Trust, summarized by Waterman in 1959 and also by Radley and posthumously published in 1971,[10] provided a foundation on which the Trust has subsequently built.

Chapters 2 and 3 have already shown how much new information has accrued from excavation of Anglian York; an even greater amount of information has been obtained through the examination of tenth-century occupation layers, particularly the excavation of 16–22 Coppergate, directed by Richard Hall (Deputy Director of the York Archaeological Trust). Some of the results of the Coppergate excavation from 1976 to 1981 have already been published;[11] other publications are in progress and should appear in print within the next few years. Some similar sites (figure

5.1) have also provided useful information about York in the Anglo-Scandinavian period, but the accumulated evidence from all these sites is not equivalent to that obtained from the single Coppergate site.

When the Great Army arrived in York in 867 it would have been confronted by a settlement in which administrative and commercial functions were combined, albeit in different areas of the town. York was also a town around which the Roman defences of the fortress and *colonia* still stood, and in which some of the Roman buildings still survived to an appreciable, and influential, extent. Some Anglo-Saxon structures such as St Wilfrid's church and other churches must have stood in masonry, built of stone quarried from Roman buildings, and there was at least one monastery of international repute. The street pattern originally laid out by the Romans within fortress and *colonia* was at least partly discernible and the bridge over the River Ouse was probably still functional. Thus at York the Scandinavians were confronted by an obviously flourishing settlement; its topography and economy was to change through their influence, but its traditions remained firmly rooted in its Roman and Anglian past.

Excavations have shown that the occupation of York by the Great Army and its civilian successors led to a modification of its topography, and in some instances a complete change. The Roman walls were refortified near the Anglian tower through clay being dumped above the previous refortifications of the Anglian period[12] and a clay and brushwood bank was built against the inner face of the Roman wall at Aldwark. At Hungate, to the south-east of the fortress, the River Foss was embanked with clay and brushwood, probably as part of a drainage scheme in that low-lying part of the town.[13] The street system of the Roman town was changed so that the main road into York from the south-west ran through the *colonia* from Micklegate in the south-west, across the Ouse Bridge into Ousegate and Coppergate, on the north-east bank of the River Ouse. This replaced the main entrance into the town in Roman times which had run further north-west, near to the modern Lendal Bridge, and effectively changed the commercial emphasis of the town.[14] Recent excavations in York have shown that in the hundred years after the arrival of the Great Army the commercial centre of the town shifted, probably from Fishergate on the far bank of the River Foss to the Ousegate–Coppergate–Pavement area, and it is from there that we have most archaeological evidence.

The first decades of Scandinavian occupation have left little evidence behind them. Some late ninth-century property boundaries and indications of the beginning of a street system have been discovered at Skeldergate on the south-west bank of the Ouse, and signs of incipient plot divisions, although no buildings, at 16–22 Coppergate. The Coppergate site may have been used as a glass-making workshop at this time for a furnace dated *c.* 860 has been found there, as have several human male skeletons.[15] There were, then, activities of one sort or another on the site before the tenth century, but it was not until *c.* 910 that intensive occupation began.

The early years of the tenth century saw a rapid development in the topography and economy of York. Rectangular plots of land bounded by wattle fences were laid out at right angles to streets (although, unfortunately, the contemporary streets have not been found), and industrial

buildings and dwellings were erected within them. Remains of plot boundaries and buildings have been discovered at a number of sites including
Coppergate, Walmgate, Pavement[16] and High Ousegate[17] on the north-east
bank of the Ouse, and Skeldergate[18] to the south-west. The most detailed
information comes from the excavations at 16–22 Coppergate, where the
front of each plot was occupied by a rectangular building, gable-end to the
street frontage, used as both dwelling and workshop. A yard at the back of
the building was the scene of industrial activities such as wood-working,
leather-working and jewellery-making. With one exception, the same types
of industries were practised in all sites so far excavated, and no specialization of crafts in particular zones of the town is apparent. The exceptional
discovery which sets Coppergate apart from the other excavated sites is that
of two early tenth-century coin-maker's dies,[19] showing that coins were
struck in this area.

The commonest types of buildings in tenth-century York were rectangular, with upright posts in the walls supporting the roof and the spaces
between them being infilled with panels of wattle. Their floors were
covered by planks or strewn with vegetation, and a hearth lay in the centre.
Raised earthen benches ran along the long walls. In plan they are reminis-
cent of the dwellings in several Scandinavian Viking-age towns, notably
Hedeby (p. 146).

At Coppergate these buildings were superseded *c*. 970 by buildings of a
completely different tradition: partly cellared (in some ways similar to the
sunken-featured buildings in England and south Scandinavia mentioned in
earlier chapters) with the cellars being lined with horizontal oak timbers.
The superstructures of these buildings have not been discovered through
archaeology, and so their external appearance is not known although we
can assume that they were simple buildings with ridged roofs which may
have protruded only slightly above ground level.[20]

Thus we can imagine that Viking-age York, at least in those areas for
which we have material remains, had a regularly laid-out system of plots
containing timber buildings and flanking streets, in many ways similar to
some of the Scandinavian towns such as Sigtuna, Oslo and Trondheim in the
late tenth and eleventh centuries. Archaeology has illustrated the standard
of carpentry employed in the construction of houses, plot boundaries and
so on, and in some cases (particularly in the late tenth-century Coppergate
sunken buildings) the skill of the craftsmen is very evident. Another branch
of archaeology, environmental archaeology, can illustrate other aspects of
the standard of living of the population of tenth-century York. The
Environmental Archaeology Unit at York has been a pioneer in this branch
of the subject and its researchers have produced results from their study of
insects, bones, seeds, parasites and so on which make serious contributions
to science and also stimulate the reader's imagination. The following quo-
tation[21] illuminates the way of life in tenth-century York much better than
any description of its buildings and crafts. York was a 'town composed of
rotting wooden buildings with earth floors covered by decaying vegetation,
surrounded by streets and yards filled by pits and middens of even fouler
organic waste', and this, no doubt, could be applied to virtually every urban
settlement in Britain and Scandinavia in the Viking age.

Nevertheless, not all York can have been so noisome and squalid, nor were the buildings of the town entirely of wood. The tenth century saw the foundation of new churches in York, constructed out of millstone grit quarried from the Roman ruins; this stone was also sent out from the town to the surrounding villages (often with names of Scandinavian derivation) where churches were also being built.[22] This expansion of church building at a time when northern England was firmly in the grip of Viking administration indicates that the Scandinavians rapidly adopted the Christian religion of England once they had settled in the Danelaw and become assimilated into the native population.

The foul 'pits and middens' of York are, however, invaluable to the archaeologist for it is in them that many of the best-preserved artifacts and organic materials can be found. Evidence from these, and from the occupation layers inside and outside buildings shows that from the early tenth century the economy of Anglo-Scandinavian York was based largely on the production of goods made from raw materials acquired from its hinterland. Combs were made from antler collected in the neighbouring woodlands; some pottery was made from local clays; cloth was woven from wool shorn from local sheep; and gravestones were carved from local stone in adaptations of Scandinavian styles. Objects were also fashioned from raw materials brought into the town from farther afield. Beads were made from glass obtained by melting down fragments of broken glass vessels; jet from the coast near Scarborough, Yorkshire, was carved into pendants and other decorations; amber from Denmark or possibly closer to home on the east coast of England was fashioned into beads and other objects of adornment. York also seems to have served as a trading centre for goods imported into England from the east, and may have been one end of a trade route emanating from Hedeby. Both utilitarian objects and luxuries were imported into York. For example, light-brown worsted twill cloth of probably Scandinavian origin and paralleled by textiles in some graves at Birka[23] must have been for everyday wear, but silk, which must have derived from Byzantium, was surely a luxury. A silk cap (figure 5.2) found at Coppergate was made from the same length of cloth as one discovered in Lincoln and suggests that individual merchants were peddling their wares around the towns of the Danelaw in the tenth century.

Some 90km to the south-east of York the Roman town of Lincoln was occupied by the Danes in 874 and subsequently became one of the Five Boroughs of the Danelaw (alongside Derby, Leicester, Nottingham and Stamford). At that time the Roman walls were still standing, as were numerous masonry buildings of Roman date and at least one church (p. 10). Like York, Lincoln has been the scene of many excavations during the past two decades (carried out by the City of Lincoln Archaeological Unit) and the Roman and medieval aspects of the city have been examined in detail. The site of greatest significance for the Scandinavian occupation of Lincoln is that of Flaxengate, at the south-east corner of the Roman colonia (figure 5.3), which was excavated from 1972–76.[24] There had already been excavations in the vicinity in the 1940s and 1960s, in which pits containing early medieval pottery, and some fragmentary building remains had been uncovered, and a kiln had also been discovered nearby at Silver Street.[25] The

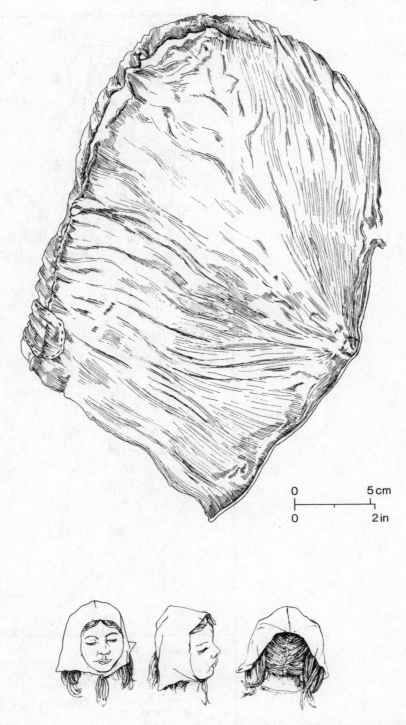

Fig. 5.2 Cap made of silk, probably from Byzantium, found at York (copyright York Archaeological Trust)

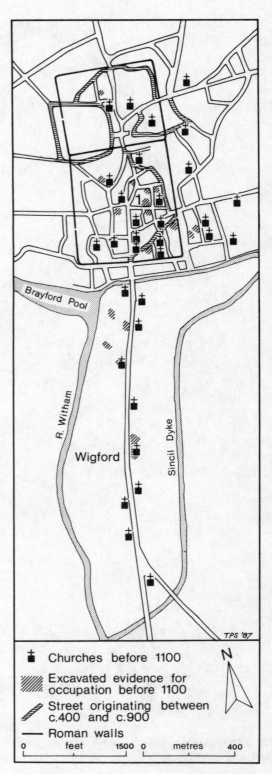

Fig. 5.3 Lincoln with (1) site
of the Flaxengate excavation
(after Perring 1981)

excavations of the 1970s, however, were of much greater extent than any previous work, and it is these which give us the best idea of the layout of a small area of Lincoln from the end of the ninth century.

The site seems not to have been inhabited until the end of the ninth century, after a gap in occupation since Roman times. Archaeomagnetic analysis of a sample from a hearth in one of the buildings gave a date of 850 ± 50 for one of the early phases of settlement.[26] A road surfaced with large and small limestone cobbling, and with several buildings along its western edge, defined the site on the east. This road remained in use, with many resurfacings but on the same alignment, until the eleventh century, but the buildings which bordered it changed radically in their arrangement during that time. They were, however, always of the same shape: rectangular, roughly 5m wide and up to 16m long. Their walls, probably clad with horizontal boards, were first built of posts set into post-holes lined with clay or stones, but by the middle of the tenth century the timbering of the walls stood on low stone foundations. Many of the buildings had a hearth in the centre of a sand-covered floor, and all were probably roofed with thatch. The number of buildings on the site increased quite rapidly over the centuries, and on one occasion they all seem to have been totally and intentionally destroyed to be replaced by a group of new buildings in a new arrangement when another street frontage (Grantham Street) was opened up. By the middle of the tenth century the buildings on the site were being used as workshops for the production of glass, textile, antler and other small objects and this continued for a hundred years or so.

No signs of property boundaries were discovered at Flaxengate, and in this it differs from the contemporary sites in York, but the excavator suggests that the whole site originally consisted of one plot under a single ownership.[27] He also argues that the site illustrates a deliberate planning of this quarter of the town which began before the incorporation of Lincoln into the Danelaw. If this is so, the origins of at least this area of the town must be attributed to its pre-Viking English inhabitants and should not be given the title of 'Viking'. Nevertheless, many of the artifacts which were discovered during the excavations at Flaxengate are similar to those found at York (glass finger-rings and beads, jet pendants, antler combs), and some of the imported objects are identical (the silk caps, for instance; see figure 5.2) and indicative of Scandinavian contacts,[28] so there must have been some considerable Scandinavian influence on Lincoln at least during the tenth and early eleventh centuries. It never, however, achieved the importance of York in the Danelaw and probably should be regarded as a town which drew from both Anglo-Saxon and Scandinavian sources for its building traditions and trading contacts.

Excavations have also taken place in Stamford, Lincolnshire, another of the Five Boroughs.[29] The archaeological evidence for the existence of Stamford during the Danelaw period is mainly drawn from pottery and pottery kilns,[30] but they suggest that the settlement had already come into prominence as a pottery-producing centre by the middle of the ninth century, before the arrival of the Great Army. Stamford's strategic situation at a ford on the River Welland where it was crossed by the Roman road (Ermine Street) still used in the early middle ages was presumably why it was chosen by the Danes as a suitable site for a defended settlement; this they founded on the north bank of the river. By doing so they gained control of the overland route between London and York and also access to the North Sea through the navigable River Welland and the Wash. Their grip on Stamford did not last long, however, for the Anglo-Saxon Chronicle records that in 920 the English king Edward the Elder 'marched with his levies to Stamford, and had a fortress built on the south bank of the river; all the people who owed allegiance to the more northerly fortress submitted to him'. Thus at that time Stamford must have consisted of two fortified centres, but unfortunately archaeology has so far failed to reveal much detail about their organization and layout. We know nothing about their ramparts or the buildings and streets which the ramparts surrounded, and few of the artifacts recovered from excavation can be attributed to Viking influence. Derby, Leicester and Nottingham have even less physical evidence for their existence as Danelaw boroughs, and even place-names are of little help, for only Derby acquired a Scandinavian name at this period (its Old English name was *Northworthy*).[31] Much still remains to be discovered about the urban settlement of this area of Scandinavian dominance at the end of the ninth and early tenth centuries.

Thetford, Norfolk, also lay in the Danelaw although it was never designated as a 'Borough'. Like Stamford, it began to develop as a pottery-making centre in the ninth century and by *c.* 850 there was a settlement of some size on the south bank of the River Little Ouse. In 870 it served as the winter quarters of the Danish troops and subsequently expanded to cover both banks of the river, the final extent of the settlement being enormous for its time: *c.* 60 hectares on the south and *c.* 15 hectares on north. Recent excavations and surveys by Andrew Rogerson of the Norfolk Archaeological Unit have shown that in the tenth century Thetford was defended by a rampart and ditch on the south bank of the Little Ouse, and a similar defence can be inferred on the north bank.[32]

Thetford's rapid development in both area and population in the tenth century was probably the result of the arrival of the Danes and subsequent industrial growth. Its main industrial activity seems to have been the manufacture of pottery which was distributed throughout East Anglia from the late ninth to the eleventh centuries and which can be found on every excavated rural and urban site known from that time (compare Ipswich and its Anglo-Saxon pottery, p. 21). Other crafts such as fine metal-working, iron smithing, and bone- and antler-working were also practised and there is some evidence of trade with the surrounding countryside. Thetford's land-locked position in the centre of East Anglia may not have encouraged the development of far-flung trading contacts (although situated on the River Little Ouse, its waterborne communications cannot have been easy) and it seems to have been a market serving a local area, not a great trading centre such as York.

There have been many excavations in Thetford, some of them such as those conducted by Group Captain Knocker from 1948–58, and by Brian Davison in the 1960s[33] being large scale. They have mainly been concentrated on the south side of the river where until recently the early medieval occupation deposits lay undisturbed for many centuries. The excavations suggest that the southern part of the town within the defences was made up of a rather haphazard arrangement of gravelled streets along which both rectangular post-built structures and sunken-featured or cellared buildings were arranged according to no very obvious plan. There is very little here to equate Thetford with other towns, either in Viking-age Scandinavia or in Anglo-Saxon England, and it seems to have had a character all of its own. We know, however, that it was regarded as a place of some significance up to the eleventh century for at that time it was the centre of a mint, the seat of a bishop, and had at least three churches. Its importance declined after the Norman conquest when it lost its diocesan position to Norwich, and the emphasis of occupation moved from the south to the north (thus leaving the undisturbed layers which have been so useful for modern archaeologists). Nevertheless, it must have maintained some status after the eleventh century as about twenty churches stood in Thetford in the thirteenth century, when it also possessed several monastic houses and friaries.

Although Thetford grew to its tenth- and early eleventh-century importance through the impetus of the Danes and the Danelaw, it is problematic whether it should be called a 'Viking town'. There can be no dispute that it was a town: defences, craftsmen's centres, mint, cathedral all underline this. What is not so certain is from where its influences came. The most satisfactory explanation for the growth of Thetford seems to be that it was an Anglo-Saxon manufacturing centre (for pottery) which was given a fillip with the arrival of the Danes, and then continued to exist and grow along non-Scandinavian lines.

Norwich, Norfolk, is another Danelaw town which began to grow in importance during the tenth century, in the period of Scandinavian dominance. Nevertheless, it can hardly be called a 'Viking' town as its origins, although still obscure, can probably be traced to the amalgamation of a group of five small, discrete Anglo-Saxon settlements alongside the River Wensum.[34] These may have been primarily rural in their economy, although the suffix *wic* in two of them (Westwick and Norwich) suggests a possible market function (but see pp. 15–16). By the tenth century there was a landing place for ships on the south bank of the Wensum[35] and possibly two defended areas: one on the north bank of the river where a rampart and ditch demarcated a roughly semi-circular area, and one to the south roughly equivalent to the later cathedral close. Excavations in 1985 in Fishergate,[36] a street flanking the north bank of the River Wensum and within the northern defended enclosure, revealed artifacts of eighth-century type including brooches and a sceatta coin of *c.* 720. These, together with quantities of imported pottery, suggest Anglo-Saxon commercial activity before the establishment of the landing place mentioned above. Tenth-century kilns for the production of pottery similar to that being produced at Thetford at the same time have been discovered along the aptly named Pottergate, and there is also archaeological evidence for other trades in Norwich although no buildings from this period have yet been discovered.[37] At about the same time the most important of the five settlements, Norwich, gave its name to the whole agglomeration.

Norwich seems to be similar to Thetford in that it originated as a settlement before the arrival of the Danes but began to grow once the

Danelaw had been established. Nevertheless, there is little archaeological evidence to indicate strong Danish presence in what was subsequently to become one of the most powerful towns of medieval England. Evidence from place-names, however, suggests that Nordic influence was more prevalent than we can see from archaeology. In particular, the suffix *gate* used in many street names (for instance, Pottergate and Fishergate) is almost as common in Norwich as in York, and the area of Tombland west of the cathedral incorporates the Scandinavian prefix *tom* = empty.[38] Thus, although excavations in Norwich have so far produced few objects which can be attributed to the Vikings, we must assume that their presence was of no little importance in the growth of the town.

The arrival of the Vikings in England obviously spurred on the development of English towns. We have seen how the Wessex kings reacted to the Scandinavian threat by founding newly defended centres or by refortifying earlier settlements and deliberately establishing some of them as urban centres. In the Danelaw, the Vikings themselves stimulated urban growth through their occupation of Roman towns such as York and Lincoln, by expanding Anglo-Saxon centres such as Thetford and Norwich, and by the few new foundations such as Nottingham. So their arrival in the ninth century had considerable influence on subsequent urban development in England, but they cannot be said to have been urban innovators. They had arrived in a country where towns were already a well-established, although not common, part of life and from a country where towns were still in their infancy; we cannot, therefore, expect the Vikings to have done more than modify what was there already. York is the best example of this for there the Scandinavian influence penetrated most deeply and lasted longest. The other places which have been mentioned in this chapter display only marginal Scandinavian influences.

Urban development in Ireland

The Vikings' most obvious influence on urban development in western Europe can be seen in Ireland where towns were unknown until their arrival. In Ireland the Scandinavians came to a country occupied by scattered rural settlements with an economy based on agricultural production and where the centres of industrial manufacture were concentrated in a few royal sites and monasteries. Thus whatever urban civilization was introduced by the Vikings was imposed on a fresh sheet, and it is in Ireland that we can look to a blueprint of what Scandinavians would have thought to be an 'ideal town'.

The Vikings who colonized Ireland came initially from Norway, a country where urban settlements (with the possible exception of the market centre of Kaupang, pp. 65–7) were unknown. It is unlikely, then, that they deliberately set out to found towns in their new colony; the towns which subsequently developed probably grew organically, perhaps almost accidentally, from simpler beginnings.

The settlement that was to become Dublin is first mentioned in written sources *c.* 840 as *Dubh Linn* (the black or dark pool), and shortly after-

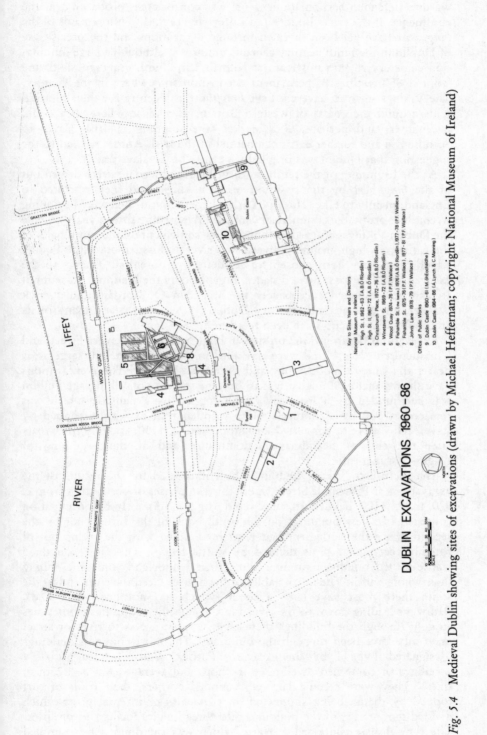

Fig. 5.4 Medieval Dublin showing sites of excavations (drawn by Michael Heffernan; copyright National Museum of Ireland)

wards a defended harbour (*longphort*) was constructed, probably near the confluence of the rivers Poddle and Liffey (figure 5.4).[39] No remains of the *longphort* have yet been revealed through excavations and the precise site of Dublin in the ninth century remains unknown, although a large inhumation cemetery *c*. 3km upstream at Kilmainham[40] with grave-goods dating from *c*. 850 testifies to permanent occupation somewhere in the vicinity. The Vikings seem to have used the *longphort* as a centre for their piratical raids around the coasts of western Britain, as a place where they could overwinter, and perhaps as a market (the shipping of Irish slaves to Scandinavia and further east documented in the Irish Annals has led to the suggestion that Dublin was originally a centre of the slave trade).

At the beginning of the tenth century the Scandinavians were driven out of the *longphort* by the coalition of Irish kings, and they retreated to England, mainly to take refuge in York where their kinsmen were beginning to conduct profitable commercial ventures. After some fifteen years of exile the Dublin Vikings returned to found a new settlement on the south bank of the Liffey, on high ground between that river and its tributary the Poddle which must have been chosen for its defensive potential. Thanks to the excavations of the past three decades, organized by the National Museum of Ireland and directed successively by Breandan Ó Ríordáin and Patrick Wallace, the site of tenth-century Dublin is well known and many of its archaeological remains have been recovered.

Excavations began in 1962 on sites in High Street, Winetavern Street, and Christchurch Place,[41] and were expanded in 1974–81 to include large areas nearer the Liffey: Wood Quay and Fishamble Street.[42] These excavations have shown that *c*. 900 what was to become the core of Viking-age Dublin was surrounded by a low earth bank topped by a palisade which was replaced *c*. 950 by a more elaborate wooden wall of wattles topped by staves. This was not converted into stone until *c*. 1100, roughly fifty years after the end of Scandinavian dominance and at the beginning of Anglo-Norman rule.

The picture of Viking Dublin is best illustrated by the results of the excavations at Fishamble Street where thirteen phases of occupation from *c*. 920 to *c*. 1100 have been uncovered (figure 5.5).[43] Initial occupation consisted of a few buildings on the south bank of the Liffey, but by the second phase the settlement had been regularized with the laying out of roughly rectangular plots defined by wattle fences. The plots contained wattle-walled buildings running along their length and sometimes filling their whole width. The north gables of the houses faced the river and to the south there must have been a street (which has not been excavated). Pathways leading down to the river ran through the properties, sometimes straight through the buildings themselves, so that access to river or street may only have been through the buildings. The most common buildings (designated Type 1 by the excavator Patrick Wallace) were probably dwellings or combined dwelling/workshops and averaged 8.5 × 4.75m in size.[44] They were rectangular with rounded corners, their roofs of turf topped by thatch being supported on two pairs of internal posts which divided the interior of the buildings into three longitudinal strips or aisles. The central aisle contained a hearth which was surrounded by trampled

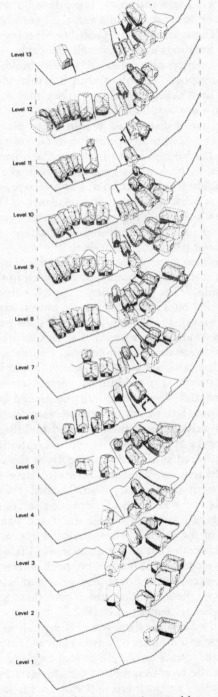

Fig. 5.5 Fishamble Street, Dublin, showing thirteen superimposed layers of buildings. Level 1 dates from the early tenth century (drawn by Michael Heffernan; copyright National Museum of Ireland)

earth, gravel, or wattle mats. The side aisles were slightly higher, their edges retained by low wattle walls and their surfaces covered by brushwood and wattle. These latter were probably sleeping areas equivalent to the side aisles of buildings in, for example, Hedeby.

The properties also contained smaller buildings (5 × 3.5m) without roof-supporting posts and often with hearths, adjuncts to the main dwellings (Type 2 in Wallace's typology). They may have been dwellings, but more probably were outbuildings.

The artifacts discovered within these properties show that Viking-age Dublin was a centre of commerce and industry, not just a defended strong-hold for the Vikings in the Irish Sea.[45] Contacts with the outside world are illustrated by finds of exotic artifacts such as a silk hairnet which must have been brought from Byzantium, and by the presence of amber from the Baltic which was made into beads and pendants at Dublin itself. Dublin may also have been a shipbuilding centre, for recent research has shown that one of the Viking-age ships discovered at Roskilde in Denmark and dated c. 1060 was made of oak grown in Ireland.[46]

Dublin's contacts with its immediate environment are less well known, although it must have been provided with foodstuffs from the surrounding countryside.[47] The only evidence for self-sufficiency comes from the preva-lence of pig bones in the occupation layers, suggesting that the families who lived in Viking-age Dublin kept their own pigs. Agricultural activities are otherwise poorly represented: the lack of querns suggests that grain was ground outside the Dublin enclave, the cattle bones discovered in Dublin suggest that cattle for slaughter were brought in on the hoof.

The Vikings also established centres elsewhere in Ireland: Limerick, Waterford and Wexford are all mentioned in contemporary documents. Archaeology has failed to discover any definite remains of Viking-age Limerick although a sunken-featured building of possible Viking-age date was found in Spring 1990. Recent excavations in Waterford and Wexford have uncovered settlements dating from the tenth and eleventh centuries. The settlement at Waterford seems to have been very similar to that at Dublin, with rectangular, wattle-walled buildings standing within plots surrounded by wattle fences. Some of the Viking-age street pattern has also been revealed, as has the huge ditch and bank which defined the Viking defences of the town.[48] These defences appear to be on a much large scale than other tenth-century defences in the Viking world, not only in Ireland, but the reason for this has not yet been determined.

Viking-age Wexford was also provided with rectangular wattle-walled buildings in plots flanking streets and these seem to reflect the pattern of Scandinavian settlement in Ireland.[49]

Thus, the Scandinavians were influential on urban development in west-ern Europe in a number of ways. Their military threat led to the foundation of defended burhs in Anglo-Saxon England in the late ninth and tenth centuries; the establishment of the Danelaw led to the growth and expan-sion of towns in northern and eastern England; and their annexation of Ireland resulted in the establishment of the only true Viking towns of the British Isles.

Chapter 6
Towns in the Slavonic-Baltic area

This chapter will deal with the areas south and east of the Baltic Sea, the homelands of the Slavonic, Baltic and Fenno-Ugrian tribes, and will examine the Scandinavians' contacts with them during the Viking age. The settlements described here are those where the archaeological evidence, from occupation deposits or graves, shows Scandinavian connections, and only occasionally will reference be made to other sites.

The west Slavonic-Baltic area (figure 6.1)

The land along the south coast of the Baltic Sea, comprising East Holstein, Mecklenburg and Pomerania (often called the land of the Wends), is of particular interest here because of its very close contact, both physically

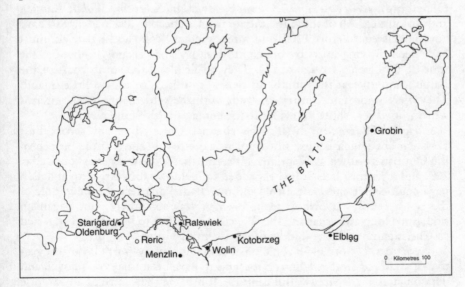

Fig. 6.1 The southern Baltic Sea showing the early medieval towns with Scandinavian connections. The site of Reric has not yet been confidently identified.

and culturally, with Scandinavia. As the Icelandic sagas and early chronicles show, it played a great part in early medieval Scandinavian history; warfare raged almost continually between the two regions, with brief interludes of peace resulting from marriage contracts and treaties.[1]

In the fifth and sixth centuries AD (the migration period) Slavonic tribes moved into the south Baltic plain in the wake of the Germanic peoples who were migrating westwards. Their colonization took the form of nucleated villages each usually protected by a neighbouring fort. The forts were generally located where rivers and lakes could provide additional defence, and were encircled by heavily timber-laced earth ramparts. Highly skilled craftsmanship is displayed in the timberwork of the ramparts, with the jointing technique of *Balkenverankerung* (anchor balks) being a specific Slavonic trait.

These villages and forts displayed embryonic social stratification and specialization which finally resulted in a change to non-agricultural settlements specializing in trade and manufacture. The precise date of this transition is difficult to pin down, but it must mainly have taken place during the period after *c.* 800 which corresponds to the Viking age, and in some cases even by *c.* 700.

The whole of the coastal belt was occupied by Slavonic tribes: the Obotrites, the Wilzians and the Ranians (on the island of Rügen) in the west and the Pomeranians in the east, and Prussians further east; each tribe having its own administrative and trading centres. Contacts between Scandinavia and these coastal sites are illustrated by their graves and grave-goods, and by the artifacts from the settlements.

There are hardly any written sources for these Slavonic sites. Wulfstan's journey from Hedeby to Truso at the end of the ninth century omits any mention of intermediate settlements such as *Starigard* (German = Oldenburg), *Reric, Arkona, Ralswiek, Menzlin, Szczecin, Wolin, Kamien* and Kołobrzeg. All of these are known from archaeological evidence to have been in existence before 1000, and some, such as Wolin and Ralswiek, must have been thriving ports by the eighth century and certainly known at the time of Wulfstan's voyage *c.* 870. They all lie along the south coast of the Baltic Sea, either at the mouths of rivers or streams or only a little inland. They were important centres for trade with the settlements of the interior which, however, show no evidence for contacts with Scandinavia.

Starigard/Oldenburg, beside the channel which then cut across East Holstein but which is now silted up, was the royal centre of the branch of the Obotrites known as Wagrians.[2] It seems that Oldenburg was founded *c.* 700, and a century later it had expanded to include a fortress, a royal hall, a pagan cult centre and craftsmen's and merchants' quarters. In the middle of the tenth century a bishop from Bremen was sent there, but paganism flourished long after that and the Wagrians seem not to have been converted to Christianity until the middle of the twelfth century.

Its fortress, of normal Slavonic type, contains heavily-burnt layers suggestive of attack or siege *c.* 800, and it seems to have been finally destroyed and depopulated in the late twelfth century. It became the centre of a bishopric *c.* 1150, but it was soon replaced by Lübeck, and today its only remains are a ringwork near the centre of the late medieval town of Oldenburg.

Excavations began in Oldenburg in 1953 under the direction of Karl Struwe, their results having recently been published by I. Gabriel and T. Kempke. The structures and artifacts which were found during the excavations show that Oldenburg was an important harbour in the Viking age, with extensive long-distance contacts. The pottery is mainly of the Slavonic Feldberg and later types (figure 6.4). Starigard and Hedeby are the most westerly outposts for objects such as glass bracelets, glazed-pottery Resurrection eggs (figure 4.24), and clay spindle-whorls imitating double-conical types made of Volhynian schist, all of which were brought from the early Russian state (p. 124). There are also a number of objects which indicate close contacts with Scandinavia: eighth- and ninth-century oval brooches, penannular brooches, and Norwegian hone stones and steatite vessels.

Reric is mentioned in the Royal Frankish Annals in connection with Godfred's activities at Hedeby and on the Danevirke in 808 (p. 56). It has so far eluded confident archaeological identification because the land of the Obotrites in which it lay is crossed by a number of rivers whose estuaries provide potential sites.[3] The small settlement and fort of Mecklenburg (meaning 'the great fort') south of Wismar could be the location of Reric, but another possible site is that of Dierkow, *c.* 50km from Mecklenburg, on the east bank of the River Warnow opposite Rostock. Occupation deposits, harbour installations, and cemeteries have been found there, together with jewellery and implements of Scandinavian origin.

Ralswiek (figure 6.2) lies on what was once an island or raised-beach ridge, *c.* 500m long, on the southern shore of a system of inlets which dissects the north of the island of Rügen.[4] A number of parallel landing places on the west side of the ridge beside a now-silted lagoon were supplemented by a concentration of buildings to the landward side, with a possible temple on the tip of the ridge to the south. Some form of suburb is present on the mainland where the Schwarzenbergen cemetery of about 400 graves, more than 300 of which have been excavated, lies. Further to the north-east there is a fort which may have been associated with the Viking-age settlement (figure 6.3).

Joachim Herrmann's excavations at Ralswiek have unearthed about a hundred buildings and many landing places. His work shows that each settlement unit in the site consisted of a number of buildings and one or two landing places. Each comprised both dwellings and craftsmen's quarters in which iron, antler and amber were worked and large quantities of pottery produced. This seems to have been one of the centres of production of the *Feldberg* and *Fresendorf* types of Slavonic pottery which were exported to Scandinavia (figure 6.4). Ralswiek was also an important ship-building centre.

A hoard of several thousand Arabic silver coins, the latest dating from the mid-ninth century, was concealed at Ralswiek during a fire which destroyed the settlement towards the end of the ninth century. As the settlement is thought not to have been rebuilt after the fire, Ralswiek can only have been in existence for about a hundred years from the middle of the eighth century even though its cemeteries seem to have been in use for another three hundred years. Most of the graves in the Ralswiek cemeteries are 'urn

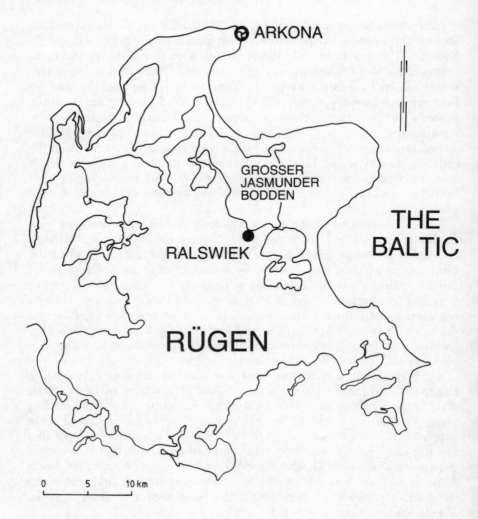

Fig. 6.2 Map of the island of Rügen with Ralswiek and the pagan temple of Arkona

burials', that is, each consists of a pottery vessel containing cremated bone buried beneath a low mound. Some of the few grave-goods which were deposited in the graves suggest that the dead were Scandinavian in origin.

South of Rügen the River Peene flows into Oderhaff, the estuary of the River Oder between the two islands of Usedom and Wolin, in what was Wilzian territory. A site similar to Ralswiek lies on a raised-beach ridge straddling the valley between Görke and Menzlin. This is the site of early *Menzlin* (figure 6.5) which stands at the north end of a ford across the river, with occupation deposits and a cemetery of boat-shaped stone-settings and mounds closely comparable to Danish Viking-age cemeteries such as Lindholm Høje in Jutland.[5] Menzlin's economic structure resembles that of Ralswiek but the site is considerably more extensive, being *c.* 10 hectares in area. *Görke* also displays an early medieval settlement but its graves are of quite a different type. The weapons and other objects which have been

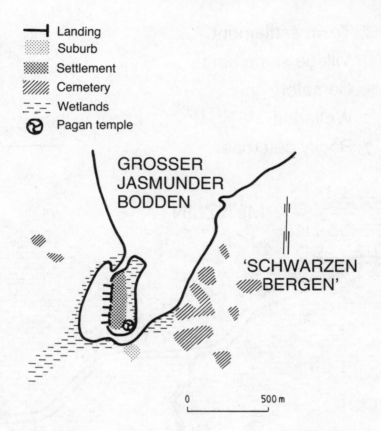

- ⊣ Landing
- Suburb
- Settlement
- Cemetery
- Wetlands
- ⊛ Pagan temple

GROSSER
JASMUNDER
BODEN

'SCHWARZEN
BERGEN'

0   500 m

Fig. 6.3 Early medieval Ralswiek, with the Viking-age shoreline (after Herrmann *et al.* 1982)

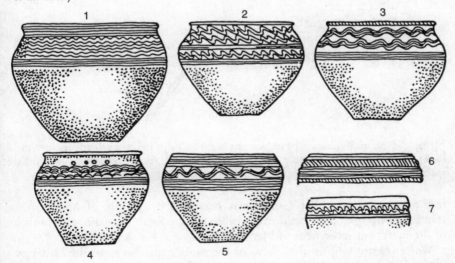

Fig. 6.4 Slavonic pottery of Feldberg (1–4) and Fresendorf (5–7) types (after Donat 1989)

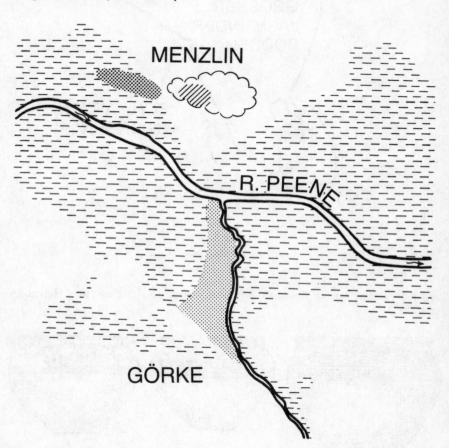

Town settlement
Village settlement
Cemetery
Wetlands
Rocky outcrops

MENZLIN

R. PEENE

GÖRKE

0   500 m

Fig. 6.5   Plan of Menzlin. The settlement lies on a ridge in the wetlands around the River Peene, with its cemetery nearby. The scattered village settlement of Görke spreads along the south side of the river (after Herrmann *et al.* 1982)

found there suggest that Görke was occupied by people of high social standing who may have been responsible for the establishment and control of the merchant settlement of Menzlin.

Wolin (figure 6.6) on the island of the same name between the estuaries of the Oder and the Dziwna, was one of the largest urban settlements along the Baltic coast, covering at least 20 hectares in all. Excavations began there

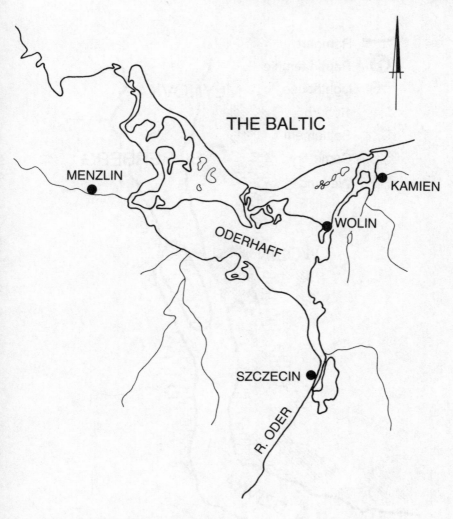

Fig. 6.6 Map of the Oder estuary with the early medieval sites mentioned in the text

at the beginning of this century under the direction of K.A. Wilde and were continued by W. Filipowiak after the Second World War.[6] They were extensive and systematic, and revealed deep occupation deposits, suggesting that this was an urban centre of considerable importance. Adam of Bremen, the late twelfth-century Danish chronicler Saxo Grammaticus, and the Iceland sagas all call the site *Jumne,*. where the pirate band of Jomsvikings lived and defended themselves during the tenth century. The Jomsvikings played an important part in Scandinavian politics during that century, finally being defeated by the Swedes and Norwegians in the 980s when their town of Jumne was ceded to the Slavonic Wends.

Wolin (figure 6.7) lies on a long raised-beach ridge between the water and the strip of marshy ground which cuts off the sand spit from the main island. In the seventh century there was a fishing settlement there which

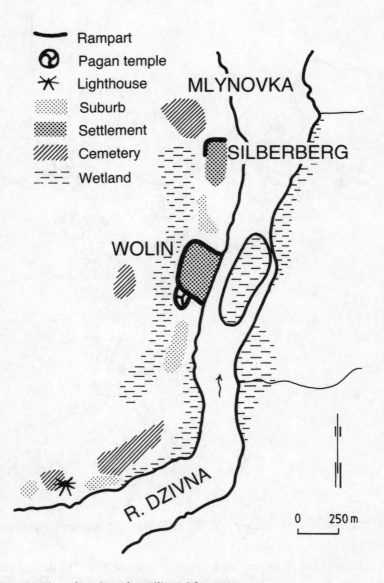

Legend:
- Rampart
- ⊘ Pagan temple
- ✳ Lighthouse
- Suburb
- Settlement
- Cemetery
- Wetland

MLYNOVKA

SILBERBERG

WOLIN

R. DZIVNA

0   250 m

Fig. 6.7   Plan of Wolin (after Filipowiak 1986)

was supplemented and finally dominated by a craftsmen's centre about 700.
In the ninth century it was enclosed by a semi-circular rampart. The town
with its suburbs at each end of the sand spit grew in importance in the tenth
century; fishermen occupied the south suburb and craftsmen a northern
one. The most northerly suburb, *Silberberg*, was also surrounded by a
rampart.

Extensive cemeteries stand on the north and south parts of the sand spit.
The northern one, *Młynówka*, comprises at least two thousand graves of the
tenth to twelfth centuries, some 1300 of which, both cremations and
inhumations, have been excavated. The southern cemetery is smaller and

was also used as the site of a beacon for shipping. A Christian cemetery has been found immediately opposite the town.

Wolin is unusual in that since the later part of the ninth century its street pattern defined regular square blocks with four houses *c.* 5 × 6m in each. The harbour has regularly laid-out quays built of halved oak logs driven vertically into the ground and fronted by horizontal planks, the whole secured and anchored to the fill behind the quayside. The types of jetties known in the west and north, at Dorestad, Hedeby and Birka for instance, do not occur at Wolin.

The stratigraphy of the settlement is of great significance for local chronology within the west Slavonic area. The artifactual evidence is sparse but the objects are basically similar to those found at Hedeby and Birka, with iron-working, smithing, ship-building, comb-making, amber-working, and leather- and textile-making tools all having been identified. Nevertheless, the pottery is almost entirely Slavonic in type.

Many settlements cluster around the mouth of the River Parsęta, east of Wolin and near modern *Kolobrzeg* (figure 6.8). Close to the estuary lie a small fortress and extensive remains of salt-pans, and several kilometres upstream there is another fortress, a harbour and a Viking-age settlement.[7] Even further upstream lies the settlement of *Swielubie* with its Viking-age occupation deposits and cemetery of about a hundred burial mounds, some of which contain Scandinavian objects of both male and female types, suggesting contacts across the Baltic Sea.

In the land of the Prussian Balts, Scandinavian grave types discovered near Elbląg have long been used as evidence for a harbour in East Prussia, east of the River Vistula and tentatively identified with the *Truso* of Wulfstan's account. The occupation deposits which have only recently been found lie near Lake Druzno, some distance away from the cemetery, and presumably pin-point the site of Wulfstan's 'lake, on the shore of which Truso stands'.

Grobin (figure 6.9) in Latvia seems also to have been a centre of Scandinavian settlement in the Baltic countries. It has a fort and at least three cemeteries, excavated by Birger Nerman[8] in the 1930s. Two of the cemeteries contained grave-goods of central Swedish type, another contained objects of Gotlandic forms. Recent excavations by V.P. Petrenko have emphasized this connection through the discovery in Grobin of a Gotlandic picture-stone. Grobin is probably the *Seeburg* in Kurland mentioned by Rimbert when describing its capture by the Svear in the mid-ninth century. The Svear then continued on to the inland town of *Apulia*, modern Apoule, five days' march from the coast, where they waged a fierce battle against the Kurlanders, only gaining victory by temporarily acknowledging Christianity. Apulia seems to have been a fortified settlement of the type frequently met with in the Slavonic lands south of the Baltic Sea and to have had no Scandinavian connections.

The Fenno-Ugrian – east Slavonic area

From the eighth to the eleventh centuries the north Russian forests, renowned for their fur-bearing animals, were inhabited by the Fenno-Ugrian

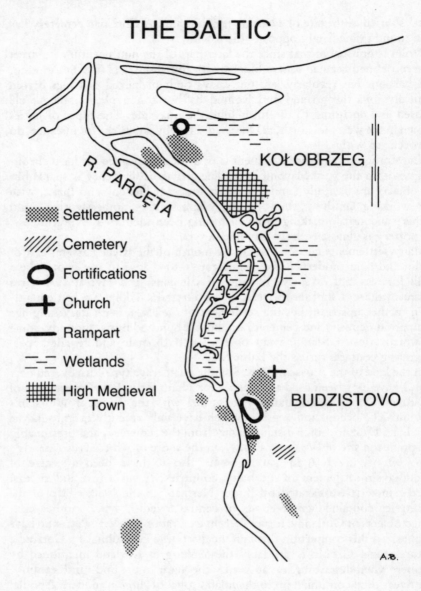

THE BALTIC

KOŁOBRZEG

R. PARCĘTA

▨ Settlement

⧄ Cemetery

O Fortifications

✛ Church

▬ Rampart

⚌ Wetlands

▦ High Medieval
Town

BUDZISTOVO

A.B.

Fig. 6.8 Plan of the Kołobrzeg area (after Filipowiak 1989)

tribes such as the Chuds, Vods, Muromas, Meryans and Veš, whose burial mounds survive today along the banks of the rivers. During the eighth and ninth centuries Slavonic tribes such as the Krivičians and Novgorod Slovenes lived a little further south. In the period corresponding to the Viking age the characteristic Slavonic agrarian settlement pattern of scattered villages began to be supplemented by fortifications. The twelfth-century Russian Primary Chronicle which records the history of the Varangians (or Scandinavians) in the formation of the ancient Russian state

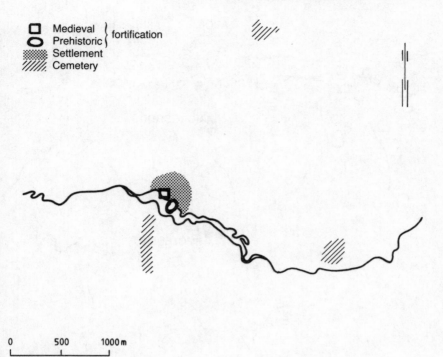

Fig. 6.9 Map of the Grobin area (after Nerman 1958)

of Kiev, repeatedly describes how the Scandinavian leaders, later to become Russian princes, settled in these fortifications which subsequently developed into towns.

The cemeteries with apparent Scandinavian connections in this region are often very large, sometimes containing thousands of burial mounds such as that at *Gnezdovo* near Smolensk, the most important junction in the tenth century for routes towards the north along the rivers Lovat and Volkhov, westwards along the River Dvina, eastwards along the Oka and Volga, and southwards along the Dnepr (figure 6.10). Controversy still rages today about how many of these burials, from Gnezdovo and from other similar cemeteries, are of Scandinavian and how many of Slavonic origin. No satisfactory consensus has yet been reached, but as the grave-goods are often identical with those found in Scandinavia, and specifically Slavonic ethnic markers such as the female hair ornaments known as *Schläfenringe* are uncommon, a Scandinavian presence cannot be discounted.

A number of the towns along the river routes also display traces of Scandinavian occupation in their earliest habitation layers. It is surprising that the Vikings, who really had no true urban culture of their own at that time (the ninth century), clearly played an important part in the development of urbanization in the East. Only a selection of the most important places will be mentioned here. Some other sites which have produced less positive evidence for Viking presence at an early stage have had to be omitted because of the inaccessibility of the published evidence.

Fig. 6.10 Map of the western parts of the Soviet Union with some of the early medieval towns with Scandinavian connections

One of the most important water routes used by the Vikings in their eastward travels was that through the Bay of Finland and Lake Ladoga, following the River Volkhov to Lake Ilmen. The plain drained by the Volkhov is surrounded by great tracts of forest and marsh, and early settlement was concentrated on the high river banks. Throughout most of its length the Volkhov was navigable to large vessels but in many places rapids necessitated extra power and skill if they were to be passed. Most of the early settlements grew up at these points, either as stations to help pilot the ships along the river or as customs posts, and many of them were

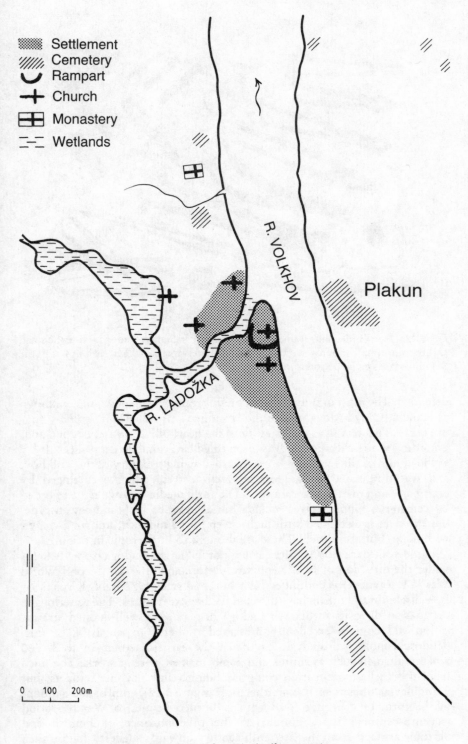

Settlement
Cemetery
Rampart
Church
Monastery
Wetlands

R. VOLKHOV

Plakun

R. LADOŽKA

0   100   200m

Fig. 6.11   Plan of Staraya Ladoga (after Kirpičnikov 1989)

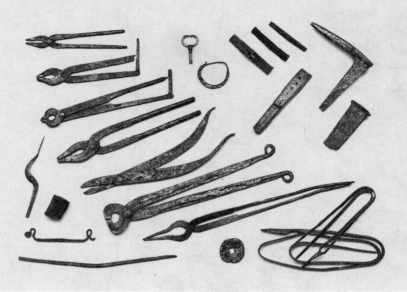

Fig. 6.12   Iron implements found in an early house in Staraya Ladoga. Note the small anthropomorphic mount with animal-head terminals which belongs to the Scandinavian Vendel period

defended. The most important point on this route was *Ladoga*, today known as Staraya (Old) Ladoga, which the Scandinavians called *Aldeigjuborg* (figure 6.11). This served as the gateway to the heart of Russia and beyond and, according to the chroniclers, was often ruled by Scandinavian princes. It lay at the mouth of the Ladożka, an eastward-flowing tributary of the Volkhov, and was dominated by a great wooden fortress which was ringed by craftmen's and merchants' suburbs.[9] The early medieval town is surrounded by cemeteries whose graves include burial mounds of Scandinavian type, but the river is also lined with high, steep burial mounds, known as *sopki*, with many burials in each. These are thought to be Slavonic in origin.

Large-scale excavations were carried out in Staraya Ladoga from 1909-13, under the direction of N.I. Repnikov. Before and after the Second World War V.I. Ravdonikas continued his work, and since 1972 A.N. Kirpičikov, E.A. Rjabinin and others have directed further excavations. The waterlogged occupation deposits in Staraya Ladoga display very well-defined stratification and contain excellently preserved timber. On the basis of this, dendrochronological analysis has dated the earliest settlement to *c.* 760 when craftsmen such as smiths and comb-makers were at work. The finds from this earliest occupation comprise Finnish and Slavonic artifacts, but Scandinavian objects such as smiths' tools (figure 6.12), combs, and a mount in the form of a bronze head with a 'horned helmet' of Vendel-period (seventh-century) type, dominate. The predominance of Finnish and Slavonic artifacts from the late tenth century onwards suggests that by then the Scandinavians had been assimilated by the local population.

Many branches of the River Volkhov flow out of Lake Ilmen, with the main ones branching out to surround a group of islands. The great medieval town of *Novgorod* (see figure 6.10), the main centre for north Russia until the seventeenth century stands on the main island. The Vikings called Novgorod *Holmgård*, 'the town on the island', but right from its foundation in *c.* 930 it incorporated areas on both sides of the west branch of the river. There was a kremlin (fort) on the west bank surrounded by craftsmen's and merchants' quarters; the original market centre with a concentration of foreign merchants stood on the east bank.[10] In the twelfth century all the different strands were brought together into one town and the earliest town wall was built.

Excavations, mainly on the west bank, before and after the Second World War by A.V. Artsikhovsky and B.A. Kolčin and subsequently by V.L. Janin, have shown that the town has occupation deposits up to 7m thick containing well-preserved timbers. Dendrochronological analyses of the street surfaces, up to thirty superimposed layers in places, have produced a remarkable set of dates enabling a precise chronology to be constructed, the earliest date being 930. Work still in progress indicates that some fine adjustments to the time-scale need to be made.

The artifacts from Novgorod are unparalleled in their quantity and quality because of the conditions of preservation of wood, textiles and leather. One of the most remarkable groups of finds is the collection of almost seven hundred high medieval letters written on birch bark in the cyrillic alphabet; they include merchants' notes, receipts, business letters and even love letters, giving a remarkable insight into daily life in the middle ages. Finds of earlier date are fewer, however, and there are no signs of occupation at Novgorod before the 930s, even though the town is named in the Primary Chronicle as the place where the Varangian (Scandinavian) Ryurik, founder of the Ryurikid dynasty, settled in the 860s.

Forts controlling the water routes stand both upstream and downstream of Novgorod, where the arms of the Volkhov divide and rejoin. The one to the south, at *Ryurikovo Gorodishche*, stands on one of the islands formed by the Volkhov, 2km upstream from the centre of Novgorod. Its occupation layers cover at least 4 hectares and discoveries there strongly suggest that this is the site of the Novgorod mentioned in the chronicle. Excavations in Ryurikovo Gorodishche began as early as 1901 and today continue under the leadership of E.N. Nosov.[11] Pottery, jewellery, beads, combs and other artifacts show that the settlement dates from at least the second half of the ninth century, but it could be even earlier. In contrast to the finds from Novgorod, some of the objects discovered at Ryurikovo Gorodishche (beads and combs, for instance) are Scandinavian in character and of an earlier date than the Novgorod finds. This, then, must be the original Holmgärd, the 'town on the island'.

Gorodishche lies at the outfall from Lake Ilmen, the lake which is considered by many scholars to have been a nodal point on the river routes east and south through Russia. The many tributaries flowing into Lake Ilmen whose sources are confusingly intertwined with those of the Volga, Dnepr and Dvina on the Valdai high plateau in the south-east, provide suitable sites for portages over which these rivers can be reached. By following them the

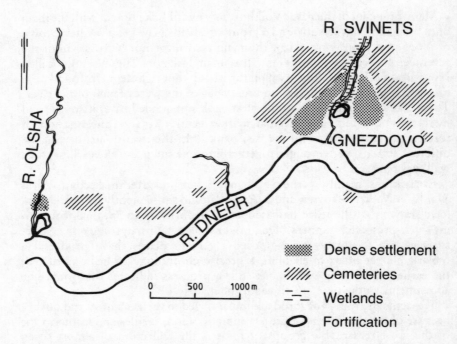

Fig. 6.13   Map of Gnezdovo on the River Dnepr (after Herrmann *et al.* 1982)

Caspian Sea and the Black Sea, entrances to both the Muslim and the
Byzantine worlds, could be reached easily.

The next important control point lies on the River Dnepr at *Gnezdovo*
(figure 6.13), *c.* 11km west of Smolensk where the rivulets Svinets and
Olsha join the Dnepr from the north. Each of the estuaries, 3km apart, is
straddled by a settlement with a neighbouring fort. The settlement on the
Svinets is the more extensive, with occupation layers up to a couple of
metres thick. It is also surrounded by huge cemeteries still containing about
2700 burial mounds.[12] About 450 of these are strung out westwards along
the Dnepr and on both sides of the mouth of the Olsha, and a group of about
100 mounds stands south of the Dnepr opposite the mouth of the Svinets. It
has proved difficult to calculate the original number of mounds in all the
cemeteries but whatever the true number, the Gnezdovo area contains the
largest cemeteries of burial mounds in eastern Europe, bigger even than
those at Birka.

The discovery at Gnezdovo in 1867 of a great silver hoard, concealed
shortly after the middle of the tenth century, stimulated interest in the site,
and many early Russian archaeologists such as V.I. Sizov and S.I. Sergejev
excavated there, particularly in the cemeteries, where about 1200 mounds
have been dug. A small part of the settlement has also been investigated.
Since 1949 large-scale excavations have been directed by D.A. Avdusin of
the University of Moscow.

The Gnezdovo settlement dates from the Viking age. It lies beside a fort
and on both sides of the river, with abundant remains of crafts (moulds,

crucibles, slag, debris from iron smithing, etc.) on the west bank. Traces of commerce and perhaps also customs control are apparent on the east bank which is probably where the silver hoard was discovered.

Excavation has, however, concentrated mainly on the cemeteries. The biggest mounds, richest in grave-goods, were excavated first, with the average-sized and small mounds not being tackled until after the Second World War. This more recent work has resulted in the number of burials without grave-goods being dramatically increased.

The mounds vary very considerably in size, from less than 50cm to 5 or 6m high. Many are surrounded by ring-ditches. Most of them are cremations, with only *c.* 120 of the 1200 excavated graves being inhumations. The cremations seem mainly to have been composed of layers of burnt bone and grave-goods, and the most common finds consist of boat rivets, weapons, and jewellery, often of Scandinavian type. Some graves contained Thor's-hammer rings, that is, neck-rings of iron with hammer-shaped pendants which were common in tenth-century central Sweden, but the greater number of graves contained very few grave-goods and so are not readily datable. They often contain only a pottery vessel of Slavonic type, but as this is often wheel-thrown it can be no earlier than the middle of the tenth century.

Since the turn of the century the finds from Gnezdovo have attracted great interest, with questions of ethnicity and date being to the fore. Some scholars have taken the types of graves and grave-goods to mean that many of the people buried there were Scandinavians, but more recently Avdusin and other Soviet scholars have suggested that most graves without grave-goods represent the Slavonic population and that only a small proportion, perhaps about forty richly furnished graves, were burials of first- or second-generation Scandinavians. Mounds surrounded by ring-ditches seem not to be Scandinavian in influence although they do occur in some parts of Sweden in the Viking age. On the other hand, the custom of using cremation layers can be associated with eastern mainland Sweden. The silver hoard from Gnezdovo also contained objects which are either of Scandinavian origin or strongly influenced by the art-styles of the Scandinavian Viking age, so the question of ethnicity remains problematic.

Dating is also problematic. The Gnezdovo graves have usually been attributed to the middle or end of the ninth century until after 1000, but the common occurrence of Slavonic wheel-thrown pottery has limited the chronological boundaries, bringing the probable earliest date of the graves to the first half of the tenth century. The conversion of the early Russian state to Christianity in 988 also provides another chronological boundary, for the latest cremations should be little later than that. If then, most of the graves are of tenth-century date, the cemeteries at Gnezdovo must represent an extremely large population. If the cemeteries were in use for less than a hundred years the population must have consisted of a minimum of 2000 individuals at any one time (cf. the calculations used at Birka and Hedeby).

The date of Gnezdovo is also important for the interpretation of Smolensk, mentioned in the Primary Chronicle as figuring in the journeys of the Varangians in the ninth century. Surprisingly, no artifacts earlier than

1000 have been discovered there and the Chronicle's Smolensk should probably be identified with Gnezdovo.

Two of the places known through their place-name (*volokh*)[13] to have been portages from the river Dvina to the Dnepr lie in the upper courses of the Olsha and the Svinets, upstream from the Gnezdovo settlements. All Russian archaeologists agree that the small settlement beside the River Olsha dates from after the Viking age. Some think that the settlement by the River Svinets (Gnezdovo itself) could be the original site of Smolensk. This conclusion is disputed by Avdusin, for he believes that the settlements of Gnezdovo and Smolensk are chronologically parallel but that Gnezdovo was superseded by Smolensk at the beginning of the eleventh century when the river routes and portages between the Dvina and Dnepr were displaced eastwards. This resulted in Smolensk becoming the pre-eminent control point on the river routes.

At the end of the ninth century Staraya Ladoga, Ryurikovo Gorodishche and perhaps even Gnezdovo were no more than small forts at points where river traffic could be both controlled and piloted. All three have yielded artifacts from occupation layers, and in two cases also grave-goods, suggesting Scandinavian presence, but the extent of the Scandinavian population is unknown, as is the degree of its assimilation into the native population.

By the end of the tenth century the forts had developed into sizeable urban settlements. At that time, Gnezdovo was one of the most important places in the whole of eastern Europe.

In contrast to these places which served as transit points along the river routes, Kiev[14] (figure 6.14) was the main destination in Russia, and the political centre of the early Russian state. According to the Primary Chronicle, Ryurik's successor Oleg had settled there before 900, initiating a great princedom which in 988, under the leadership of the Prince Vladimir, adopted the Byzantine form of Christianity.

Kiev stands on and at the foot of a steep escarpment forming the edge of the high plateau to the west of the River Dnepr. There was a settlement there long before the Viking age, but this was probably of rural character. About the year 900 Kiev began to expand dramatically: a fortress was built on Starokievskaja Gora, and an extensive settlement began to grow up in the low-lying Podol. Craft-production and trade were concentrated in Podol, with Starokievskaja Gora being primarily the administrative centre which also contained cemeteries, mainly of an aristocratic character.

After 988 when Vladimir introduced Christianity the defended area of Starokievskaja Gora was enlarged, and it became an ecclesiastical centre. Influential monastic houses, such as the Monastery of the Caves in the south, were then founded around the town.

There is regrettably little information about the activities in these areas, although we know that one of the most important industries to develop there was that of glass-working whose products were distributed from *c.* 1000 onwards throughout all the Rus' towns and even as far as Sigtuna and Hedeby. The demand for glazed tiles and mosaics for the churches built after the 988 conversion brought Greek craftsmen to Kiev, where they remained to initiate the important glass workshops, of which many have been found during the excavations.[15]

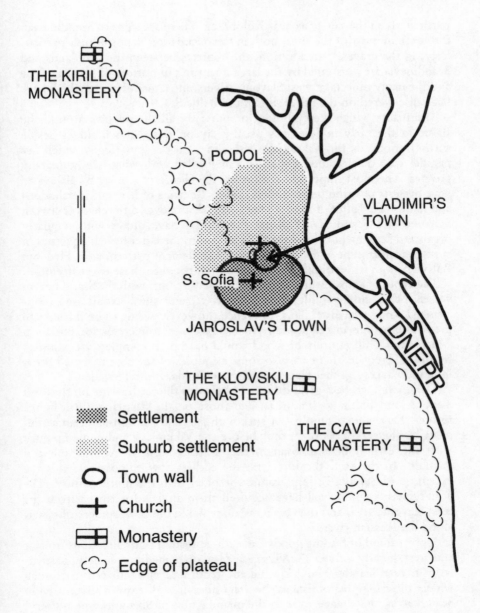

THE KIRILLOV
MONASTERY

PODOL

VLADIMIR'S
TOWN

S. Sofia

JAROSLAV'S TOWN

R. DNEPR

THE KLOVSKIJ
MONASTERY

Settlement

Suburb settlement

⬭ Town wall

✚ Church

⊞ Monastery

◌⊃ Edge of plateau

THE CAVE
MONASTERY

Fig. 6.14 Map of Kiev including the tenth- and eleventh-century churches and monasteries (after Toločko 1989)

Summary: the Baltic, east and west

With the exception of Wolin and Menzlin, the many places on the southern Baltic coast known to have had Scandinavian connections seem to have been minor harbours with small populations. Their limited economic activities were often associated with some type of local resource, such as the salt which was produced in many places inland from the Baltic coast, but particularly in the salt-pans near Kołobrzeg. There are signs of Scandinavian influence in most of the sites, both in the occupation deposits and, particularly, in the graves.[16] In addition, the contacts between the Slav lands and Scandinavia are illustrated by the large quantities of pottery of Slavonic type and the many objects of west Slavonic silversmiths' manufacture which have been discovered on the other side of the Baltic Sea.[17]

The places which were chosen for ports by all the peoples around the Baltic in the early middle ages usually lay on raised-beach ridges beside small lagoons in the Viking-age shoreline, or on low ridges which lay parallel with or straddled a shallow valley filled with what is now marshy ground. The most important reason for the choice of site seems always to have been its position on seabound routes. Remains of harbour installations and ships are often found. There are distinctive differences between Slavonic and Scandinavian ports: the former have quays with regularly organized settlement behind them, as at Wolin, the latter have long jetties of west European type and a more irregular settlement pattern, as at Hedeby. Ralswiek with its landing places seems to fall between these two extremes.

The types of ships seem also to have been different, with the Scandinavian vessels being clinker-built using iron rivets, and the Slavonic ones constructed using trenails.[18] This difference, however, seems to be difficult to prove as most remains of Scandinavian ships come from cremation burials in which ships built entirely of wood would have been completely consumed by fire. Moreover, there are also some examples of sewn or trenailed boats in Scandinavia, e.g. that from Tuna in Badelunda, central Sweden.

There seems to be a great difference between the settlements on the west Slavonic and Baltic coastal areas, and those on the Russian rivers. In the former there were a number of sites with specialized, non-agrarian settlement by the eighth century, thus before the Viking age and contemporary with the earliest Scandinavian market centres such as Åhus, Ribe and Paviken. In the east, the forts and the earliest towns, possibly with the exception of Staraya Ladoga, cannot be older than the ninth century. The Scandinavians could well have acquired their models for towns from the west Slavonic area, and then been instrumental in the development of towns along the Russian rivers.

A great flood of trading goods and skills spread in both directions, to east and west, greatly influencing Viking-age and early medieval society, particularly in east Scandinavia.[19] During the tenth and eleventh centuries such widely differing phenomena as the great quantities of eastern silver used in Scandinavia, the change-over to the manufacture of Slavonic-type pottery, and the transition in central Sweden to a probably Byzantine-influenced Christianity can be seen as the most important results of these contacts.

The conversion in 988 was very influential not only on Russia but also on east Scandinavia which seems to have become Christian shortly afterwards. The central Swedish conversion to Christianity is indicated by the adoption there of east-west oriented inhumations without grave-goods and the use of runic stones decorated with crosses; but written sources in the west, such as Adam of Bremen's history, suggest that Sweden was not fully Christian even as late as the 1070s. The marriage in *c.* 1017 of Ingegerd, daughter of the Svea king Olov Skötkonung, to Prince Jaroslav, son of Vladimir, further underlines the Russian–Swedish connection. Her portrait, and that of her daughters, still stand as a wall painting in the cathedral of St Sophia in Kiev; they are some of the earliest known likenesses of people of Scandinavian descent.

Chapter 7

Towns in north, east and west: their physical structure and economy

This chapter will deal with a number of problems common to the early towns of the Viking age in all the areas dealt with in previous chapters: topography, the choice of site and its relationship with communication systems, street plan and plot arrangement, building types, institutions, defences, burials, churchyards and population. It will also include a consideration of Viking-age economy in the form of trade, industry, environment and hinterland.

Topography, hinterland and communications

Towns in the early middle ages could only develop if there were support systems in the form of settlements in the hinterland, and a network of communications. Defensibility seems to have been a secondary consideration.

Almost all the towns which have been discussed in chapters 4, 5 and 6 lie in direct connection with waterways, often by the sea coast and on inlets but in some cases along rivers and other waterway systems. Water transport must, therefore, have been of prime importance for urban economy in the Viking age even though some places were also served by overland routes.

When the urban settlements were on virgin sites, locations near the sea coast were often chosen for their harbours which offered shelter for shipping in bad weather. They often lay upstream of an estuary, or, in the virtually tideless Baltic Sea region, on the coast itself or beside a lagoon protected by sand banks or gravel spits. Further from the sea, an island in an inlet or the confluence of several rivers might be selected, particularly where there was a promontory which could be easily delimited on its landward side.

Birka, Hedeby and Wolin, the biggest Viking-age trading sites in the Baltic region, have a rather unusual situation in that all three are on inlets at a considerable distance from the open coast. In contrast, the towns in inland Russia all stand on river banks.

The topography of Viking-age towns on coasts or inlets is sometimes rather difficult to establish today because water levels and the position of shorelines have changed in the intervening centuries. Some European coastlines have silted up, others have been subjected to erosion, and in Scandinavia isostatic land upheaval and eustatic water-level changes have led to dramatic variations.[1]

Another important reason for the choice of site must have been the presence in the vicinity of a rural population which could supply the town with provisions, fuel, hay, and raw materials, and which would also provide a market for the manufactured and traded products originating in the towns. The potential of the hinterland may also have influenced the need for industrial and other specializations in a town.

Until recently there have been few studies of the interaction between towns and their hinterland, although Jankuhn and Müller-Wille have researched into Hedeby and its surroundings.[2] Jankuhn was unable to establish any definite connection between Hedeby and the rural settlements in the province of Angeln. His conclusions reiterated those arrived at by earlier research, that is, that Hedeby, Birka and other settlements of their type were components of an international trading and transport system rather than places which provided services for their rural hinterland. Müller-Wille's more recent and continuing research has produced more positive evidence of a connection between the town and its surroundings.

One place where we can now see that Jankuhn's conclusions must be at least partly wrong is the Mälaren valley where the well-preserved field monuments in the countryside illustrate the ancient landscape and provide excellent evidence for the way its population increased and its rural settlements expanded in the early middle ages.[3] The settlement pattern of this area in the years up to 1000 was one of isolated farmsteads strung out along the cultivable valleys, each farm with its adjacent family cemetery of burial mounds. Excavations have showed that the grave-goods in the burials often include manufactured items such as knives and other small iron tools, combs, and simple imported objects like glass beads, all of which could have been obtained in the markets of the contemporary centre of Birka. As our knowledge of the topography of this rural area has increased it has become ever more obvious that Birka acted as a stopping point and exchange centre on the route leading from the northern forests with their abundance of raw materials to the lands of the Baltic Sea and central Europe.[4] So it had a dual role: a service centre for its immediate hinterland and a node in long-distance routes stretching from western Europe to the lands of the Russians, Greeks, and Moslems in the east.

In the British Isles, the hinterlands of Viking-age towns such as York and Dublin, and of the earlier Hamwic, are coming under scientific scrutiny, and we are beginning to understand how closely related were town and countryside in the early middle ages. All three depended on their surroundings for food and building materials.[5] In contrast to the Mälaren valley, it is not

Fig. 7.1   Reconstructed Skuldelev ships under sail. The *knarr* (merchantman) is in the foreground (Photo Skibs Historisk Laboratorium, Roskilde)

so clear what the rural settlements received in return although the distribution of building stone from the Roman ruins of York for reuse in village churches suggests a reciprocal exchange.[6]

The main means of transport in the Viking age was waterborne. Until fairly recently most of our knowledge of Viking ships came from vessels such as those excavated from the burial mounds of Oseberg and Gokstad in Norway,[7] or from the rusty rivets which are often all that remain in the ground to represent ships, for example, the boat burials of Ladby in Denmark,[8] or Vendel[9] and Valsgärde[10] in Sweden. The state of knowledge increased dramatically with the excavation of the Skuldelev ships from Roskilde fjord on Zealand, Denmark, which began in the early 1960s; through this excavation a completely new picture of the variety of Viking-age vessels has emerged.[11] The Skuldelev 1 (figure 7.1), for instance, was a merchantman (*knarr* in Old Norse) with a character quite different from that of a warlike longship. Ole Crumlin-Pedersen's researches into the Skuldelev find and other Viking-age discoveries in Denmark and elsewhere have shown that there were many different types of ships designed for specific functions, and that there were also regional variations in the shipbuilding tradition of the time. Sea trials of replica vessels have also increased our understanding of the manoeuvrability and use of the originals.

Fig. 7.2 A reconstruction of one of the boats used along the central Swedish rivers and around the islands of the archipelago, from the remains discovered in grave 14 at Valsgärde (Photo Björn Ambrosiani)

Small, shallow draught, ships up to 12-15m long, were common both in the Baltic Sea and in Scandinavia in general in the Viking age (figure 7.2). These all-purpose vessels built in Nordic clinker-built technique were designed for sailing or rowing along rivers and between islands, and they could also be dragged easily through portages which straddled promontories or circumvented waterfalls, dangerous currents, or other obstacles. Many place-names with the elements *drag*, *ed*- and *bor*- show that these portages were common in Scandinavia.

In some cases portages must have been specially constructed, with a ditch over a watershed being lined with timber to facilitate the passage of the ships which had to be manhandled through them. The north-south route via Birka relied on two portages, one by *Tälje* (modern Södertälje) and the other by *Draget* (between Lake Mälaren and Ullvifjärdarna on the way to Uppsala).[12] Building development in Södertälje at the south end of the Tälje portage has recently revealed a clay-filled ditch along the line of the medieval main street to the market place, below the Viking-age water level (figure 7.3). The clay represents the silting of a possibly man-made canal from whose northernmost end it was only a couple of hundred metres to the Viking-age water level on the Mälaren. At Draget the portage was longer, perhaps between 500 and 1000m, and lined with timber. Similar portages are known elsewhere, particularly between the river·systems of the Dvina, Volkhov-Lovat, Volga and Dnepr in Russia[13] (figure 6.10). The siting of Gnezdovo (p. 117) must have been entirely dependent on the existence of portages, and place-names with the element *volokh*, indicate portages in the upper reaches of the rivers Swinets and Olsha.[14]

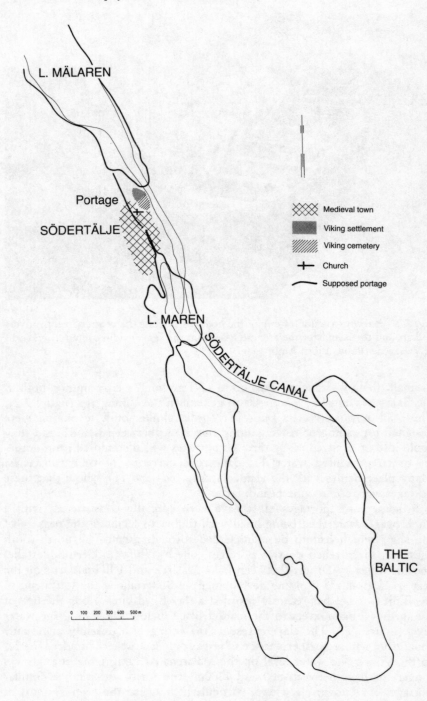

Fig. 7.3 The portage 15km south of Birka lies in the centre of Södertälje, on a narrow isthmus between lake Mälaren and an inlet of the Baltic. The shoreline here is the present 5m contour (sea-level in the Viking age). In the Viking age Lake Mälaren was still an inlet of the Baltic, not a lake.

The presence of portages on the Russian rivers implies the use of small vessels as transports to and from Byzantium and Arabia. They may have been locally-built expanded dug-out boats (constructed of a hollowed-out log supplemented by planks as gunwales), some remains of which have been found in excavations at Novgorod.[15] Some Byzantine written sources indicate that such boats were modified for travel across the Black Sea to the Bosphorus.

Heavy sea-going vessels such as the *knarr*, and later the *cog*[16] could not have been dragged overland through portages, and they would have had to sail around headlands and peninsulas. The transition from light clinker-built vessels to these larger ships in the late tenth or early eleventh century must have entailed a change in waterborne routes, and this may have been one of the reasons why some settlements were abandoned at that time.

In the Viking age the main shipping routes followed the coast, for example, the Norwegian route to and from the north kept as far as possible to the straits between the islands and the mainland. Travel probably took place only during the daylight hours with overnight stops in safe anchorages. This is shown by the ninth-century description of Ottar's journey from north Norway,[17] and also by high medieval sources which mention indispensable night anchorages on the route to Finland and the Baltic States.[18]

The high seas were crossed only when it was absolutely essential (the saga mentions of sea crossings underline their unusual nature), but then there were well-known navigational landmarks, points of departure, and established routes for the hazardous journeys across the North Sea and the Atlantic. These long-distance journeys must have been undertaken by vessels larger than those used in the Baltic where the archipelagos and long stretches of river could only be navigated by rowing.

The common belief that Viking ships were beached by being dragged up on to the shore must now be revised in the light of new discoveries. All the places where Viking-age waterfront sites have been excavated have shown that they were provided with quays and other revetments parallel to the shore, or with jetties built on piles out into the water. Quays seem to have been particularly common in western Europe and the west Slav areas, while jetties are found in Scandinavia, as at Kaupang, Birka and Hedeby for example, but also at Dorestad.[19] There is as yet no evidence for any of these structures along the Russian rivers.

It must not be forgotten that in the Baltic Sea region, and particularly in the north, winter ice was a positive advantage for communications. It was possible, by horse and sledge or on skates, to travel more quickly over long distances in the winter than in the summer.[20] During the high middle ages great winter markets were common, well documented, for example, in Uppsala and other central Swedish towns. One sign of this winter traffic in the Viking age comes from the many hundreds of ice skates made from the long-bones of cattle or horses which were discovered in the Black Earth of Birka (figures 7.4, 7.5). Interestingly, bone skates are also known from Anglo-Scandinavian York.[21] It is unlikely that the British climate at that time was severe enough either for communications along frozen rivers or for the holding of winter fairs on ice, and we must conclude that skating was more likely to have been a leisure pastime of the York Vikings.

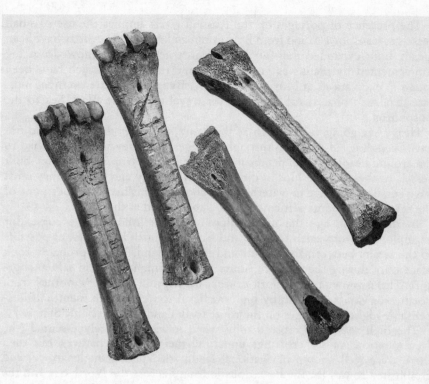

Fig. 7.4 Hundreds of bone skates were discovered during excavations of the Black Earth at Birka. They are polished on the underside, where they came in contact with the ice, and roughened above to give a grip for shoes (Photo Mats Spett)

Fig. 7.5 Bone skates in use. This illustration from Olaus Magnus 1555 shows skates of an exaggerated length, probably because of a misunderstanding by Olaus' south European draughtsman

Fig. 7.6   The hollow ways at Timmele, west Sweden, are still more than 4m deep and represent parts of the main route from Denmark to Västergötland and central Sweden which was in use from the stone age (Photo Björn Ambrosiani)

Another sign of winter travel comes from the ice-nails for horses' hoofs which have been discovered in innumerable Scandinavian Viking-age graves.[22] Overland travel by horse in winter could only have been possible if they were used.

The location of Hedeby entailed a combination of water and land transport, for cargoes destined for the west must have been carried across the Jutland peninsula by wagon or packhorse[23] (see figure 4.10). According to Jankuhn, people and goods from the east arrived at Hedeby by boat, but then would have had to cross the *c.* 15km overland route to Hollingstedt, or its predecessor on the River Treene, to reach the west coast of Jutland whence boats could set out across the North Sea to the British Isles, or south-westwards to the mouths of the Elbe, the Rhine and beyond. Hedeby's westerly contacts have, though, been disputed by Schietzel because virtually no objects of western derivation have been found in his recent excavations. Ships travelling between the Baltic and North Seas could also have used the Limfjord in north Jutland. In the Viking age there was a northerly passage from Limfjord to Skagerrak in addition to the east-west strait used today,[24] but travel around the north point of Jutland (Skagen) was generally avoided because of dangerous currents and shifting sandbanks.

Waterborne transport clearly took priority over land transport in Viking-age Scandinavia. There is little information about the latter and the road system seems to have been very undeveloped, as it was in Sweden until the seventeenth century, and even later in Norway. But a few stretches of

Fig. 7.7 Road systems often used earth and stone causeways to cross wetlands. Sometimes wooden bridges were built. This bridge at Ravning enge near Jelling, Denmark, was built of heavy oak timbers and has been dated by dendrochronology to 978–980. It formed part of the *Hærvejen* through Jutland (Flemming Bau)

road in Sweden still traceable today might have been used in the Viking age; these are represented by bridlepaths or hollow ways (figure 7.6), occasionally using bridges or causeways to cross marshy ground. Many eleventh-century rune stones in central Sweden were erected to commemorate their construction. A system of hollow ways also ran from Danish Halland (modern south-west Sweden) through Västergötland and Östergötland to central Sweden, its route being marked by rune stones which show that it was in use in the eleventh century.[25]

A linked system of hollow ways can also still be traced along the Hærvejen in Jutland, from Viborg to Hedeby.[26] The bridge at Ravning (figure 7.7) spanning the Vejle valley south of Jelling formed part of this system. It was built of heavy oak posts which supported a planked carriageway, and has been dated by dendrochronology to 979–80. The recent discovery of a Viking-age causeway leading to a timber bridge across the River Hull at Skern, Humberside[27] in England has given us some information about tenth-century communications in that country, but England differs from Scandinavia in that it had a well-developed system of Roman roads which, although no doubt in a poor state of repair, remained in use throughout the middle ages.

Town foundation and administration

The processes leading to the foundation or growth of towns have long been controversial issues (see, for example, Christophersen 1989). The spontaneous growth of a town on the site of an earlier market or agricultural nucleus to which specific functions accrued is one popular explanation, but a town could also be a place founded by a king, noble, or bishop, which acquired special privileges, defences, a mint, etc. Divergent opinions of historians and archaeologists have led to the formulation of differing definitions of what is a town. As shown in the introduction (p. 3), we have chosen for this book to use an historical-geographical and social definition rather than an historical-legalistic one. The different regions in which Viking-age towns are known show many parallel models leading to the type of society which we call urban.

In England and western Europe many early medieval towns grew out of their Roman predecessors and often developed through royal or ecclesiastical patronage. Some also depended on commerce and industry for their origins but even those seem to have been closely associated with royal, aristocratic, or ecclesiastical overlords.[28] They are, therefore, different in their origins from the Viking-age towns in the non-Romanized parts of Europe.

Many towns in the Slavonic areas around the Baltic (see figure 6.1) show an association with tribal centres (such as Oldenburg: p. 108) which developed *c.* 700 into places with non–agricultural activities, but towns such as Wolin, with its early fishing settlement, or Ralswiek,[29] seem to have been more closely connected with the coast and seafaring. Menzlin, and neighbouring Görke, is similar to Swielubie/Kołobrzeg, where a nobleman could have been responsible for deliberate foundation. In Russia, most Viking-age towns seem to have developed from native or Varangian hillforts; economic activities were first concentrated within the forts, with commercial and industrial suburbs developing in the tenth century.

It is becoming more and more clear that in Scandinavia market and urban functions were usually associated with royal, or occasionally aristocratic or, later, ecclesiastical, settlements, and that they formed part of the infrastructure of royal or other high-status estates (often called early medieval manors by Scandinavian archaeologists). This was perpetuated in the towns when they became the purveyors of trade, grew to be responsible for fees and tolls, and acted as monopolistic controllers of imported goods.

Scandinavia has many examples of towns founded on land which, when written sources begin, belonged to royal estate centres or manors: Birka, Sigtuna, Lund and Kaupang, for example.[30] In this they are similar to many towns in western Europe. Royal or aristocratic initiative probably explains why property divisions, sometimes demarcated by ditches, were often laid out on initial occupation; they signify a deliberate foundation of the market place/town (see the next section).

Another aspect of towns which may result from the mechanisms of foundation is the continuity or discontinuity of occupation on urban sites. Continuity from the Viking age to the present day can be traced in many towns in western Europe (Dublin, for example), and continuity with even earlier urban settlements is also clear (the towns with Roman origins in Gaul or England) but we also have evidence for towns which changed their sites over the intervening centuries. In the Mälaren valley, for instance, Viking-age Birka was abandoned in the tenth century to be replaced by Sigtuna which, by the thirteenth century, had lost its economic and administrative importance to Stockholm. In western Sweden at a later date Lödöse was replaced by Nya Lödöse which was then superseded by the forerunners of Gothenburg, and finally by Gothenburg itself. A similar movement of centres of population can also be seen in Scania where early medieval Åhus moved to its present site in the high middle ages.[31]

Similar discontinuity can be traced in other areas. For example, Hedeby was replaced by Schleswig although there was a short period of simultaneous existence,[32] and at Ribe the Viking-age settlement on the north bank of the river subsequently became merely a suburb of the high medieval town on the south bank. In Norway, Kaupang was probably overtaken by Tønsberg or Skien,[33] and in Russia we have seen that Gorodishche was replaced by Novgorod, and Gnezdovo by Smolensk (pp. 121–4).

Although the movement of early medieval centres of population is not so obvious in western Europe, the same phenomenon can also be seen there. For instance, the eighth-century settlement of Hamwic (p. 35) was replaced by Southampton sometime in the ninth century, and the commercial centres of London and York which flourished up to the ninth century were finally resited elsewhere.

The reasons for these shifts in site during the early middle ages are complex and there cannot be any one simple explanation for this obvious discontinuity. Changing methods of transport and routes of communication must be one explanation; as mentioned above (p. 133), the development of bigger ships demanded more elaborate harbours with deeper-water access, and this could account for some of the changes. Also, until the end of the tenth century Scandinavian towns were built entirely of timber and their movement would not have entailed much capital loss to their founders or overlords. Once they were replaced by towns with masonry buildings such as churches or (later) monasteries, friaries, and castles they could not have been moved with such ease and so the towns of the post-Viking age have remained on the same sites up to the present day. This explanation does not necessarily hold good for the non-Scandinavian towns of this period, for Hamwic had a stone church (St Mary) during its period of occupation, and York and London were probably in the same situation.

Street plan and plot arrangement

These aspects of Viking-age towns are very difficult to describe in general terms as so little of the total area of any town has been excavated, and the dwelling surfaces have often been disturbed by later agricultural use, or are still occupied. In no case has a complete town plan from the Viking age been retrieved. In some instances the original core of what is still a town today may be traced in a semi-circular zone representing the original boundary or defended unit, for example at Visby[34] and Århus,[35] although it is by no means certain that the plan of any modern town truly reflects its original layout.

Also, no study of early town plans can be complete because the areas which have been archaeologically excavated are small, at best comprising no more than a few per cent of the total occupied area (0.125 per cent in York and 5 per cent in Hedeby, for example). This makes it difficult to discover how the overall street systems were laid out and to be certain of the original shape of the plots and the arrangement of buildings which stood within them. The sites of public buildings such as churches are known in many west European Viking-age towns and their permanent nature can help to elucidate general urban plans, but they do not necessarily give us much information about the specifics of town organization in the Viking age.

Many Viking-age towns seem to have consisted of one main street, parallel to the shore or a riverbank, sometimes with narrow lanes running back from it at right angles. Excavations of early levels at Dublin[36] (see figure 5.5) seem to show a typical example of this form, as do those at Sigtuna,[37] but unfortunately it is always difficult to be sure whether the earliest plan revealed by excavation is really the original one. The best archaeological evidence for a 'high street' and right-angle lanes so far available may be from late tenth-century Sigtuna (see figure 4.23) but even there it is rather doubtful, for *Stora gatan* (the high street) has not been excavated to its lowest levels, and the 'narrow lanes' which have been discovered recently could equally well be long, narrow yards along one side of and within the building plots, or merely eavesdrips. At Sigtuna the plots themselves have been shown to date from the initial period of settlement, at the end of the tenth century, when they were separated from each other by shallow ditches cut into the subsoil. The original position of the ditches was perpetuated by the fences which replaced them. Soon after the foundation of the town some plots were abandoned to form a churchyard and the high street was laid out. The same plot pattern is also found in Ribe as early as the eighth century and in tenth-century Dublin and York.

Some Scandinavian inland towns which lay beside neither river nor coast seem to have had one long street along which the plots were laid out much as in an agricultural village. Andrén's interpretation of the earliest settlement in Lund shows just such a pattern.[38]

Hedeby differs from the above in having a much less regular street system, with streets criss-crossing at all angles, and with few signs of parallelism[39] (figure 7.8). Wolin[40] had a more right-angular, chequer-board street system, and the plots there seem to have been more regular and organized. In this way Wolin clearly differs from contemporary towns in Scandinavia.

There seems to be a significant difference between east and west in the materials used for street surfaces. Most west European towns seem to have had streets with gravel metalling (Hereford, Winchester,[41] Lincoln and so on), whereas those in Scandinavia and east Europe were made of planks and

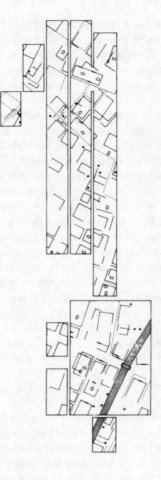

Fig. 7.8 The street and plot pattern discovered by excavations at Hedeby (Schietzel 1981)

split logs laid transversely on a longitudinal timber framework. In Novgorod,[12] for example, the timber-surfaced streets were frequently renewed, with the result that there are now up to thirty superimposed layers of timber street surfaces, the first of which dates from the early tenth century.

The laying out of street systems must have been accompanied by the division of the land into habitable plots. Much still remains to be discovered about plot shape and size, for large-scale excavations are essential if the shape of the plots, the organization of buildings on them and possible continuity of occupation since earliest times are to be discovered. A few sites such as Hall's excavations in York, Jankuhn's and Schietzel's excavations in Hedeby, and Artsikhovsky's and others' excavations in Novgorod, have been of the requisite area. When medieval towns were growing up in Scandinavia during the eleventh century and later, long narrow plots were laid out at right angles to streets, and small shops or workshops stood on the street frontages. The dwellings were situated towards the rear. Sigtuna, Oslo,[43] Trondheim and Bergen have provided good evidence of this arrangement in the eleventh century, but it also seems to have been present earlier in other places, in tenth-century York, for example, where excavations at Coppergate have revealed rectangular plots with workshops and dwellings,[44] and in Dublin from the early tenth century onwards.[45] As mentioned above, some early Viking-age towns such as Ribe and Hedeby seem to have been laid out from the initiation of occupation, in the eighth century in the case of Ribe, with plot boundaries marked out by shallow ditches.[46] This suggests that from the start of a settlement the right to a plot was regulated by the owner, or by permission from an overall landowner who might have been the founder of the town. The lack of order and parallelism shown in the plots and streets in the excavated parts of Hedeby may indicate that this town grew piecemeal from an early, more highly organized, centre, not yet discovered, with new areas being taken into occupation when necessary and not following the original pattern.

Plot boundaries seem to have been permanent from the earliest levels as fences and other demarcations can often be traced in the same position through the occupation deposits right up to the present day. This may mean that ownership or usage always protected the boundaries from encroachment by neighbouring plots. There is no evidence for plot divisions at Birka although the plans of the 1870s' excavations show parallel rows of stones cutting through the deposits in the Black Earth and running down towards the shore. They may represent plot boundaries. Excavations which began in summer 1990 should elucidate this.

Apart from Wolin, none of the Scandinavian or Slavonic towns of the Viking age had the chequer-board street pattern known from Anglo-Saxon towns such as Winchester.[47] The predominance of linear arrangements in the towns of the Baltic region probably stems from their coastal or riverine positions.

Excavations in many towns show that plot boundaries were permanent urban features from their foundation. The first step towards laying out a town must have been the establishment of a plot system, with the property boundaries marked by ditches or fences. They show that most Viking-age towns were deliberately founded and did not grow up organically around an earlier agricultural centre. Ribe may be an exception as the accumulation of manure and objects of simple agrarian character found in the earliest levels suggest that a farm or cattle market was its initial nucleus.

Building types

Buildings in urban settlements in the Viking age seem to have derived from earlier rural equivalents, with modifications probably the result of the economic demands placed on buildings in towns. Like rural buildings, they were constructed of wood, for in the early middle ages masonry was used only for buildings of exceptional significance, for example churches, or occasionally high-status structures such as the 'palace' at Northampton (p. 37).

By the beginning of the Viking age the characteristic buildings in the rural settlements of continental Europe and Scandinavia (those with internal roof-supporting posts and accommodation for both people and animals: figure 7.9:A) were being replaced by structures where the weight of the roof was carried by sturdy posts in the walls. The advantage of this type of building is that there is more unobstructed space within the body of the building (figure 7.9:C), and the so-called 'Trelleborg' buildings found in the tenth-century villages and ring-forts of Denmark[48] are of this basic form (figure 7.10). In Anglo-Saxon England a variant of this type of building was the norm on rural sites at least from the early sixth century, but it was supplemented, perhaps for economic and industrial purposes, by sunken-featured buildings (figure 7.9:B), also known from other parts of early medieval Europe, especially the Slavonic areas. This tradition continued in a modified form up to the end of the tenth century in some places, being known, for instance from excavations in York, London and Thetford in the late tenth century, and in Århus in Denmark, and throughout the southern Baltic region.

Although buildings in 'corner-timbering' or 'blockhouse' technique[49] are known from later medieval (but not Viking-age) Scandinavia, particularly in urban and rural settlements from the eleventh century onwards, they are of Fenno-Ugrian origin and were the usual domestic and industrial structures in the urban sites of Russia during the Viking age (figure 7.11a).

Excavations have shown the types of buildings erected and used in some Viking-age towns. The buildings in Hedeby, Sigtuna and Lund were usually 4-6m × 5-10m in size, consisting of a dwelling space with a hearth, and a storage and working area. Usually all that remains of these buildings is a wooden beam sunk into the earth (ground-sill) or sometimes a low stone foundation which supported walls of wattle-and-daub or stave construction (figure 7.11b). The lowest horizontal timbers of blockhouse buildings have also been discovered in Sigtuna, but as mentioned above they are commonest in the east where they have been found at Staraya Ladoga and Novgorod, for instance.

Because of the nature of the archaeological evidence the appearance of buildings above the original ground surface is hardly ever known. Hedeby is an important exception here, for its waterlogged deposits have preserved parts of the superstructures of buildings, and in one case complete walls including an entire gable[50] (figure 7.12).

Thanks to this fortunate chance it has been possible to reconstruct the whole building including the angle of slope of the roof (figure 7.13), and dendrochronology (figures 7.13, 7.14) has dated it to the mid–ninth century. This building was *c.* 5 × 12m in size, built of frame-construction on a timber ground-sill, with walls of wattle-and-daub along the outside of which sloping buttress posts supported the tops of the walls and counteracted the thrust of the roof. Its interior was divided into three rooms, the central one

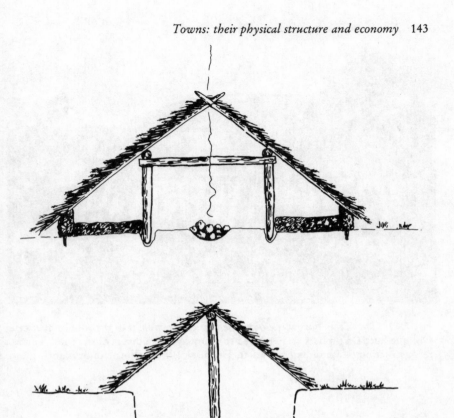

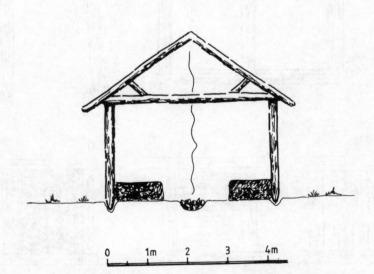

0	1m	2	3	4m

Fig. 7.9 Cross-sections of the most common types of buildings of the Viking age
top: aisled building with the weight of the roof carried by internal posts
centre: sunken-featured building
bottom: hall house with the weight of the roof carried by sturdy walls, no internal posts.

Fig. 7.10   The 'Trelleborg' type of house carried the weight of the roof on the walls. Oblique buttress timbers were needed to counteract the thrust of the roof. This is a reconstruction of a building at Fyrkat, Denmark (Photo Björn Ambrosiani)

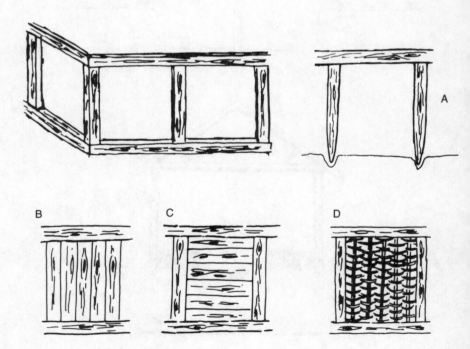

Fig. 7.11a   The walls of Viking-age buildings were constructed in a number of different ways: (A) timber framing forming panels filled with (B) upright planks or staves, (C) horizontal planks or (D) wattle and daub

Fig. 7.11b Corner timbering, a technique which originated in the north Russian forest zone.

Fig. 7.12 The collapsed wattle walls of a house at Hedeby. Archaeological excavations usually reveal only the foundations of buildings, and the preservation of these walls is exceptional. The reconstruction of the building is shown in figure 13 (Photo Archäologisches Landesmuseum, Schloss Gottorf)

being the dwelling with a large hearth in the centre of the floor and clay-built benches along the walls. One of the gable rooms originally contained a baking oven which was later replaced by a trough. The other gable room was a stable or, more likely, a storeroom throughout its existence. The baking oven in this Hedeby house is very unusual for in the Viking age cooking, heating and lighting were normally provided by open fires on a hard-burnt slab of clay or a stone paving.

The dendrochronological dating of this house at Hedeby gives us some idea of how long it stood before it needed to be repaired. The timbers used

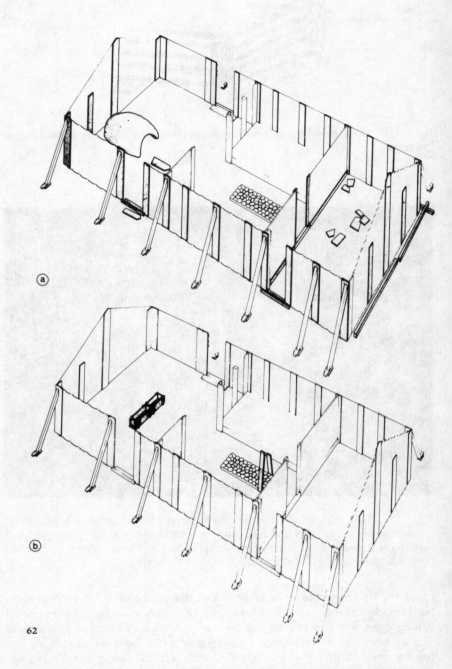

Fig. 7.13 The Hedeby house: reconstruction and dendrochronology. The house was built in 870 and repaired in 882. Some of the wedges under the buttresses were of wood felled in 848 and must have originally been used elsewhere (Schietzel 1981)

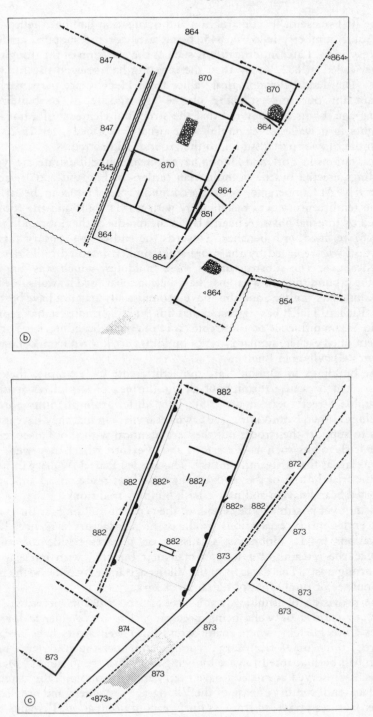

Fig. 7.14 Ground plan of the two phases of the Hedeby house showing the dendrochronological dates (Schietzel 1981)

in the first phase of its construction and occupation had been felled in 870 with older timbers, felled in 845, being used for the supports under the buttress posts. Later modifications, such as the insertion of the trough, used timber felled in 882, so by then the building had been in use for twelve years. The dendrochronological values from Hedeby are particularly important for our understanding of the age and repair of buildings in Viking-age towns for they tell that the structural elements of a house (the uprights in a wall, for example) were usually replaced after 15-20 years when their lower parts, sunk into the ground, had rotted.

Excavations in York and Dublin have done much to illustrate the types of buildings erected by the Scandinavian settlers in England and Ireland respectively. At Coppergate, York, the common type of house in the early part of the tenth century was rectangular, with wattle walls and the roof supported by internal posts. A hearth lay in the middle of the floor and the long walls were lined with benches. Towards the end of the century this construction was replaced by the more solid sunken-featured buildings mentioned above. The substructure of these buildings, which was dug down into the ground to form what may have been a cellar, had its walls lined with horizontal oak timbers, and the above-ground walls may not have been very high. Richard Hall[51] has suggested that this building tradition may represent Anglo-Saxon influence on the architecture of Anglo-Scandinavian York for, as mentioned earlier, similar types of buildings are known from contemporary sites elsewhere in England.

The buildings of Dublin[52] are quite different; for example, they were constructed of wattle throughout all the thirteen phases of occupation at Fishamble Street[53] (see figure 5.5). They differ from all other forms of buildings known from Viking-age towns elsewhere in that they have internal posts to support their roofs but they are identical with those discovered in other Irish towns such as Waterford and Wexford where they were being built as late as the thirteenth century. This has led Patrick Wallace to suggest that the Irish houses of the tenth century and later represent an amalgam of imported Scandinavian and native Irish building traditions.

It is not yet possible to be certain of the types of buildings at Birka as the nineteenth-century excavations produced no satisfactory evidence. Recent excavations by L. Holmqvist–Olausson on terraces beside the rampart revealed the remains of a long, rectangular building with internal roof-supporting posts. This dates from the Viking age and may indicate the partial continuance of rural types of buildings at Birka.[54]

The provision of drinking water was also essential in any town, with access to springs or wells being necessary. The best evidence for wells comes from Hedeby where many wood-lined well shafts have been discovered, often made from large wooden containers such as wine barrels which had been adapted for use by being sunk into the ground.[55] Many of the wells preserved at Hedeby have been dendrochronologically dated to a late (late tenth century) phase of the Viking-age settlement and are the only timber features preserved from its final years of occupation. Remains of the houses contemporary with the wells have disappeared because of the generally poor preservation of the topmost occupation layers at Hedeby (the waterlogged conditions leading to good preservation, p. 59, apply only to its lowest levels). The water from these wells must have been contaminated by the domestic rubbish and sewage which accumulated in the town, to form its thick occupation deposits now so useful to the archaeologist.

Institutions

Late medieval towns had a well-developed system of public buildings: town halls, guildhalls, churches, monasteries and hospitals. These are virtually unknown in Viking-age towns in Scandinavia, although churches are a feature of west European towns such as York in England and many continental sites with Viking affinities. The churches which were built in Scandinavia during the Viking age, such as the ones at Hedeby, Ribe and Birka recorded as having been founded by Ansgar,[56] were constructed of wood and perhaps, as we can see from the still preserved but ruined stone churches of twelfth-century Sigtuna and Visby or those from Kiev, they were situated on the periphery of the town. None of Ansgar's churches has yet been identified on the ground although a 'church' is noted on Stolpe's 1888–9 map of Birka.[57] Its position near the Viking-age shoreline suggests that the stone feature which Stolpe believed to be a church was the landward foundation of a jetty, such as that excavated from 1969–71. A rectangular crop-mark on the edge of Birka's 'Black Earth' near the valley leading to Björkö village may have surrounded a building or enclosed a churchyard, but it has not as yet been investigated and is only known from aerial photographs.

The only places in Sweden where we have some idea of the siting of churches are the late Viking-age towns of Sigtuna and Lund.[58] In Sigtuna six churches and monasteries from the twelfth and thirteenth centuries stood in a semi-circle around the settlement, defining its medieval limits (see figure 4.23). Another, St Gertrude, lay in the centre of the town, founded on top of the remains of earlier timber secular buildings which must have been deliberately destroyed when the church was built. The date of this church is still problematic, but it was probably established before the other six and may have been the church of the bishop, first mentioned in the mid-tenth century. In Lund there are no primary churches in the earliest, east-west, settlement (as defined by Andrén[59]) but south of it large stave-built churches and, slightly later, stone churches and churchyards stood in what was the expanded area of the eleventh-century town. Lund, therefore, presents a more prosperous picture than Sigtuna as there the town grew beyond the boundary marked by its churches.

The situation is rather different in the British Isles and western Europe where ecclesiastical foundations played a crucial part in urban life after the end of the Roman empire. Churches and monasteries are well known in all the major towns, some from physical remains, others from documentary sources,[60] and the arrival of the Vikings did little to change this. Indeed, the Scandinavians seem to have adopted Christianity very soon after their arrival in these already Christian countries, and in places such as York they soon began to build churches of their own. The discovery of Viking graves in country churchyards in the Danelaw underlines the rapidity with which

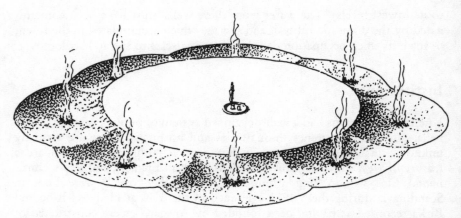

Fig. 7.15 Pagan temples or cult centres have left few remains but the excavation of the temple of the god Perun, at Novgorod, showed that there the god was represented by a wooden pole. His representation was surrounded by a ring of sacrificial pits (Sedov 1982)

the Scandinavians adapted to the traditions and religion of the lands which they were colonizing.[61]

Several heathen temples are known from contemporary records, although the most famous at Arkona on the island of Rügen and at Uppsala in Sweden were not in Viking-age towns. Historical sources and recent archaeological literature also record temples in Slavonic towns such as Oldenburg/Starigard, Ralswiek, Wolin and Novgorod.[62] At Novgorod V.V. Sedov has excavated the god Perun's temple south of the town: a circular site containing an idol in the form of a wooden post and surrounded by a ring of pits for sacrificial fires (figure 7.15).

Defences

Towns have always been obvious targets for attack and plunder, not least in the turbulent times of the Viking age. This was even true in the comparatively peaceful Viking homeland where internal conflicts and external wars often disrupted economic life. Attacks such as those described in Rimbert's *Life of Ansgar* and the Icelandic sagas often resulted in *brandskattning* (the exaction of ransom for not burning a town, the equivalent of the Danegeld levied in England) as at Birka, or in the total destruction of towns by fire as at Hedeby in *c.* 1050.[63]

Although the earliest coastal Viking-age towns in the Baltic region had no encircling defences, a hillfort or other type of defensive structure often stood nearby. Examples of these can be found at places such as Helgö. Hedeby, Birka, and probably Ralswiek and Sigtuna. They are usually simple in their construction: a low single or double rampart of stone and earth built only where necessary to block access points to a hill. This type of construction, with discontinuous ramparts, was common in Scandinavia in all prehistoric periods and about a thousand are known from Sweden alone.[64] In

Fig. 7.16   Aerial view of the Birka hillfort from the north-west. This is probably the hillfort mentioned by Rimbert in the ninth century (Photo Björn Ambrosiani)

Sweden this type of defence was particularly suitable, for there the broken and mountainous terrain provided innumerable hills which could be adequately defended through the minimum expenditure of labour. The forts at Helgö and Sigtuna are examples of these common features, but the hillfort of Hedeby[65] is more unusual as the flat lands of south Scandinavia has few hills which could be defended in such a simple manner.

The Birka hillfort (figure 7.16) is somewhat different from the fairly modest structures built elsewhere. The hill on which it stands is naturally defended on the south-west where a steep cliff faces the lake, but on the landward side the hill slope is more gentle, necessitating the construction of a substantial earth and stone rampart with only a couple of entrances. The rampart is tallest where it faces the town: *c.* 4m high on its outer and *c.* 3m high on its inner sides. The stretch of the rampart confronting the unoccupied parts of the island is lower but still well constructed, with a level top suggesting that it had a wall walk.

Some terraces outside the Birka hillfort were excavated by Holger Arbman in the 1930s.[66] The charcoal, soot and iron artifacts which he found suggest a military presence and he interpreted the area of his excavations as the headquarters of a garrison and a signalling station whose beacons produced the charcoal and soot. There were no signs of occupation inside the hillfort itself although, as at Hedeby, it contained some graves.[67] At Hedeby the graves within the hillfort probably date from the time before the foundation of the town but those at Birka date from the ninth century, that is, from a period early in the history of Birka as a town.

In the tenth century, as towns in Scandinavia and the Baltic became wealthier or otherwise important, they began to acquire defences around

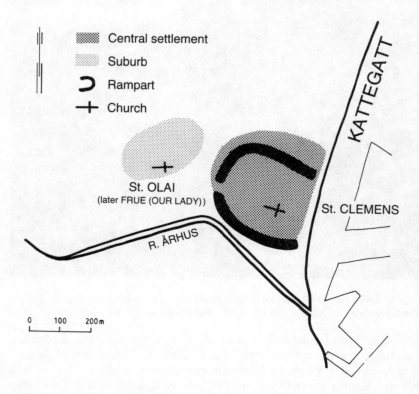

Fig. 7.17 Århus in Denmark is a good example of a town which acquired a fortification in the late tenth century (after Andersen *et al.* 1971)

their settled areas, often a semi-circular rampart suggesting that potential danger came from the land. Viking-age semi-circular defensive walls have been found at Hedeby,[68] Århus,[69] Västergarn near Paviken[70] and Löddeköpinge[71] in Scandinavia, and at Wolin.[72] Many of them were supplemented by an underwater palisade to defend the shore (figure 7.17).

At the same time defended settlements began to grow up along the Russian rivers. Staraya Ladoga, the earliest site of Novgorod at Ryurykovo Gorodishche, and Gnezdovo were all walled in their earliest phases.

When ramparts began to be built around Viking-age towns earth and stone were used as the building materials. Although these ramparts did not have the heavily-timbered defences of contemporary Slavonic forts they must have been supplemented by palisades and other timber structures, perhaps towers. Their front faces were not necessarily revetted with timber and it is perhaps here that their difference from Slavonic fortifications can best be appreciated.

The Hedeby rampart is exceptional in its size, and in its final form it could have been defended without additional timberwork (figure 7.18). It was

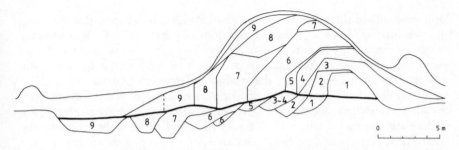

Fig. 7.18 Section through the Hedeby rampart showing at least nine phases of building (after Jakuhn 1986)

built up in many stages, as many as nine separate phases being represented in the northern section.[73] It was encircled by a dry moat, a feature otherwise only known from Waterford.

There were usually only a few gateways through the ramparts: two parallel to the coast and one opening inland. Birka is an exception to this for its communications were predominantly waterborne, and danger was unlikely to threaten from the land. So the rampart had a large number of gateways opening on to the cemeteries of Hemlanden (see figure 4.21), and the south-east valley between Hemlanden and the hillfort has no discernible fortifications. Birka's rampart gives the impression of being a boundary rather than a defensive feature; nevertheless it was rebuilt at least once, and then possibly in some haste, for it then straddled earlier grave mounds, perhaps deliberately to give it added height.

Some Viking-age sites were never defended, the best example being Kaupang. The reason for this is almost certainly because of the date of the occupation there, for in Scandinavia walled towns are a tenth-century phenomenon and any settlements abandoned before 900 cannot have had a defensive rampart. The towns which the Vikings visited, attacked or occupied in western Europe, however, were defended by walls or ramparts before this date and it is possible that they influenced the defence of Viking-age settlements in the homeland. In York, for example, the Roman walls must still have been serviceable in the ninth and tenth centuries, and may have been refurbished two hundred years earlier. The Viking immigrants merely supplemented them with a low earth bank. By the ninth century other west European towns were being defended by earth and timber ramparts, many of them defining a roughly semi-circular area: Hereford and Norwich in England, for example, and Ghent in Belgium.[74] In Ireland, however, defended towns were unknown before the arrival of the Vikings, although the early medieval monasteries were surrounded by a boundary wall (*vallum monasterii*). So the settlements of Dublin and Waterford must have been defended from scratch by their Scandinavian founders in the tenth century. Waterford[75] was provided with an earth rampart and wide ditch; Dublin was surrounded by a less substantial earthen wall.

The semi-circular walls of Scandinavian Viking-age towns followed the pattern of some of their west-European predecessors by defending the landward side of the settlements. In some cases, such as Birka, this was only the confined space of an island. But as both cargo transports and military threats were usually waterborne a landward-facing wall would have provided only limited protection if it were not supplemented by waterside defence. As mentioned above, the landward defences of Birka and Hedeby were supplemented by palisades in the water, some of them having been revealed by underwater survey.[76] Adam of Bremen[77] mentions man-made underwater obstacles which protected Birka, but these were probably the skerries, islands and dangerous shallows of the archipelago around the entrance to Lake Mälaren. Foreigners found these natural obstacles difficult to negotiate, and so they formed an ideal defence.

Graves, cemeteries and churchyards

The evidence used in this section is taken mainly from Scandinavia where there has been the most excavation of datable Viking-age graves. In western Europe our knowledge of grave types and burial customs is very limited for this period; conversion to Christianity led to the tradition of burial without grave-goods, and there have also been few excavations in Christian churchyards. The Russian material has also been omitted here because it has been impossible to gain full access to the evidence (see chapter 6).

The populations of all settlements are reflected in their graves, for the dead must be buried. In Viking-age Scandinavia many of the dead were commemorated by a monument in the shape of a mound or an arrangement of stones (stone-setting). The custom of burying the dead with their personal equipment and clothing means that the graves can give us useful dating points, often more precise than the dating from settlements. Occupation deposits in towns accumulated gradually and the objects which they contain represent a considerable timespan, but graves represent a single point in time, the time when the burial was consigned to the ground. Cemeteries also provide data which can be used to calculate the size of a population at any given time, but the statistics depend on knowledge of the original number of burials.

In Scandinavia, the cemeteries and churchyards of Hedeby, Helgö, Birka, Sigtuna, Köpingsvik, Visby, Kaupang and the slightly later Lund all provide information about the beginning and end of the settlements, continuity, and chronological distribution; they also give a minimum value for the average number of inhabitants at any given time.

Although inhumation had become the predominant burial rite in Denmark and on Gotland by the beginning of the Viking age, rural central Sweden and Norway continued to practise cremation until the end of the tenth century.

A comparison of the burial rites in different settlements may be used as an indicator of urban or rural societies. The presence of inhumations at Kaupang and Birka (figure 7.19), for instance, tell us either that their native inhabitants had abandoned their traditional pagan beliefs, or that the inhumation graves were those of foreigners, probably merchants and craftsmen. Although the introduction of Christianity presupposes inhumations, the

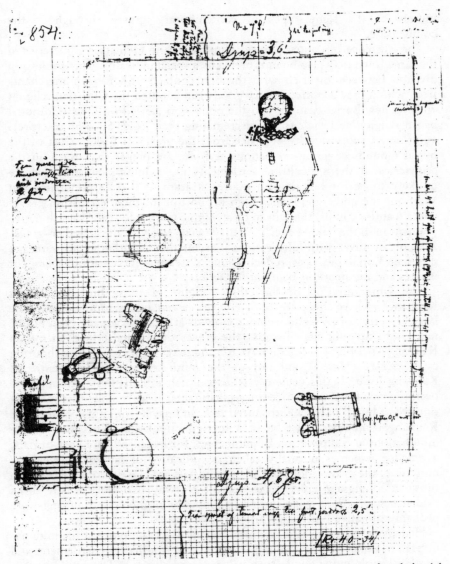

Fig. 7.19 Stolpe's drawing of a chamber grave at Birka (grave 854), a female burial of the ninth century (Antikvariskt Topografiska Arkivet, Stockholm)

presence of inhumations does not necessarily indicate Christianity. Many of the north-south oriented inhumation burials in Birka, Hedeby or Wolin, for example, may have been of Islamic or pagan ethnic groups such as Slavs or Balts. Some of the inhumation burials in Birka contain two bodies, one of them undoubtedly a victim sacrificed to accompany the main burial.[78] These cannot have been Christian interments as Christianity did not countenance human sacrifice. But many of the east-west oriented coffin–graves at Birka and Hedeby probably contained Christians, and Sigtuna's eleventh-century cemeteries of coffin graves are also likely to have been for Christian burials of the same types as contemporary graves throughout the countryside.[79]

The existence of contemporary inhumation and cremation cemeteries in the same town may also be interpreted as a social indicator. This could be a division between the rich who through contact with foreign merchants from whom they acquired luxury goods had adopted the Christian religion with its new burial custom, and the poor who carried on their traditional pagan religion and the custom of cremating their dead. Such an interpretation is not supported by evidence from the graves at Birka. Most of the burial mounds covering cremations at Birka are bigger than those in the cemeteries of the agricultural settlements in its hinterland and thus are unlikely to be the burials of a poorer stratum of Birka's population. In addition, the grave-goods in a high proportion of these cremation graves contain antler combs, thought to be an ethnic marker for the Swedish native population in the Viking age.[80] As they occur rarely in the chamber–graves and coffin–graves with inhumations it seems that at Birka, at any rate, the different burial practices reflect ethnic differences: cremations being of natives and inhumations being of foreigners.

The same question of the ethnic origins of those buried arises at Kaupang[81] where there are both cremation and inhumation burials. The large cemetery of cremations under mounds at North Kaupang need not be taken into account here because the graves date from a time later than Kaupang's period of occupation (p. 67) and may belong to the neighbouring estate centre (*Husby*) and not to the ninth-century market centre of Kaupang itself. If this cemetery is discounted, inhumation seems to have been the rule for the ninth-century inhabitants. If we assume that inhumation was a burial practice introduced to Scandinavia from outside, then the Kaupang cemeteries must be of a foreign population. But most of the inhumations at Kaupang (on Bikjholberget, for instance) were boat-burials, a practice which is normally taken as indicative of native Norwegians; moreover, the grave-goods in the boat-burials are closely comparable with those in Viking-age graves elsewhere in Norway. Contrary to the Birka evidence, then, the people buried in inhumation graves at Kaupang were probably of native Norwegian origin.

Hedeby provides yet another interpretation. There, most of the inhumations in chamber-graves lie along a 'funeral way' south of the settlement, and contain simple grave-goods such as spear and shield.[82] The similarity between these grave constructions and those of the chamber-graves at Birka has resulted in their being interpreted as burials of a tenth-century Swedish garrison at Hedeby (p. 61). They differ in their grave-goods, however, for the chamber-graves of Birka are extremely rich and, of course, seem to be burials of foreigners. So it is extremely unlikely that the chamber-graves at Hedeby are those of Swedish warriors. This example shows that burial customs cannot be interpreted in the same way on every site; they have to be looked at in their local context.

Graves can also be used to estimate the number of inhabitants in a settlement, but it must be remembered that the estimated population size arrived through analysis of burials can only be a *minimum*. The number of burials which we know now cannot be the original total, for preservation and discovery are biased by factors such as the degree of accidental destruction and the techniques of modern archaeology. In addition, children's graves are often absent from or very rare in pagan cemeteries and thus the numbers discovered in modern times are unlikely to be representative of the actual number of children in an early community. Adult burials are probably more representative, although some sectors of early populations may never have been buried in any formal manner.

Only Birka and Hedeby have provided sufficient evidence for calculations to be attempted, and they have been used as the examples here.

The following points have been observed in this attempt to calculate original population size from burials: the annual average death rate has been used, with no attempt to estimate generations or to count only adult burials. The method chosen produces more precise figures than if speculative factors such as lengths of generations are included and is based on the statistics provided by Kurth and Gejvall,[83] whose work on early medieval populations has shown that an average annual death rate of 40 per 1000 of population was the norm. Studies of the eighteenth-century death rate in the same area suggest that 30 per 1000 was the norm. An annual death rate of 40 per 1000 of population would mean that only 40 per cent of all individuals reached adulthood; if the death rate were 30 per 1000 of population then 55 per cent reached adulthood. In practice the results are very close and within the boundaries of error. For ease of calculation, the former death rate has been used here.

The formula used in the present calculation is

$$\frac{40P}{1000} = \frac{2.5 \times G_{ad}}{time}$$

P = population
G_{ad} = adult burials = 40% of total individuals

Birka has a minimum of 3000 burials, discounting graves with more than one body but including a certain proportion of graves of children (although they make up no more than 15-20 per cent of the inhumations and a smaller percentage of the cremations). If the multiple burials are included and the children discounted they probably largely cancel each other out, thus the number of adult burials can be assumed to be > 3,000. Using the formula,

$$\frac{40}{1000}P = \frac{2.5 \times 3000}{200}$$

then P = 900, that is, the average population throughout 200 years is at least *c.* 900 individuals, including children.

It is more difficult to establish the number of graves at Hedeby. Jankuhn and Steuer have estimated a minimum of 3000 and a maximum of 7000 burials on the two large cemeteries of *Südsiedlung* and in the area inside the rampart.[84] The graves further north and in the hillfort must be added to this total. If the maximum of 7000 burials is taken, Hedeby's average population, using the above formula, would be *c.* 1500 individuals throughout its period of occupation.

These figures can only be approximations but may be used for a further calculation based on an assumption of average family size. Six people per household in the Viking age has been taken as the norm here. This figure has been used because iron-age farm cemeteries in the Mälaren valley which have been evaluated statistically show that an average family consisted of six to eight individuals, comparable to that of seventeenth-century families in the same area where written evidence is available. Thus, if there were an average of six people per household in the Viking age there would have been at least 150 households in tenth-century Birka, and at least 270 households in tenth-century Hedeby. This sum can be converted into surface area, for at Hedeby the average size of the excavated household plots was *c.* 300m^2, and for comparative purposes we shall assume that they were much the same at Birka. Thus, the 150 plots at Birka would have occupied *c.* 45,000m^2, and the 270 households at Hedeby would have occupied 80,000m^2, about half the postulated settlement areas within the ramparts of each site. This seems an acceptable estimate as the population must have fluctuated in size throughout the long period of occupation, at some times occupying much more, and other times much less, than this average of inhabited space.

Although all the above calculations are extremely hypothetical the figures arrived at by archaeological means may be reasonably accurate. A useful comparison can be made with nineteenth-century Swedish towns. In the middle of that century many of them had a population of less than a thousand.

In conclusion, it must be said that the population of the Viking-age towns was very limited and that the hypothetical estimate of six people per household would have left much free space within the tenth-century walled areas. Even though the number of households may have fluctuated considerably throughout the period of occupation of the towns there was always plenty of room to accommodate them in the areas which are now known archaeologically. At Hedeby the cemeteries must originally have been appreciably more extensive than are known today, and a much larger population could have been housed within the area of the town.

In other Viking-age towns much less is known about the original number of burials, and their populations cannot even be guessed at.

Economy, manufacture and trade

One of the criteria used to define a town is that its economy must have been based on non-agricultural pursuits. In all the towns described in chapters 4, 5 and 6 there are signs of such non-agricultural economy, and only slight traces of rural activities. Metalworking, the processing of bone, antler and horn, and the production of glass beads took place in almost all Viking-age towns in all regions. Iron smithing, and in some cases smelting, were also practised although the latter was largely confined to rural areas where bog iron and other suitable raw materials could be found alongside the necessary fuel. Archaeological excavations in towns unearth vast quantities of artifacts: occupation layers contain domestic rubbish accumulated over long periods of time and waste arising from craft production. The organic waste represented by animal bones, fish remains, etc., results in high phosphate and pH-values in areas of intensive occupation, so the conditions of preservation of skeletal and metal artifacts on urban sites are better than those found in less heavily populated rural occupation deposits or in graves.

There is a considerable difference between wet and dry occupation layers. When water is present alongside high phosphate and high pH-values it leads to good preservation, not only of bone but also of organic materials such as wood, leather and textiles. Excavations in towns are difficult because the sites are often deeply stratified, and they are further complicated by the necessity of retrieving and recording enormous quantities of finds. The recovery of small fragments of artifacts, and minute evidence such as fishbones and seeds, demands techniques such as flotation, water sieving and scrupulous cleaning, but the results can be most revealing. Changes in the proportions of different types of finds between layers and features can be statistically established, and a highly detailed stratigraphy and analysis of the functions of specific areas within the whole site worked out.

As mentioned above (p. 154), one important difference between occupation and burial evidence is that the latter represents one point in the time-scale; occupation material is inevitably less chronologically precise. There is also another difference: the objects in a grave illustrate consumption while occupation deposits, particularly in towns, also show production. The evidence from burials and occupation deposits, therefore, is seldom comparable although the consumption represented by grave-goods can also indicate artifact production and distribution.

Many types of craftsmanship were practised in Viking-age towns. Textile production is mainly reflected in spindle-whorls, loom-weights, wool shears and needles and needle cases, with the final product of textiles only being preserved occasionally, usually on waterlogged sites such as Hedeby and Dublin but sometimes on dry sites as in the graves at Birka.

Large quantities of textiles have been recovered from the harbour at Hedeby.[85] They consist of bales of cloth from discarded clothing, and rags which had been used as luting between the planks in the clinker-built ships. Well-preserved fragments of cloth have also been discovered in the excavations at Viking-age Dublin, York and Lincoln in the British Isles, and on east Baltic sites. In all cases woollen cloth predominates and this fabric was probably locally produced, but imported textiles, particularly silk, are also present.

Strangely enough, we know most about dress in the Viking age from research into textiles discovered on a dry site: Birka.[86] In some of its graves cloth still adhered to the grave-goods (mainly female jewellery) when they were excavated (figure 7.20). Agnes Geijer analysed the remains, and established the types of textiles represented, and the styles of dress of those buried. She showed that their clothing was usually made of fine and coarse woollen fabrics but that linen and silk were also worn. Some of the clothes were embellished with borders worked in gold and silver thread.

Tanning of leather and shoemaking is also well represented in early towns where the waterlogged conditions often preserve the evidence extremely well. Large wooden vats which were used for tanning, leather-working

Fig. 7.20 The remains of a pleated linen undergarment and other clothing preserved inside oval brooches from Grave 517, Birka (Photo Antikvariskt Topografiska Arkivet, Stockholm)

Fig. 7.21 Leather shoe, one of the hundreds of a similar type found at York and characteristic of footwear in Scandinavian and Baltic towns of the Viking age (copyright York Archaeological Trust)

tools, and many half-finished wares and waste,[87] all illustrate the importance of this activity in early medieval towns (figure 7.21).

Furs are found less often, although we know that they formed one of the luxury commodities traded throughout the Viking world. Some remains have been found in the Birka graves where they, like textiles, were discovered attached to bronze jewellery.[88] Unfortunately they have not yet been analysed in detail.

Horn, antler and bone were very important raw materials in the Viking age. Horn from cattle, sheep and goat was used very extensively but is hardly ever preserved in archaeological layers, the main evidence for it

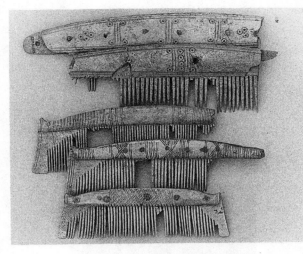

Fig. 7.22a Tenth-century antler combs from Birka (Photo Finn Martner)

being the horn cores which were discarded once their outer surface was removed for use. Antler from red deer, reindeer and elk is commonly found in Viking-age towns in Scandinavia,[89] but in the British Isles red deer antler was predominant although some elk antler is recorded from York.[90] Enormous quantities of finished and unfinished objects made of antler, plus the waste from the production of many types of artifacts such as combs, pins, playing pieces, dice and spindle-whorls have been discovered in all the Viking-age towns of northern and western Europe. The excavated area of Hedeby, for example, revealed more than 5000 burrs of red deer, mostly from antlers which were shed in the autumn and collected in local woodlands.[91] Similar evidence has been discovered in other places where the manufacture of artifacts from antler was commonplace until the end of the eleventh century.

Surprisingly, almost identical objects of antler were made in all the Viking-age towns so that it is virtually impossible to distinguish a comb found in York or Dublin from one found in Hedeby, Birka, or Staraya Ladoga (figures 7.22a, 7.22b). But raw materials differed from place to place, as did their accessibility; for example, red deer antler was usually used for the manufacture of combs in Hedeby whereas elk antler was used in Birka[92] and Sigtuna. Recent research has suggested that itinerant craftsmen travelled between the towns, using the local raw materials. This would explain the similarity between the combs, and the dissimilarity of the raw materials.

In Scandinavia and the British Isles, bone does not seem to have been used for making combs until much later in the middle ages. The availability of antler was clearly sufficient for the demand throughout the Viking age but it must have become a more precious commodity with the establishment of royal forests in the second half of the eleventh century. At that point the hunting of deer and the collection of their shed antlers became a royal perquisite, and so combs had to be made from the more easily acquired bones of cattle and sheep.

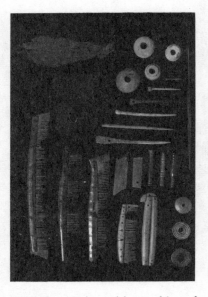

Fig. 7.22b   Tenth-century antler combs and bone objects from York (Photo York Archaeological Trust)

Fig. 7.23   Ivory comb from Sigtuna. A number of these so-called liturgical combs have been found during the current excavations at Sigtuna (Photo Mats Pettersson)

The Vikings also used the bones from cattle, sheep and pig to make a multitude of other implements, from pins to ice skates, the latter being fashioned from long bones of cattle and horses. Ivory, mostly walrus ivory, was used only occasionally, for decorated objects such as combs, chessmen or other luxury items, and elephant ivory is very rarely found although some elaborately decorated combs, probably for liturgical use, have recently been discovered at Sigtuna (figure 7.23).

Metalworking was one of the most important urban industries. Its scope ranged from the manufacture of iron tools to the production of jewellery in gold, silver and bronze. Archaeological evidence of this industry consists of tools, unfinished objects, raw materials in the form of metal scrap, slag, moulds and crucibles, and iron, bronze and precious-metal objects. All such objects have been discovered in abundance in Viking-age occupation layers, but they are particularly significant for the pre-Viking settlements of Helgö, Åhus and Ribe where artifacts and workshops have been found.[93] At Ribe, the workshops were better preserved than at Helgö and consisted of open-air clay floors each with a central hearth surrounded by manufacturing refuse.

The many fragments of moulds, often for casting artifacts which have not been found as finished products elsewhere, indicate the manufacturing centres of particular objects. For example, Berdal brooches (figure 7.24), elaborate oval brooches which were originally thought to have been made in Viking-age Norway because that is where they are most commonly found in archaeological contexts, have been shown to have been manufactured in Ribe.[94]

During the early middle ages metalworking was often associated with the making of glass beads, with the same craftsman perhaps being responsible for both activities. Until recently no urban production centres were known, with the possible exception of a glass workshop excavated by Jankuhn at Hedeby and a glass furnace at York[95] but some have now been positively identified, although mainly in the pre-Viking markets of Ribe, Åhus, and Paviken[96] where raw materials (pieces of glass mosaic, thin multicoloured glass rods and sherds of broken glass) and simple tools have been found. Similar material has been discovered in Hedeby and York,[97] but there is very little evidence of bead-making at other important Viking-age sites such as Birka and Wolin.

Although glass vessels do not seem to have been made in the Viking-age towns of Scandinavia, the Baltic or the British Isles, the glass industry did produce one product other than beads; finger-rings of green or yellow glass. These have been discovered in many towns such as Hedeby and York, and also at Lincoln[98] where crucibles coated with glass containing a high proportion of lead indicate manufacture on site. From the end of the tenth century, green and yellow finger-rings were made in enormous quantities in Kiev and distributed from there throughout Russia and the Baltic region where they flooded the market.[99] Large numbers of them have been found, for instance, in the eleventh- and twelfth-century levels at Sigtuna.

Beads and rings may not have been the only things manufactured in places where large quantities of scrap glass have been found, for enamel could also be made from the same raw material. An interesting point which may illustrate this comes from one of the most important eighth-century glass-working centres so far found: Åhus in Scania. As early as the 1940s, long before Åhus was discovered, Greta Arwidsson suggested[100] that the tradition of using enamel on certain early eighth-century bronze objects (those decorated in so-called Vendel Style D) probably originated in the southern Baltic region; perhaps Åhus was one of the centres of production for the enamel.

The fashioning of amber into jewellery and amulets was very common around the Baltic coast where the raw material occurs naturally, but there is

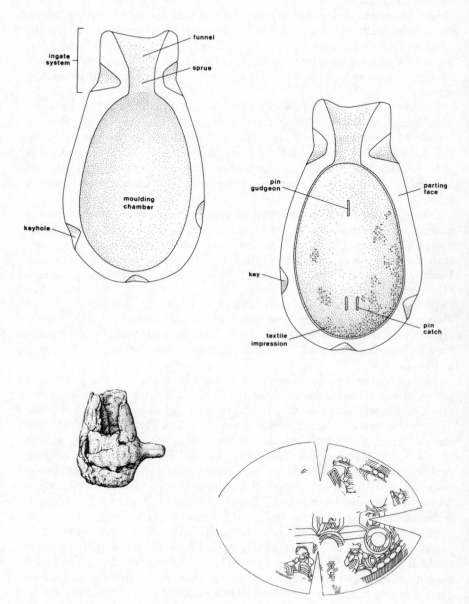

Fig. 7.24 Moulds and crucibles discovered at Ribe show that metalworking was an important activity on the site. Oval brooches of the Berdal type (shown here), commonly found in Denmark and Norway in the late eighth and early ninth centuries, were probably made in Ribe (Helge Brinch Madsen 1984)

also evidence for amber carving in virtually every Viking age town, even as far west as Dublin where every scrap of amber must have been imported. Staraya Ladoga in the east provides an interesting sidelight on craft specialization, for there amber jewellery was made in the same building as that in which antler combs were being produced; perhaps the same craftsman or craftsmen worked in these two very different materials.[101] Jet was also fashioned into decorations, with Dublin, York and Lincoln[102] all being centres for this aspect of jewellery making in the late tenth and early eleventh centuries.

Pottery-making must also have been important, and potsherds are the most common finds in many towns. Different centres of pottery manufacture during the Viking age can be distinguished, particularly in the British Isles, the Rhineland and the Slavonic area.

The Danelaw region of England contained many such centres, mainly producing unglazed but wheel-thrown and kiln-fired vessels of the so-called Thetford type (p. 100) and its derivatives. This has been discovered on virtually all tenth-century sites, both urban and rural, in the Danelaw but seems not to have been exported further afield. Another very distinctive form of pottery, with a pale yellow glaze and a fine white fabric, was made at Stamford (p. 99) and seems to have been in greater demand abroad. Sherds of this very easily recognizable pottery have been discovered in Viking-age towns as far apart as Dublin[103] and Lund.[104]

The pinkish-yellow Badorf ware[105] was widely distributed from its manufacturing centre in the Rhineland throughout the lands bordering the North Sea. It reached Hedeby but otherwise is uncommon in the Baltic region. At Birka, for example, it and Tating ware (also from the Rhineland) together make up only 1 per cent of the total pottery assemblage.[106]

Pottery was also manufactured at Hedeby. The dark grey, unglazed, globular cooking-pots had only a fairly local distribution outside Hedeby itself, mainly to settlements in the Jutland peninsula, with the pottery used in the Baltic area as a whole being predominately of the Slavonic/Wendish type in its Feldberg and Fresendorf variants. A local hand-made imitation of Slavonic/Wendish pottery was made in eastern Sweden during the Viking age; pottery from elsewhere is hardly represented at all in Viking-age sites there.

A characteristic type of pottery was also made in Finland in the Viking age. It consisted of well-fired round-bottomed vessels, its exterior burnished to make a polished surface into which simple linear or cord decoration was impressed.

Although much of the pottery found on Viking-age sites must have been used as table ware or cooking vessels, many of the pots probably served as containers for storing commodities (such as salt, wine or honey) which can no longer be traced in archaeological finds. Many of these goods will have been brought from far afield in their containers, so the presence of foreign pottery on a site may be used as an indicator of trading connections and exchange of perishable goods.

One of the most important of these consumables was wine. Barrels made of wood from the Rhineland and elsewhere have been discovered at Hedeby, for example, where they were reused as linings for wells, but they

Fig. 7.25 Ceramics found in some Birka graves: from the left, a locally produced pot, a Tating jug, a pot influenced by Slavonic prototypes, and a bowl made in Finland (Photo Sören Hallgren)

must originally have been containers for wine brought to the North from Germany and France. Some of the finer pottery vessels may also have accompanied the wine, and it has been suggested that the Rhenish Tating-ware jugs (figure 7.25) were consecrated containers for communion wine. Their presence in at least eight of the graves at Birka (chamber-graves, coffin-graves and cremation burials), and in everyday contexts elsewhere indicate that they must also have been in secular use.

Ship building and ship repairing must also have been very important crafts. Ship repairing is better represented in the archaeological record. At Paviken and Wolin,[107] for example, there are innumerable examples of chopped-up rivets extracted from ships' planking so that the strakes of the clinker-built ships could be replaced, and excavations at Paviken also unearthed a crowbar used in the removal of rivets.[108] A simple stone structure at right angles to the Idån stream at that site may be the foundations for a ship-repairing wharf. Ralswiek seems to have been a ship building centre (mainly for ships of the Slavonic type in which no iron rivets were used), and as sea communications were so important during the Viking age we can expect more finds of this type in the future.

Manufacture played an important part in the trade and exchange which were centred on early medieval towns. The interchange between town and hinterland can be seen particularly clearly in the Mälaren area where foodstuffs, fuel, hay, and raw materials were brought from the countryside into Birka. At Birka the raw materials were converted into simple jewellery,

Fig. 7.26 Drawing of the inscription on an Ulfberth sword found at Hulterstad, Öland (SHM 3104:1). It is one of five sword blades discovered there, all of which were imported from Francia for hilting in Scandinavia (drawing by Anders Eide)

tools and sophisticated iron objects such as knives, arrow-heads and craftsmens' tools, examples of which have been found in Viking-age graves in the farms of Birka's hinterland.

So the Viking-age towns played a crucial part in commercial interchange with their surroundings, and acted as service centres for their agricultural neighbours. Raw materials in demand in foreign countries were assembled in the towns and then exported in exchange for foreign goods. Only a few of these imports found their way to the peasants living in the countryside, for the most precious and valuable luxuries must have been destined for the merchants' households in the towns; most of them have been found in the rich graves in the cemeteries of Birka or Hedeby, or in the occupation layers of other towns.

As mentioned above, the hinterlands provided raw materials which were converted into finished products, but they could also be exported in an unprocessed state to far-flung destinations. For example, the Scandinavian countryside was the source of commodities which were in demand on the Continent. Iron, tar, timber, feathers, down and furs came from the east Scandinavian forests; iron, hone stones[109] and soapstone were important products of the west Scandinavian mountains. Many of the goods carried from country to country in the Viking age were organic materials and as such were either consumed at the time or have since decayed away in the ground, so they are impossible to trace archaeologically. One of the present authors[110] has shown, for example, that in the well-documented high middle ages most of the commodities traded between England and the Baltic have since disappeared without archaeological trace. The same must be true of trade goods in the less well-documented earlier periods.

Not all the goods which were transported around the Viking world were raw materials and other utilitarian necessities. Silk and other valuable goods such as slaves, sword blades, and silver were important features of long-distance trade. Recent research has shown that although silk could have come from China along the Silk Road it is more likely to have been brought from no further east than Byzantium: the peace treaty between the Rus' and Byzantines in 945 limiting the value of the silk cloth which could be acquired by Viking or Rus' merchants suggests that this precious cloth originated there.

Slaves are mentioned occasionally in written sources. For example, *Vita Rimberti* recounts how Rimbert freed a nun from slavery in Hedeby (at the price of his horse)[111] and one of the Icelandic sagas tells of the purchase of an Irish princess in a slave tent beside the Göta älv on the west coast of Sweden. Prisoners of war from both east and west Europe contributed to the labour force as slaves, and the *longphort* of Dublin is often described as a centre of the slave trade.

Sword blades had intrinsic value as capital. Swords with hilts decorated in characteristic Nordic art styles have been found throughout north and east Europe but their blades, particularly those inlaid with the name *Ulfberht*, indicate that they were made in the kingdom of the Franks[112] (figure 7.26). The fact that these sword blades have been found over the whole of what was then a pagan region shows that high-quality weapons were exported to the Franks' Viking enemies despite the prohibitions laid upon this trade. Once arrived in Scandinavia, the sword blades were hilted by native Scandinavian craftsmen, hence the local styles of decoration.

In Scandinavia the Viking period is sometimes known as 'the silver age'. Enormous quantities of silver coins, jewellery and bullion have been found from Viking-age contexts, but we still do not really know how the Vikings obtained their silver. Many hoards of silver dating from the Viking-age (figure 7.27) have been discovered on Gotland,[113] in other parts of Scandinavia, in eastern Europe, and the British Isles, mostly consisting of jewellery, arabic coins, or chopped-up fragments of silver objects (*hacksilver*). Great quantities of silver were brought to Scandinavia from the Volga region[114] in the form of coins or as spiral bracelets (the so-called Permian type; figure 7.28). Most of the ninth-century hoards are composed of coins and complete jewellery, but the tenth-century hoards contain coins and jewellery only in the form of hacksilver.

The role of silver, specifically whether it was used in commercial transactions or regarded as a purely capital investment, is one of the great subjects of contention between archaeologists, historians and numismatists.[115] The date of the latest coin in a hoard is used to establish when the hoard was concealed and, consequently, to define periods of unrest when peasants and merchants hid their wealth for safekeeping but were unable to retrieve it later. Some scholars see the large quantities of silver represented by the hoards as booty from a few piratical raids which had no importance in daily life or commercial transactions. Hacksilver, particularly from tenth-century hoards, and the occurrence of scales and weights for the weighing of precious metals (many weights have been discovered in tenth-century Dublin[116] and on Gotland, for instance) suggest that silver was in common circulation during most of the Viking age and played a part in everyday commercial life; and recent research on Gotland has shown that most of the silver hoards on that island were concealed in Viking-age settlements (perhaps as some sort of 'savings bank'), not hidden in the countryside during times of trouble.[117]

Many silver coins have also been found in early medieval occupation layers in Scandinavian towns such as Ribe and Birka[118] (figure 7.29A). These

Fig. 7.27 Silver hoard discovered at Birka. Two hoards were found during Stolpe's excavations in the Black Earth at Birka. They contained arm-rings, kufic coins and Byzantine coins, the latest date of each being *c.* 960. Using these, the end of Birka has been dated *c.* 970 (Photo Sören Hallgren)

Fig. 7.28   The silver hoard from Asarve, Hemse parish, Gotland (SHM 11930). Some silver bracelets of native type are seen in the foreground, behind them bracelets of Permian type, imported from the Volga region (Photo Antikvariskt Topografiska Arkivet, Stockholm)

coins seem to have been treated by the Vikings as bullion rather than as currency, and scales and weights are common finds in most of the north and east European trading centres. With the exception of an early mint at Hedeby in the ninth and tenth centuries (figure 7.29B), and in Sigtuna *c.* 1000, there were no mints in Scandinavia until well on in the eleventh century,[119] and then they were only in Denmark (Lund, Odense, Roskilde and Viborg) and Norway (Oslo and Trondheim). The minting of coins was more commonplace in western Europe during the Viking age (figure 7.30); this underlines the more advanced urban development of these areas which has been outlined in earlier chapters.

Most of the silver in circulation in Viking-age Scandinavia came from the silver mines of Transoxania. Minted silver was probably more common than is apparent today for much Viking-age silver jewellery must have been made from melted-down coins. By the middle of the tenth century the source of eastern silver dried up, to be gradually replaced by German silver from the mines in the Hartz mountains. There was obviously no shortage of silver in Scandinavia or in the British Isles at any time in the Viking age. In the late tenth and early eleventh centuries Scandinavian coffers were replenished by Danegeld of thousands of pounds of silver, paid by the English kings to the once more marauding Vikings.

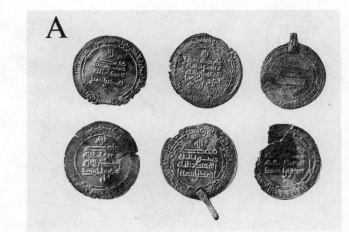

Fig. 7.29   Coins of many different origins circulated in Scandinavia during the Viking age: (A) arabic kufic coins imported into Scandinavia in great numbers in the ninth and tenth centuries; (B) coins minted at Hedeby, the only place in Scandinavia where coins were struck before the second half of the tenth century (Photos Antikvariskt Topografiska Arkivet, Stockholm)

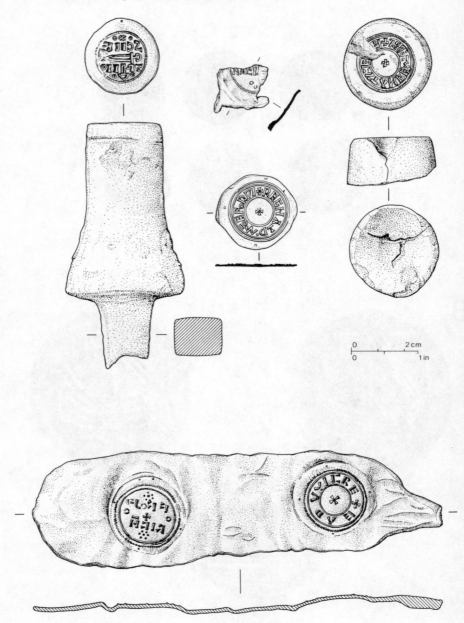

Fig. 7.30 Two coin-making dies (above) and a lead strip used as a trial piece (below) from York (copyright York Archaeological Trust)

Chapter 8

Current questions and future work

The previous chapters have outlined the origin, development, physical structure, and economy of towns in northern and western Europe from the fifth to the eleventh centuries, with the emphasis on Scandinavia and the Baltic in the Viking age. The huge area and timespan which have been covered have revealed some similarities in the progress of urbanization in the early middle ages, but also some quite fundamental regional differences. The survey has also illustrated the importance of archaeology to the study of early towns. Contemporary written evidence has been mentioned where appropriate, but it is noticeable that these non-archaeological sources tell us little about the physical appearance of towns, their economic role, or even their date of origin. Recent archaeological excavations have given substance to these aspects, and without archaeology our knowledge of early medieval towns would be scanty indeed.

Nevertheless, much still remains to be learned about early towns, and our concluding chapter assembles some of the still unanswered questions. We must depend on future excavations to provide many of the answers, although as some questions are resolved, others will undoubtedly arise.

The fundamental thread which runs through the whole of this book is the question of why and how towns began to grow up in the early middle ages, particularly in those parts of northern Europe uninfluenced by Roman predecessors. Added to this we can debate whether towns *developed* in the strict evolutionary sense, that is, did all the towns mentioned in this book necessarily go through a pre-urban stage (a farm with additional non-agricultural activities) before evolving into purely non-agricultural, commercial or administrative units. The evidence that we have at present suggests that this was not the case, and that deliberate foundation with specific urban functions in mind led to true urbanism. The following pages will expand this view in the light of our present archaeological evidence and the gaps in that evidence.

It is now clear that there were several generations of towns (or settlements with urban potential) in Scandinavia and the Baltic region during the first millennium AD. Some settlements such as Dankirke and Gudme in Denmark seem to have been fundamentally rural sites whose agricultural activities were supplemented by trade and industrial production. Neither of these sites developed into a fully-fledged town, if we use the definition of a town quoted in chapter 1, being occupied from the fourth century until their abandonment just before or around the year 800. They are representatives of the earliest stages of town formation in the North but are also examples of arrested urban development as they never grew beyond the stage of small, semi-agricultural units. Their desertion *c.* 800 is not yet fully understood, but they must have lacked urban potential: the resources of their hinterlands may not have been sufficient to support a larger and less agricultural population; their communications with the outside world may have been insufficient to allow the expansion of external trade; even, perhaps, they did not stand on land under the control or ownership of a central authority through whose influence an urban place could grow.

Chronological successors of these earliest sites can be seen in Ribe (only a few kilometres north of Dankirke), Hedeby *Südsiedlung*, Åhus in Scania, perhaps some of the Scanian *köpingeorter*, Paviken on Gotland, and Grobin on the eastern coast of the Baltic, all of which seem to have been deliberately founded on virgin sites without earlier farm-like settlements. At these sites we can discern an emphasis on industry and commerce rather than on agriculture; this indicates a more positive step towards urbanization. All of these were founded in the eighth century, slightly before or just at the beginning of the Viking age, and certainly before the beginning of the Viking raids.

Ribe, Hedeby and the south Baltic sites continued as towns throughout the Viking age proper when they were supplemented by, among others, Kaupang in Norway, Birka in Sweden, and Russian towns such as Staraya Ladoga. Others were abandoned and superseded by neighbouring, newly founded, settlements (for instance, Hedeby *Südsiedlung* was replaced by the central settlement of Hedeby).

In the late tenth century the final generation of Viking-age towns were founded, also on virgin sites. Most of them have continued as towns to the present day. Sigtuna in central Sweden seems to have begun *c.* 980; Oslo and Skien in Norway were founded at about the same time; and Lund (then Danish but now in Sweden) has evidence from the same period. The Danish towns of Århus, Viborg and Odense are other late tenth-century foundations which grew to importance later in the middle ages and which are still in existence.

This bald outline of the expansion of urbanism in north and north-east Europe conceals a multitude of questions, some of which are presented below.

One of the questions which has been touched upon is why, and under whose or what influences, towns began to grow up during the early middle ages. In the countries of western Europe with an urban legacy from the Roman world the reoccupation of towns began under royal or ecclesiastical patronage during the sixth and seventh centuries. At that time the former Roman towns were used mainly as administrative centres for kingdoms or dioceses. These royal or ecclesiastical presences were gradually supplemented by a population whose main occupations concentrated on commerce and industry until, by the eighth century, there was a network of trading communities over much of northern Gaul and lowland England. These towns seem still to have been controlled by royal or clerical over-lords, and the role of some such ruling authority seems to have been instrumental in the foundation of new towns as well as in the continuance of occupation in towns with Roman roots.

Much scholastic research has gone into the investigation of the extent of royal or ecclesiastical influence on town foundation in these areas, and the same is true of Scandinavian and Baltic urban development. The consistent presence of a controlling authority in the foundation of towns is now accepted throughout the area discussed in this book, but the extent to which such an authority directed the course of urbanization is still far from clear. Reference has been made in several of the preceding chapters to the juxtaposition of 'royal manor' and 'town'. In the comparatively well-documented urban settlements of western Europe this connection can be demonstrated fairly easily, but it is more difficult in those areas where written evidence is sparse or non-existent. In Scandinavia, place-names have been used as evidence for royal authority; for instance, the presence of a *husby* name, usually at a place where there is also a group of high-status burial mounds, near an archaeologically attested early medieval commercial centre has been taken to illustrate a royal connection. Where place-names are lacking, concentrations of high-status burials adjacent to early towns have been taken as evidence for royal control of those towns. In Sweden and Denmark, too, later medieval traditions of royal associations must be taken into account.

The towns of the south Baltic coast are similarly lacking in contemporary written sources which could underline a royal connection, and archaeology is the prime evidence for hypotheses about town foundation. In those areas a tribal rather than a royal influence may have been the rule. In all the areas discussed in this book, research into the connection between royal power, other forms of central authority, and commercial centres continues.

The question of who was responsible for the economic development of towns brings us to another characteristic of early medieval urbanism: the growth of the merchant class. Who were the people who conducted both long-distance and local trade, who perhaps commissioned some of the industrial production, and who acted as middlemen? Scraps of information can be picked up from some west European written sources, but the bulk of our evidence is archaeological. In one or two Viking-age towns, particularly Birka, the presence of numerous burials with rich grave-goods acquired from virtually all over the then known world suggests that the merchants were a class set apart from the normal native population: they were richer, more eclectic in their absorption of foreign traditions and accumulation of personal possessions. They probably were members of a semi-independent and supra-national group responsible only to the king or administrator of the town in which they were living or trading at any given time.

Another tantalizing subject crying out for further work is the question of continuity or discontinuity of urban settlements. Over the past few years it has become clear that many Viking-age towns were abandoned after several centuries of occupation and then re-established in new positions on 'green-field sites', often with new names yet only a short distance away from the original. This is not true of all the sites which have been discussed here for some, particularly those of the final generation of Viking-age foundations, have remained inhabited to the present day; but there are enough examples of shift in site to make it seem a common phenomenon of the eighth, ninth and tenth centuries. Explanations have been suggested for this (silting waterways, developments in shipping, destruction by outside forces and so on) but the topic remains beset by intriguing questions. Can archaeology tell us why some towns remained fixed and flourishing, and others did not? Does the date of initial foundation have any significance for urban stability? Do the economic or social roots of a settlement have a bearing on its permanence? Do physical features such as the presence or absence of masonry buildings and well-built fortifications influence the permanence of a settlement? We have seen that the Scandinavian towns which were founded in the late tenth century have continued as towns up to the present day, whereas those which began earlier did not. Why is this? There must be a fundamental difference between the final generation of Viking-age towns and those which flourished earlier. Ribe is one of the few examples of a town founded in the eighth century still to be in existence today; this must tell us something, but what? Viking-age Ribe lay on the north side of the river; medieval and modern Ribe, concentrated around the cathedral, stands on the south bank. Is there, therefore, a continuity of occupation? Once again, further research is needed. Urban continuity remains an unresolved problem.

Many other questions will have occurred to the reader during the course of the previous pages. For instance, how much do we really know about town plans *in toto*? In none of the settlements described above has more than 5 per cent of the total area been excavated, and in most cases a good deal less. In some towns, but by no means in all, we know about individual plots and buildings in great detail, but how far can these be extrapolated to the town as a whole? Any superficial survey of a modern town shows that there are enormous differences between one area and another: commercial sectors, residential zones (with their own social stratification), centres for communal activities. Were things different in the Viking age? And if they were not, are we justified in drawing any overall conclusions? We have here tried to summarize present knowledge about the size, layout, and economic base of towns in the Viking age, but we are aware that our information is limited and reliant on archaeological evidence from a tiny sample of individual towns. Ideally, if we are to understand the social and economic significance and physical organization of any one Viking-age town the whole town should be excavated, but as this is patently impossible we have here tried to draw some general conclusions based on the present evidence, however sparse.

The origin and development of defences are further points for debate. In western Europe, those early medieval towns which grew up in former Roman centres had ready-made defences which were reused and in some places (York, for example) refurbished in the eighth century or even earlier. By the end of the ninth century newly constructed ramparts surrounded the Anglo-Saxon *burhs* of Wessex and Mercia; early tenth-century Dublin was defended by a bank and palisade, and at a slightly later date Waterford was provided with a massive rampart and ditch. The situation seems, however, to have been somewhat different further east and north where urban settlements appear to have remained open and undefended until well on in their histories. Some of the towns in Scandinavia and the Baltic grew up beside already existing hillforts which must have provided some protection, but the occupation areas themselves did not acquire defences until the second half of the tenth century. Obvious questions include why urban ramparts suddenly became necessary after several centuries without them. Were towns then more prone to attack than they had been before? Were the defences status symbols rather than necessities? Did thë Vikings take back to Scandinavia ideas of defence which they picked up during their forays westwards?

Until recently archaeologists have tended to view towns as isolated phenomena, divorced from their rural hinterland and with no connection with the countryside. Now, however, we are beginning to see increasing research emphasis on placing a town in its setting. The view that the countryside was a provisioning resource for towns and a reservoir of raw materials is now axiomatic and, indeed, the site of a town may have been selected because of the potential of its hinterland. Research into the environment of towns has been a well-established branch of urban archaeological science, but it is now used to illustrate the environment of the countryside as well as of the town. Evidence for the types of crops grown, the breeds of animals reared and the wildlife of the countryside can all be culled from the analysis of plant and animals remains preserved in rubbish pits and middens in towns.

The commodities which were sent out from the towns in exchange for essential raw materials can also be traced. Up to now most of this evidence has been discovered in the form of grave-goods in pagan graves beside rural settlements (as in the Mälaren valley where Birka's commercial contacts have been illustrated by this means). But the past couple of years have seen the emergence of research projects, centred on Ribe or Hedeby, for instance, investigating settlement finds and features rather than grave-goods. This research is still in its infancy, but preliminary results augur well for the future.

Other fundamental questions will only be answered through future excavations and syntheses of existing knowledge. The density and size of urban populations has been tackled for a couple of Viking-age towns; statistics could be worked out for some others (notably the Russian examples) where datable burial grounds exist, but there is as yet little sign of this being done. By contrast, the industrial and commercial aspects of early medieval towns have aroused much interest and research, but even for these topics questions still remain. For example, how much did towns depend on their routes of communication for their economic life, and how far was their existence dependent on long-distance trade rather than local commerce and exchange? What commodities were traded over long and short distances and how much can we recover from the archaeological record? Can we reconstruct the proportion of perishable materials carried along trade routes which are archaeologically pin-pointed by the presence of non-perishable goods?

The remaining questions are legion and mostly unanswerable in the present state of knowledge. Happily, excavations and research into towns in the Viking age still continue. In the British Isles, information is continually being retrieved through rescue excavations, particularly in York, Lincoln and Waterford. In Denmark, Ribe and Hedeby are thriving centres of hinterland research. In Sweden, a five-year campaign of excavations began at Birka in May 1990. Further east, the Latvian and Lithuanian towns of Grobin and Wiskiauten (Višnevo) are being investigated, and Novgorod and Staraya Ladoga in the Soviet Union are currently the subject of intensive research projects. Other towns, about which we today know nothing, will undoubtedly produce new and exciting information over the next decade.

The subject of towns in the Viking age is, therefore, one of current concern throughout the whole area dealt with in the present book. That being so, many of the questions left unanswered in here will certainly be resolved in the not too distant future.

Notes

2 North-west European towns up to the end of the seventh century

1. *Gregory of Tours.*
2. Galinié 1988, p. 61.
3. Bonnet 1986, 1987.
4. Joris 1965; Verhulst 1989, p. 17.
5. Declercq and Verhulst 1989; Verhulst 1989.
6. Reece 1980, p. 77.
7. Biddle 1983, p. 112; Brooks 1986; Macphail 1981, 1983; Yule 1990.
8. Biddle 1972; Yorke 1982.
9. Gilmour 1979; Morris 1983, pp. 38-9.
10. *Bede* II:16.
11. Barker *et al.* 1974.
12. Carver 1987, p. 46.
13. *Bede* II:14.
14. Phillips 1985, p. 47.
15. Youngs *et al.* 1986, pp. 154-6.
16. Tatton-Brown 1988, pp. 213-15; Tatton-Brown and Macpherson-Grant 1985.
17. Vince 1988, p. 91; Vince 1990.
18. *Bede* II:3.
19. *St Wilfrid* XVI.
20. Ottaway 1984.
21. Biddle 1970, pp. 317-21; Biddle and Kjølby-Biddle forthcoming.
22. Biddle 1976, pp. 289-92.
23. Biddle 1975, pp. 303-10.
24. Hinton *et al.* 1981, pp. 47-9; Qualmann 1986.
25. Clarke 1988, pp. 247-50; Vince 1989, pp. 136-43.
26. Ekwall 1964.
27. Coutts and Worthington 1986; Hill *et al.* 1990.
28. Sutherland 1948.
29. *Bede* IV:1.
30. *St Wilfrid* XXV.
31. van Es and Verwers 1980; Verwers 1988.
32. Capelle 1976; Jankuhn 1958, 1986, pp. 25-6.
33. Capelle 1978.
34. Lebecq 1983, pp. 145-6.

35. Wade 1988.
36. Hurst 1976, pp. 299-303.
37. Rumble 1980.
38. Brisbane 1988; Holdsworth 1976, 1980.
39. Andrews 1988.
40. Tatton-Brown 1988, pp. 213-21.

3   North-west European towns in the eighth and ninth centuries

1. *Anglo-Saxon Chronicle* 793.
2. Sawyer 1982, pp. 78-97.
3. Wilson 1986, p. 222.
4. van Es and Verwers 1980.
5. Stenton 1971, p. 221.
6. Capelle 1976.
7. Capelle 1978.
8. van Es and Verwers 1985.
9. Besteman 1974, 1989.
10. Haarnagel 1984.
11. Brandt 1985.
12. Claude 1987, pp. 51-3; Verhulst 1985, p. 334
13. van der Walle 1961; Frans Verhaeghe pers. comm.
14. Janssen 1985, pp. 220-4.
15. Reynolds 1987, p. 295
16. Biddle 1984; Milne 1989; Milne and Goodburn 1990; Vince 1984.
17. Vince 1988.
18. Tatton-Brown 1986.
19. Hall 1988, pp. 235-8; Kemp 1987.
20. Phillips 1985, p. 46.
21. Addyman 1974, p. 207; Buckland 1984; Cramp 1967; Tweddle 1986.
22. Kenward *et al.* 1986, pp. 276-7.
23. Palliser 1984.
24. Hall 1984a, pp. 34-42.
25. Dunmore *et al.* 1975; Wade 1978, 1988.
26. Brisbane 1988.
27. Andrews 1988.
28. Brisbane 1988, p. 106.
29. Bourdillon 1988.
30. Williams 1984a, pp. 31-3, 1984b; Williams *et al.* 1985.
31. Williams 1979.
32. Rahtz 1977.
33. *Bede* II:14.
34. Hope-Taylor 1977.
35. Hinchcliffe 1986.
36. Rahtz 1979.
37. Heighway 1984.
38. Mason 1985.
39. Keevil 1989.
40. Blackburn and Bonser 1984, 1985.
41. Rogerson and Dallas 1984.

42. Kilmurry 1980, pp. 144-50; Mahany and Rolfe 1983.
43. Shoesmith 1980, 1982.

4 Towns in the Viking homelands

1. Callmer 1986; Grøngaard-Jeppesen 1981.
2. Ambrosiani 1974, 1981, 1983.
3. Arbman 1955; Bolin 1939; Pirenne 1939; Schück 1926.
4. Thorvildsen 1972.
5. Thrane 1987.
6. Rimbert 1986; *Royal Frankish Annals*.
7. *Adam of Bremen*.
8. Bencard 1978; Bencard 1981- ; Frandsen and Jensen 1988; Stig Jensen pers. comm.
9. Feveile *et al.* 1990.
10. Callmer 1982; Rosenberg 1984.
11. Jankuhn 1986; Schietzel 1969- .
12. Andersen *et al.* 1976.
13. Andersen 1985.
14. Hoffmann *et al.* 1987.
15. Vogel 1983- .
16. Jankuhn 1986, p. 23.
17. Andersen *et al.* 1971.
18. Viborg: Krongaard-Kristensen 1987; Odense: Christensen 1988.
19. Wihlborg 1984.
20. Andrén 1980, 1984, 1985; Blomqvist and Mårtensson 1963; Mårtensson 1976.
21. Strömberg 1978; Tesch 1983.
22. Jacobsson and Wallin 1986.
23. Cinthio 1980; Ohlsson 1976.
24. Lund 1984.
25. Blindheim 1975; Blindheim *et al.* 1981.
26. Myrvoll 1986.
27. Andersson 1981.
28. Ambrosiani 1974, 1981, 1983.
29. Lundström 1988.
30. Ambrosiani 1985a, 1988a.
31. *Birka* I-V; Ambrosiani *et al.* 1973; Ambrosiani 1988b, 1988c; Gräslund 1985.
32. Ambrosiani, K. 1981; Davidan 1982.
33. Thordeman 1920; Rydh 1936.
34. Floderus 1941; Tesch 1989a, 1989b.
35. Damell 1989.
36. Malmer 1989.
37. Ambrosiani 1990.
38. Hagberg 1985.
39. *Corpus Nummorum* I- .
40. *Gutasagan* 1983.
41. Engeström *et al.* 1989; Westholm 1985.
42. Lundström 1974, 1981, 1985.
43. Lundström 1983.
44. Carlsson 1987.
45. Carlsson 1988 and pers. comm.

46. Schulz 1988; Schulz and Schulz 1989.
47. Andrén 1985; Cinthio 1975, 1982.

5 The Vikings in Britain

1. Hill 1969.
2. Biddle and Hill 1971.
3. Biddle 1972, pp. 248-52.
4. Smyth 1977.
5. *William of Malmesbury*, p. 139.
6. Fellows Jensen 1981; Sawyer 1971, pp. 154-69.
7. Smyth 1975-1979.
8. Smith 1937, pp. 280-300.
9. Dolley 1978; Hall 1981, p. 95, 1984a pp. 60-3.
10. Radley 1971; Waterman 1959.
11. Hall 1982, 1984a, 1984b, 1988; Mainman 1990.
12. Webster and Cherry 1972, pp. 165-7.
13. Richardson 1959.
14. Andrews 1984; Moulden and Tweddle 1986, p. 8.
15. Hall 1984a, pp. 43-8.
16. Addyman 1974, pp. 218-24; Hall 1978; Radley 1971, pp. 40-2.
17. Radley 1971, pp. 42-3.
18. Moulden and Tweddle 1986, pp. 37-52.
19. Hall 1984a, pp. 61-3.
20. Hall 1984b.
21. Kenward *et al.* 1978, p. 67.
22. Addyman 1984, p. 20; Wenham *et al.* 1987.
23. MacGregor 1982, p. 102.
24. Colyer and Jones 1979, pp. 50-61; Gilmour 1988; Mann 1982; O'Connor 1982; Perring 1981.
25. Coppack 1973; Wacher 1979.
26. Perring 1981, p. 36.
27. Perring 1981, p. 43.
28. Mann 1982, p. 47.
29. Mahany and Rolfe 1983.
30. Kilmurry 1980.
31. Hall 1989.
32. Rogerson and Dallas 1984; Andrew Rogerson pers. comm.
33. Davison 1967.
34. Carter 1978.
35. Ayers 1988; pp. 165-6.
36. Youngs *et al.* 1986, p. 159
37. Carter *et al.* 1977.
38. Sandred and Lindström 1990.
39. Clarke 1977; Wallace 1985, pp. 107-9.
40. Briggs 1985.
41. Ó Ríordáin 1971, 1976, 1981; Wallace 1988.
42. Wallace 1985, 1987b.
43. Wallace 1985, p. 110-30.
44. See also Murray 1983.
45. Wallace 1987b.
46. Crumlin-Pedersen 1989c.

47. Mitchell 1987; Wallace 1987b, pp. 201-5.
48. Youngs *et al.* 1988, p. 299.
49. Patrick Wallace pers. comm.

6 Towns in the Slavonic-Baltic area

1. Lund 1984.
2. Gabriel 1989a, 1989b; Kempke 1989a, 1989b; Struwe 1989.
3. Herrmann 1989.
4. Herrmann 1978, 1985; Herrmann *et al.* 1982; Warnke 1978, 1985.
5. Schohknecht 1977, 1978.
6. Filipowiak 1981, 1985, 1986, 1989.
7. Filipowiak 1989.
8. Nerman 1958.
9. Davidan 1970, 1982; Kirpičnikov 1989; Raudonikas 1930.
10. Janin 1989, Yanin 1990; Kolčin 1989; Rybakov 1982; Sedov 1982.
11. Nosov 1987.
12. Avdusin 1970, 1977; Mühle 1989.
13. Udolph 1987.
14. Tolocko 1989.
15. Noonan 1989b.
16. Callmer 1989.
17. Duczko 1985.
18. Crumlin-Pedersen 1989a, 1989b.
19. Jansson 1989; Stalsberg 1989.

7 Towns in north, east and west: their physical structure and economy

1. Ambrosiani 1985b; Miller and Hedin 1988.
2. Jankuhn 1961, 1986; Müller-Wille 1988.
3. Ambrosiani 1983.
4. Ambrosiani 1985a.
5. Bourdillon 1988; Kenward *et al.* 1978; Wallace 1987b, pp. 201-5.
6. Addyman 1984, p. 20.
7. Brøgger and Shetelig 1953, pp. 104-72.
8. Thorvildsen 1957.
9. Stolpe and Arne 1912.
10. Arwidsson 1977.
11. Olsen and Crumlin-Pedersen 1978.
12. Ambrosiani 1990.
13. Crumlin-Pedersen 1989a.
14. Udolph 1987.
15. Crumlin-Pedersen 1989a, 1989b.
16. Ellmers 1972.
17. Lund 1984.
18. Cederlund 1989.
19. Herteig 1985; Milne and Hobley 1981; van Es and Verwers 1980.
20. *Olaus Magnus* 1555, XX:17.
21. MacGregor 1978, p. 48; Radley 1971, pp. 55-7.
22. Arwidsson 1986a, 1986b.

23. Jankuhn 1986, pp. 117-30 (but note also Schietzel's recent observation, p. 62 above).
24. Møller 1986.
25. Ambrosiani 1985c.
26. Sawyer 1988, p. 91.
27. Dent 1984.
28. Christophersen 1989; Reynolds 1977.
29. Herrmann 1985, 1989; Herrmann *et al.* 1982.
30. Ambrosiani 1987; Andrén 1985.
31. Ambrosiani 1977.
32. Schietzel 1985.
33. Lidén 1977; Myrvoll 1986.
34. Westholm 1989.
35. Andersen *et al.* 1971.
36. Wallace 1985, 1987b.
37. Tesch 1989a.
38. Andrén 1984.
39. Schietzel 1981.
40. Filipowiak 1981, 1986.
41. Biddle 1983, pp. 122–6.
42. Rybakov 1982.
43. Schia 1987.
44. Hall 1984a.
45. Wallace 1987b.
46. Frandsen and Jensen 1988; Feveile *et al.* 1990.
47. Biddle 1983, pp. 122-6.
48. Hvass 1985; Schmidt 1977.
49. Hinz 1989.
50. Schietzel 1981, pp. 61-4.
51. Hall 1984b.
52. Murray 1983.
53. Wallace 1985.
54. Holmqvist-Olausson pers. comm.
55. Schietzel 1981, pp. 47-8.
56. *Rimbert* 1986.
57. *Birka* I.
58. Andrén 1984; Tesch 1989a.
59. Andrén 1984.
60. Wenham *et al.* 1987.
61. Graham-Campbell 1980; Wilson 1967.
62. Filipowiak 1986; Gabriel 1989b; Herrmann *et al.* 1982; Sedov 1982.
63. Jankuhn 1986.
64. Ambrosiani 1978.
65. Jankuhn 1986, pp. 68-9.
66. *Birka* I, p. xx.
67. Jankuhn 1986, pp. 68-9.
68. Jankuhn 1986, pp. 65-8.
69. Andersen *et al.* 1971.
70. Elfwendahl 1989; Lundström 1974.
71. Ohlsson 1976.
72. Filipowiak 1986.
73. Jankuhn 1986, p. 67.
74. Decavele 1989, p. 50.

75. Clare Walsh pers. comm.
76. Ingelman-Sundberg 1972.
77. *Adam of Bremen* I:60.
78. *Birka* I.
79. Tesch 1989a, 1989b.
80. Ambrosiani, K. 1981.
81. Blindheim *et al.* 1981.
82. Jankuhn 1986, pp. 100-14.
83. Kurth 1963.
84. Jankuhn 1986; Steuer 1984.
85. Hägg 1984.
86. Geijer 1938; Hägg 1974.
87. MacGregor 1982, pp. 136-43.
88. Hägg 1974.
89. Ambrosiani, K. 1981; MacGregor 1985.
90. Addyman 1984, p. 19.
91. Ulbricht 1978.
92. Ambrosiani, K. 1981.
93. Holmqvist *et al.* 1972; Brinch Madsen 1984.
94. Brinch Madsen 1984.
95. Hall 1984a, p. 44; Jankuhn 1986.
96. Lundström 1981, pp. 96-100.
97. Radley 1971, pp. 49-50.
98. Mann 1982, p. 1.
99. Noonan 1989b.
100. Arwidsson 1942.
101. Davidan 1982.
102. Mann 1982, p. 46.
103. Wallace 1987a, p. 217.
104. Mårtensson 1976, p. 267.
105. Hübener 1959; Janssen 1987.
106. Ambrosiani and Arrhenius 1973; Selling 1955.
107. Filipowiak 1981; Lundström 1981, pp. 74-81.
108. Lundström 1981, p. 79.
109. Blindheim 1987a; Resi 1979, 1987.
110. Clarke 1985.
111. Jankuhn 1986, pp. 141ff.
112. Kirpičnikov 1970.
113. Stenberger 1947-58.
114. Noonan 1989a.
115. Lebedev 1982; Sawyer 1982.
116. Wallace 1987a, pp. 206-15.
117. Östergren 1989.
118. Bendixen 1981; Kyhlberg 1973; Linder–Welin 1973; Wiséhn 1989.
119. Malmer 1966, 1989.

Bibliography

Abbreviations

Antiq. Jnl.	*Antiquaries Journal*
Archaeol. Jnl.	*The Archaeological Journal*
BAR	British Archaeological Reports
Bede	*Venerabilis Baedae. Historìam Ecclesasticam Gentis Anglorum* (ed. Plummer 1896)
Berichten ROB.	*Berichten van de Rijksdienst voor het Oudheidkundig Bodemonderzoek*
CBA Res. Rep.	Council for British Archaeology Research Reports
Corpus Nummorum	*Corpus nummorum saeculorum IX-XI qui in Suecia reperti sunt*
E. Anglian Archaeol.	*East Anglian Archaeology*
Jnl. R. Soc. Antiq. Ireland	*Journal of the Royal Society of Antiquaries of Ireland*
KVHAA	Kungliga Vitterhets Historie och Antikvitets Akademien
Lincs. Hist. Archaeol.	*Lincolnshire History and Archaeology*
Med. Archaeol.	*Medieval Archaeology*
Oxford Jnl. Archaeol.	*Oxford Journal of Archaeology*
Pop. Archaeol.	*Popular Archaeology*
RAÄ	Riksantikvarieämbetet
SHM	Statens Historiska Museet

Adam of Bremen, 1959, *History of the Archbishops of Hamburg-Bremen*, translation with an introduction and notes by Francis J. Tschan, Records of Civilization Sources and Studies LIII, New York.

Addyman, P.V., 1974, 'Excavations in York 1972-1973', first interim report, *Antiq. Jnl.* 54:2, 200-231.

Addyman, P.V., 1984, 'York in its archaeological setting', in P.V. Addyman, and V.E. Black, (eds), 1984, 7-21.

Addyman, P.V. and Black, V.E. (eds), 1984, *Archaeological Papers from York Presented to M.W. Barley*, York.

Almqvist, B. and Greene, D. (eds), 1976, *Proceedings of the Seventh Viking Congress*, Dublin.

Ambrosiani, B., 1974, 'Neue Ausgrabungen in Birka', in Jankuhn, H. *et al.* (eds), 1973-74, *Vor- und Frühformen der europäischen Stadt in Mittelalter*, 1-2. Abh. der Akademie der Wissenschaften in Göttingen, 83, 84, 58-63, Göttingen.

Ambrosiani, B., 1977, 'Urban archaeology in Sweden' (with a contribution on western Sweden by Hans Andersson), in M.W. Barley (ed.), *European Towns. Their Archaeology and Early History*. London-New York-San Francisco, 103-26.

Ambrosiani, B., 1978, 'Burg, 29-31: Schwedische, finnische und norwegische', in *Reallexikon der Germanischen Altertumskunde*, Berlin.

Ambrosiani, B., 1981, 'Birka – a planted town serving an increasing agricultural population', in Bekker-Nielsen *et al.* (eds), *Proceedings of the Eighth Viking Congress*, Medieval Scandinavian Supplements 2, Odense, 19-23.

Ambrosiani, B., 1983, 'Background to the boat-graves of the Mälaren valley', in *Vendel Period Studies*, ed. by J.-P. Lamm and H.-Å. Nordström, SHM Studies 2, Stockholm.

Ambrosiani, B., 1985a, 'Specialization and urbanization in the Mälaren Valley – a question of maturity', in Lindquist, S.O. (ed.), *Society and Trade in the Baltic during the Viking Age*, Acta Visbyensia VII, Visby, 103-12.

Ambrosiani, B., 1985b, 'Jetties in Birka and Stockholm and the changing water levels in the Mälaren area', in Herteig (ed.), 66-8.

Ambrosiani, B., 1985c, Adams Nordenbild, in *Västergötlands äldre historia*, ed. by G. Behre and E. Wegraeus, Vänersborg, 25-40.

Ambrosiani, B., 1987, 'Royal manors and towns in central Sweden', in Knirk, J. (ed.), *Proceedings of the Tenth Viking Congress, Larkollen, Norway, 1985*, Universitetets Oldsaksamlings Skrifter, Ny rekke 9, Oslo, 247-53.

Ambrosiani, B., 1988a, 'Helgö or Bona on Helgö', in A. Lundström (ed.), 14-19.

Ambrosiani, B., 1988b, *Birka on the Island of Björkö*. Stockholm.

Ambrosiani, B., 1988c, 'The prehistory of towns in Sweden', in Hodges R. and Hobley, B. (eds), *The Rebirth of Towns in the West AD 700-1050*, CBA Res. Rep. 68, London, 63-68.

Ambrosiani, B., 1990, 'Birka: its waterways and hinterland', in *Maritime Scandinavia AD 200-1200*, ed. by O. Crumlin-Pedersen and K. Hansen, Roskilde.

Ambrosiani, B. *et al.*, 1973. *Birka. Svarta Jordens Hamnområde. Arkeologisk undersökning 1970-1971*, RAÄ Rapport, C 1 1973, Stockholm.

Ambrosiani, B. and Arrhenius, B., 1973, 'Keramik', in Ambrosiani *et al.*, 115-48.

Ambrosiani, K., 1981, *Viking Age Combs, Comb Making and Comb Makers*. Stockholm Studies in Archaeology, 2.

Andersen, H.H., 1985, 'Hedenske danske kongegrave og deres historiske baggrund – et forsøg på en syntese', *Kuml*, 11-34.

Andersen, H.H. *et al.*, 1971, *Århus Søndervold*, Jysk Arkæologisk Selskabs Skrifter, IX, Århus.

Andersen, H.H. *et al.*, 1976, *Danevirke*, Jysk Arkæologisk Selskabs Skrifter, XIII, Århus.

Andersson, H., 1981, *Kungahälla*. Rapport Medeltidsstaden, 29, Stockholm.

Andrén, A., 1980, *Lund*. Rapport Medeltidsstaden, 26, Stockholm.

Andrén, A., 1984, *Lund, tomtindelning, ägostruktur, sockenbildning*. Rapport Medeltidsstaden, 56, Stockholm.

Andrén, A., 1985, *Den Urbana Scenen. Städer och samhälle i det medeltida Danmark*, Acta Archaeologica Lundensia, Series in 8°, 13.

Andrews, G., 1984, 'Archaeology in York: an assessment', in Addyman and Black (eds)., 173-208.

Andrews, P. (ed.), 1988, *Southampton Finds Volume I. The Coins and Pottery from Hamwic*, Southampton.

Anglo-Saxon Chronicle, translated by G.N. Garmonsway, London, 1977.

Arbman, H., 1955, *Svear i österviking*, Stockholm.

Arwidsson, G., 1942, *Vendelstile, Email und Glas im 7.-8. Jahrhundert*, Valsgärde-Studien 1, Uppsala.

Arwidsson, G., 1977, *Valsgärde 7*, Uppsala.

Arwidsson, G., 1986a, 'Die Eissporen', *Birka II:2*, 111-12.

Arwidsson, G., 1986b, 'Pferdeeisnägel', in *Birka II:2*, 136.

Avdusin, D.A., 1970, 'Material culture in the towns of Ancient Rus', in Hannestad *et al.* (eds), *Varangian Problems*, Scando-Slavica, Supplementum I, Copenhagen, 95-106.

Avdusin, D.A., 1977, 'Gnezdovo – der Nachbar von Smolensk', *Zeitschrift für Archäologie*, Berlin, 263-90.

Ayers, B., 1988, 'Excavations at St Martin-at-Palace-Plain, Norwich, *E. Anglian Archaeol.*, 37.

Barker, P.A. *et al.*, 1974. 'Two burials under the refectory of Worcester cathedral', *Med. Archaeol.*, 18, 146-51.

Barley, M.W. (ed.), 1977, *European Towns, Their Archaeology and Early History*, London–New York–San Francisco.

Bekker-Nielsen, H. *et al.* (eds), 1981, *Proceedings of the Eighth Viking Congress*, Medieval Scandinavia Supplements 2. Odense.

Bencard, M., 1978, 'Ribe i tusind år', *Tidskriften Bygd*, Esbjerg.

Bencard, M. (ed.), 1981-, *Ribe Excavations 1970-76*, Vol. 1–, Esbjerg.

Bendixen, K., 1981, 'Sceattas and other coin finds', in Bencard (ed.), 1, 63-101.

Besteman, J.C., 1974, 'Carolingian Medemblik', *Berichten ROB*, 24, 43-106.

Besteman, J.C., 1989, 'The pre-urban development of Medemblik: from an early medieval trading centre to a medieval town', in Heidiuga, H.A. and van Regteren Altena, H.H. (eds), *Medemblik and Monnickendam*, Amsterdam, 1-30.

Biddle, M., 1970, 'Excavations at Winchester, 1969: eighth interim report', *Antiq. Jnl.*, 50:1, 277-326.

Biddle, M., 1972, 'Winchester: the development of an early capital', in Jankuhn *et al.* (eds), 229-61.

Biddle, M., 1975, 'Excavations at Winchester, 1971: tenth and final report II', *Antiq. Jnl.*, 55:2, 295-337.

Biddle, M., 1976, *Winchester in the Early Middle Ages*, Winchester Studies 1, Oxford.

Biddle, M., 1983, 'The study of Winchester: archaeology and history in a British town, 1961-1983', *Proc. British Academy*, 69, 93-135.

Biddle, M., 1984, 'London on the Strand', *Pop. Archaeol.*, 6:1, 23-7.

Biddle, M. and Hill, D., 1971, 'Late Saxon planned towns', *Antiq. Jnl.*, 511, 70-85.

Biddle, M. and Kjølby-Biddle, B., forthcoming, *The Anglo-Saxon Minsters in Winchester*, Winchester Studies 4, Oxford.

Birka I-V, 1938-1989, ed. by H. Arbman and G. Arwidsson, KVHAA, Stockholm.

Blackburn, M.A.S. and Bonser, M.J., 1984, 'Single finds of Anglo-Saxon and Norman coins 1', *British Numismatic Journal*, 54, 68-73.

Blackburn, M.A.S. and Bonser, M.J., 1985, 'Single finds of Anglo-Saxon and Norman coins 2', *British Numismatic Journal*, 55, 55-78.

Blindheim, C., 1975, 'Kaupang by the Viks Fjord in Vestfold', in Herteig *et al.*, *Archaeological Contributions to the Early History of Urban Communities in Norway*, Oslo, 125-73.

Blindheim, C., 1987a, 'Internal trade in Viking age Norway', in Düwel *et al.* (eds), *Untersuchungen zu Handel und Verkehr der vor- und frühgeschichtlichen Zeit in Mittel- und Nordeuropa IV*: Der Handel der Karolinger- und Wikinger- zeit Göttingen, 758-72.

Blindheim, C., 1987b, 'Introduction', in Knirk (ed.), 27-42.

Blindheim, C. *et al.*, 1981, *Kaupang-funnene* I, Norske Oldfunn XI, Oslo.

Blomqvist, R. and Märtensson, A. (eds), 1983, *Thulegrävningen 1961*, Archaeologica Lundensia, II, Lund.

Bolin, S., 1939, 'Muhammed, Karl den store och Rurik', *Scandia*, XII, 181-222.

Bonnet, C., 1986, *Geneva in Early Christian Times*, Geneva.

Bonnet, C., 1987, 'The archaeological site of the cathedral of Saint Peter (Saint-Pierre), Geneva', *World Archaeol*, 18:3, 330-40.

Bourdillon, J., 1988, 'Countryside and town: the animal resources of Saxon Southampton', in Hooke, D. (ed.), *Anglo-Saxon Settlements*, Oxford, 177-95.

Brandt, K., 1985, 'Medieval harbour settlements in the marshlands between Ems and Weser, northwestern Germany', in Herteig (ed.), 99-105.

Briggs, C.S., 1985, 'A neglected Viking burial with beads from Kilmainham, Dublin, discovered in 1847', *Med. Archaeol.*, 29, 107-22.

Brinch Madsen, H., 1984, 'Metal-casting', in Bencard (ed.), II, 15-189.

Brisbane, M., 1988, 'Hamwic (Saxon Southampton): an 8th century port and production centre', in Hodges and Hobley (eds), 101-8.

Brøgger, A.W. and Shetelig, H., 1953, *The Viking Ships*, Oslo.

Brooks, D.A., 1986, 'A review of the evidence for continuity in British towns in the 5th and 6th centuries', *Oxford Jnl. Archaeol.*, 5:1, 77-102.

Buckland, P., 1984, 'The "Anglian" Tower and the use of Jurassic limestone in York', in Addyman and Black (eds), 51-7.

Bullock, P. and Murphy, C. (eds), 1983, *Soil Morphology* I, Oxford.

Callmer, J., 1982, 'Production site and market area. Some notes on fieldwork in progress', *Meddelanden från Lunds Universitets Historiska Museum 1981-1982*, 135-65.

Callmer, J., 1986, 'To stay or to move', *Meddelanden från Lunds Universitets Historiska Museum 1985-1986*, 167-208.

Callmer, J., 1989, 'Slawisch-skandinavische Kontakte am Beispiel der slawischen Keramik in Skandinavien während des 8. and 9. Jahrhunderts', in Müller-Wille, M. (ed.), 1989, *Oldenburg–Wolin–Staraja Ladoga–Novgorod–Kiev. Handel und Handelsverbindungen im südlichen und östlichen Ostseeraum während des frühen Mittelalters*, Bericht der Römisch-Germanischen Kommission, 69, Mainz, 654-74.

Capelle, T., 1976, 'Die frühgeschichtlichen Metallfunde von Domburg auf Walcheren 1 and 2, *Nederlandse Oudheden 1976*.

Capelle, T., 1978, 'Die karolingischen Funde von Schouwen', *Nederlandse Oudheden 1978*.

Carlsson, D., 1987, Äldre hamnar – ett hotat kulturarv', *Fornvännen*, 82, 6-18.

Carlsson, D., 1988, 'Vikingatida hamnar på Gotland', *Populär Arkeologi*, 1988, 2.

Carter, A., 1978, 'The Anglo-Saxon origins of Norwich', *Anglo-Saxon England*, 7, 175-204.

Carter, A. *et al.*, 1977, 'Excavations in Norwich – 1973. The Norwich Survey, third interim report', *Norfolk Archaeol.*, 36, 37-71.

Carver, M., 1987, *Underneath English Towns*, London.

Cederlund, C.-O., 1989, 'Sjövägarna vid svenska Östersjökusten på 1200-talet, *Marinarkeologisk Tidskrift*, 1989:3, 8-15.

Cherry, J.F. *et al.* (eds), 1978, *Sampling in Contemporary British Archaeology*, BAR 50, Oxford.

Christensen, A.S., 1988, *Middelalderbyen Odense*, Århus.

Christophersen, A., 1989, 'Royal Authority and early urbanization in Trondheim during the transition to the historical period', *Arkeologiske Skrifter fra Historisk Museum Bergen*, 5, 91-135.

Cinthio, E., 1975, 'Köping och stad i det tidigmedeltida Skåne', *Ale*, 1.

Cinthio, E., 1982, 'Den sydskandinaviska 1200-tals staden – ett kontinuitets- och omlandsproblem', *Bebyggelsehistorisk Tidskrift*, 3, 33-40.

Cinthio, H., 1980, 'The Löddeköpinge Investigation III. The early medieval cemetery', *Meddelanden från Lunds Universitets Historiska Museum, 1979-1980*, 112-31.

Clarke, H., 1985, 'English and Baltic trade in the middle ages – an evaluation of the evidence', in Lindquist (ed.), 113-20.

Clarke, H., 1988, 'Seasonally-occupied settlements and Anglo-Saxon towns', in B. Hårdh *et al.* (eds), *Trade and Exchange in Prehistory*, Lund, 247-54.

Clarke, H.B., 1977, 'The topographical development of early medieval Dublin', *Jnl. Royal Soc. Antiq. Ireland*, 107, 29-51.

Clarke, H.B. and Simms, A. (eds), 1985, *The Comparative History of Urban Origins in Non-Roman Europe*, BAR Int. Ser. 255, Oxford.

Claude, D., 1987, 'Aspekte des Binnenhandels im Merowingerreich auf Grund der Schriftquellen', in Düwel *et al.*, *Untersuchungen zu Handel und Verkehr der vor- und frühgeschichtlichen Zeit in Mittel- und Nordeuropa III:* Der Handel des frühen Mittelalters, Göttingen, 9-99.

Colyer, C. and Jones, M.J., 1979, 'Excavations at Lincoln. Second interim report: excavations in the lower town 1972-1978', *Antig. Jnl.*, 59:1, 50-91.

Coppack, G., 1973, 'The excavation of a Roman and medieval site at Flaxengate, Lincoln', *Lincs. Hist. Archaeol.*, 8, 73-114.

Corpus Nummorum 1975- , ed. by B. Malmer, Stockholm.

Coutts, C. and Worthington, M., 1986, 'The early medieval pottery from Quentovic – an interim note', *Med. Ceramics*, 10, 23-7.

Cramp, R., 1967, *Anglian and Viking York*, Borthwick Papers 33.

Crumlin-Pedersen, O., 1989a, 'Vikingernes "søvej" til Byzans – om betingelser for sejlads ad flodvejene fra Østersø til Sortehav', *Ottende tværfaglige Vikinge-symposium*, Århus, 33-51.

Crumlin-Pedersen, O., 1989b, 'Schiffe und Schiffahrtswege im Ostseeraum während des 9.-12. Jahrhunderts', in Müller-Wille (ed.), 530-63.

Crumlin-Pedersen, O., 1989c, 'Et irsk langskib?', *Nyt fra Nationalmuseet*, 45, 4-5.

Damell, D., 1989, 'Fornsigtuna', in Tesch (ed.), 20-34.

Davidan, O., 1970, 'Contacts between Staraja Ladoga and Scandinavia', in Hannestad *et al.* (eds), 79-91.

Davidan, O., 1982, 'Om hantverkets utveckling i Staraja-Ladoga', *Fornvännen*, 77, 170-9.

Davison, B.K., 1967, 'The late Saxon town of Thetford', *Med. Archaeol.*, 11, 189-208.

Decavele, J. (ed.), 1989, *Ghent. In Defence of a Rebellious City*, Antwerp.

Declercq, G. and Verhulst, A., 1989, 'Early medieval Ghent between two abbeys and the count's castle', in Decavele (ed.), 37-59.

Dent. J., 1984, 'Skerne', *Current Archaeology*, 91, 251-3.

Dolley, M., 1978, 'The Anglo-Danish and Anglo-Norse coinages of York', in R.A. Hall (ed.), *Viking Age York and the North*, CBA Res. Rep., 27, London, 26-36.

Donat, P., 1989, 'Archäologisch-kulturelle Gebiete und materielle Kultur in der slawischen Stammesgebieten vom 8-13 Jh.', in J. Herrmann (ed.), *Archäologie in der Deutschen Demokratischen Republik*, Berlin.

Dornier, A. (ed.), 1977, *Mercian Studies*, Leicester.

Duczko. W., 1985, *The Filigree and Granulation Work of the Viking Period. An analysis of the Material from Björkö*, *Birka* V, KVHAA, Stockholm.

Dunmore, A., *et al.*, 1975, 'The origin and development of Ipswich: an interim report', *E. Anglian Archaeol.*, 1, 57-67.

Düwel, *et al.* (eds), 1985, *Untersuchungen zu Handel und Verkehr der vor- und frühgeschichtlichen Zeit in Mittel- und Nordeuropa* III: Der Handel des frühen

Mittelalters, Göttingen.

Düwel, *et al.* (eds), 1987, *Untersuchungen zu Handel und Verkehr der vor- und frühgeschichtlichen Zeit in Mittel- und Nordeuropa* IV: Der Handel der Karolinger- und Wikingerzeit, Göttingen.

Ekwall, E., 1964, *Old English Wic in Place-names*, Lund.

Elfwendahl, M., 1989, *Arkeologi på Gotland, Fyra undersökningar i Västergarn*, Rapport, RAGU 1989:1, Visby.

Ellmers, D., 1972. *Frühmittelalterliche Handelsschiffahrt in Mittel- und Nordeuropa*, Neumünster.

Engeström, R. *et al.*, 1989, *Visby*, I-II. Rapport Medeltidsstaden, 71-2, Stockholm.

Faull, M.L. (ed.), 1984, *Studies in Late Anglo-Saxon Settlement*, Oxford.

Fellows Jensen, G., 1981, 'Signposts to settling', in Roesdahl *et al.* (eds), *The Vikings in England*, London, 79-82.

Feveile *et al.*, 1970, 'Ansgars Ribe endelig fundet – rapport over en udgravning ved Rosenallé i Ribe 1989', *By, Marsk og Geest*, 1:1988, 29-53.

Filipowiak, W., 1981, 'Wolin, Poland', in Milne and Hobley (eds), 61-9.

Filipowiak, W., 1985, 'Die Bedeutung Wolins im Ostseehandel', in Lindquist (ed.), 121-38.

Filipowiak, W., 1986, *Wolin–Wineta*, Rostock–Stralsund.

Filipowiak, W., 1989, 'Handel und Handelsplätze an der Ostseeküste Westpommerns', in Müller-Wille (ed.), 690-719.

Floderus, E., 1941, *Sigtuna. Sveriges Äldsta Medeltidsstad*, Stockholm.

Frandsen, L.B. and Jensen, S., 1988, 'Hvor lå Ribe i vikingetiden? Et bidrag til Ribes topografi fra 8 til 11 århundrede, *Kuml* 1986, 21-35.

Gabriel, I., 1989a, 'Hof- und Sakralkultur sowie Gebrauchs- und Handelsgut im Spiegel der Kleinfunde von Starigard/Oldenburg, in Müller-Wille (ed.), 103-291.

Gabriel, I., 1989b, 'Zur Innenbebauung von Starigard/Oldenburg', in Müller-Wille (ed.), 55-86.

Galinié, H., 1988, 'Reflections on early medieval Tours', in Hodges and Hobley (eds), 57-62.

Geijer, A., 1938, *Die Textilfunde aus den Gräbern, Birka* III, KVHAA, Stockholm.

Gilmour, B., 1979, 'The Anglo-Saxon church at St Paul-in-the-Bail, Lincoln', *Med. Archaeol.*, 23, 214-18.

Gilmour, L.A., 1988, *Early Medieval Pottery from Flaxengate, Lincoln*. Archaeol. of Lincoln XVII:2.

Graham-Campbell, J.A., 1980, 'The Viking-age burials of England – some problems of interpretation', in Rahtz, P.A. *et al.* (eds), *Anglo-Saxon Cemeteries 1979*, BAR 82, Oxford, 379-82.

Gräslund, A.-S., 1980, *The Burial Customs. A Study of the Graves on Björkö, Birka* IV, KVHAA, Stockholm.

Gregory of Tours, History of the Franks, translated by Ernest Brehaut, 1973, New York.

Grøngaard-Jeppesen, T., 1981, *Middelalderlandsbyens opståen. Kontinuitet og brud i den fynske agrarbebygggelse mellem yngre jernalder og tidlig middelalder*, Fynske Studier, XI.

Gutasagan, 1983, in I. Jansson (ed.) *Gutar och Vikingar*, Stockholm, 470-80.

Haarnagel, W., 1984, 'Die frühgeschichtliche Handelssiedlung Emden und ihre Entwicklung bis zum Mittelalter', in Jankuhn *et al.* (eds), 114-35.

Hagberg, U.E., 1985, 'Ports and trading places on Öland and in the Kalmarsund area', in Lindquist (ed.), 139-48.

Hall, R.A., 1978, 'The topography of Anglo-Scandinavian York', in Hall (ed.), 31-6

Hall, R.A. (ed) 1978, *Viking Age York and the North*, CBA Res. Rep. 27, London.

Hall, R.A., 1981, 'Markets of the Danelaw', in Roesdahl *et al.* (eds), 95-9.

Hall. R.A., 1982, 'Tenth-century woodworking in Coppergate, York', in S. McGrail (ed.), *Woodworking Techniques before A.D. 1500*, BAR Int. Ser, 129, Oxford, 31-6.

Hall, R.A., 1984a, *The Viking Dig*, York.

Hall, R.A., 1984b, 'A late pre-conquest building tradition', in Addyman and Black (eds), 26-36.

Hall, R.A., 1988, 'York 700-1050', in Hodges and Hobley (eds), 125-32.

Hall, R.A., 1989, 'The Five Boroughs of the Danelaw: a review of present knowledge', *Anglo-Saxon England*, 18, 149-206.

Hägg, I., 1974, *Kvinnodräkten i Birka*, Aun 2, Uppsala.

Hägg, I., 1984, *Textilien aus dem Hafen von Haithabu*. Berichte über die Ausgrabungen in Haithabu, 20, Neumünster.

Hannestad, K. *et al.* (eds), 1970, *Varangian Problems*, Scando-Slavica, Supplementum I, Copenhagen.

Hårdh, B., *et al.* (eds), 1988, *Trade and Exchange in Prehistory*, Lund.

Heighway, C., 1984, 'Anglo-Saxon Gloucester to A.D. 1000', in M.L. Faull (ed.), *Studies in Late Anglo-Saxon Settlement*, Oxford, 34-53.

Herrmann, J., 1978. 'Ralswiek auf Rügen – Ein Handelsplatz des 9. Jahrhunderts und die Fernhandelbeziehungen im Ostseegebiet', *Zeitschrift für Archäologie*, 163-80.

Herrmann, J., 1985, 'Hinterland, trade and craftworking in the early trading stations of the North-western Slavs', in H.B. Clarke and A. Simms (eds), *The Comparative History of Urban Origins in Non-Roman Europe*, BAR Int. Ser., 255, Oxford, 249-66.

Herrmann, J., 1989, 'Zur Struktur von Handel und Handelsplätzen im Südwestlichen Ostseegebiet vom 8.-10. Jahrhundert', in Müller-Wille (ed.), 720-39.

Herrmann, J. *et al.*, 1982, *Wikinger und Slawen. Zur Frühgeschichte der Ostseevölker*, Neumünster.

Herteig, A. (ed.) 1985, *Conference on Waterfront Archaeology in North European Towns 2, Bergen 1983*, Bergen.

Hill, D., 1969, 'The Burghal Hidage: the establishment of a text', *Med. Archaeol.*, 13, 84-92.

Hill, D. *et al.*, 1990, 'Quentovic defined', *Antiquity*, 64:242, 51-8.

Hinchcliffe, J. 1986, 'An early medieval settlement at Cowage Farm, Foxley, near Malmesbury', *Archaeol. Jnl.*, 143, 240-59.

Hinton, D.A. *et al.*, 1981, 'The Winchester reliquary', *Med. Archaeol.*, 25, 45-77.

Hinz, H., 1989, 'Ländlicher Hausbau in Skandinavien vom 6. bis 14. Jahrhundert: Stova – Eldhus – Bur.' *Zeitschrift für Archäologie des Mittelalters*, 5.

Hobley, B., 1988. Saxon London: *Lundenwic* and *Lundenburh*: two cities rediscovered, in R. Hodges and B. Hobley (eds) *The Rebirth of Towns in the West AD 700-1050*, CBA Res. Rep. 68, London, 69-82.

Hodges, R. and Hobley, B. (eds), 1988, *The Rebirth of Towns in the West AD 700-1050*, CBA Res. Rep. 68, London.

Hoffmann, D. *et al.*, 1987, *Hollingstedt – Untersuchungen zum Nordseehafen von Haithabu/Schleswig*. Berichte über die Ausgrabungen in Haithabu, 25, Neumünster.

Holdsworth, P., 1976, 'Saxon Southampton: a new review', *Med. Archaeol.*, 20, 26-61.

Holdsworth, P., 1980, *Excavations at Melbourne Street, Southampton, 971-76*, CBA Res. Rep. 33, London.

Holmqvist, W. *et al.*, 1961, *Report for 1954–1956*, Excavations at Helgö, I, Stockholm.

Holmqvist, W. *et al.*, 1972, *Workshop, Part I*, Excavations at Helgö, IV, Stockholm.

Holt, J.C. (ed.), 1987, *Domesday Studies*, Royal Historical Society, London.

Hooke, D. (ed.), 1988, *Anglo Saxon Settlements*, Oxford.

Hope-Taylor, B., 1977, *Yeavering*, Dept. of Environment Archaeol. Reports 7, London.

Hübener, W., 1959, *Die Keramik von Haithabu*. Die Ausgrabungen in Haithabu, 2. Neumünster.

Hurst, J.G., 1976, 'The pottery', in D.M. Wilson (ed.), *The Archaeology of Anglo-Saxon England*, London, 283-348.

Hvass, S., 1985, 'Viking Age villages in Denmark – new investigations', in Lindquist (ed.), 211-28.

Ingelman-Sundberg, C., 1972, 'Undervattensarkeologisk undersökning utanför Birka', *Fornvännen*, 67, 127-35.

Jacobsson, B. and Wallin, L., 1986, *Trelleborg under vikingatid och medeltid*, Riksantikvarieämbetet UV-Syd's skriftserie, 7, Lund.

Janin, V.L., 1989, 'Das frühe Novgorod', in Müller-Wille (ed.), 338-43.

Jankuhn, H., 1958, 'Die frühmittelalterlichen Seehandelsplätze in Nord- und Ostseeraum', in T. Mayer (ed.), *Studien zu den Anfängen des europäischen Städtewesens. Reichenau-Vorträqe 1955-1956*, Vorträge und Forschungen, 4, Lindau and Konstanz, 451-98.

Jankuhn, H., 1961, 'Die Entstehung der mittelalterlichen Agrarlandschaft in Angeln', in *Morphogenesis of the agrarian cultural landscape, Papers of the Vadstena Symposium at the XIXth International Geographical Congress August 14-20, 1960*, ed. by Staffan Helmfrid. Geografiska Annaler, XLIII:1-2, 151-64.

Jankuhn, H. *et al.* (eds), 1973–4, *Vor- und Frühformen der europäischen Stadt in Mittelalter*, 1-2. Abh. der Akademie der Wissenschaften in Göttingen, 83, 84, Göttingen.

Jankuhn, H., 1986, *Haithabu. Ein Handelsplatz der Wikingerzeit* (8th ed.), Neumünster.

Janssen, W., 1985, 'The origins of the non-Roman town in Germany', in Clarke and Simms (eds), 217-35.

Janssen, W., 1987, *Die Importkeramik von Haithabu*. Die Ausgrabungen in Haithabu, 9, Neumünster.

Jansson, I. (ed.), 1983, *Guter och Vikingar*, Stockholm.

Jansson, I., 1989, 'Wikingerezeitlicher orientalischer Import in Skandinavien', in Müller-Wille (ed.), 564-647.

Jones, M. and Dimbleby, G.W., 1981, *The Environment of Man*, BAR 87, Oxford.

Joris, A., 1965, *Huy, Ville Medievale*, Brussels.

Keevil, G., 1989, *Carlisle Cathedral Excavations 1988. Interim Report*, Carlisle.

Kemp, R., 1987, 'Anglian York – the missing link', *Current Archaeology*, 104, 259-63.

Kempke, T., 1989a, 'Zur Chronologie der Keramik von Starigard/Oldenburg', in Müller-Wille (ed), 89-102.

Kempke, T., 1989b, 'Zur überregionalen Verbreitung der Pfeilspitzentypen des 8.-12. Jahrhunderts aus Starigard/Oldenburg', in Müller-Wille (ed), 292-306.

Kenward, H.K. *et al.*, 1978, 'The environment of Anglo-Scandinavian York', in Hall (ed.), 58-70.

Kenward, H.K. *et al.*, 1986, *Environmental Evidence from a Roman Well and Anglian Pits in the Legionary Fortress*. Archaeol. of York 19/4.

Kilmurry, K., 1980, *The Pottery Industry of Stamford, Lincs*, BAR 84, Oxford.

Kirpičnikov, A.N., 1970, 'Connections between Russia and Scandinavia in the 9th and 10th centuries, as illustrated by weapon finds', in Hannestad *et al.* (eds), 50-76.

Kirpičnikov, A.N., 1989, 'Staraja Ladoga/Alt-Ladoga und seine überregionalen Beziehungen im 8.-10. Jahrhundert', in Müller-Wille (ed.), 307-37.

Knirk, J. (ed.), 1987, *Proceedings of the Tenth Viking Congress, Larkollen, Norway*,

1985. Universitetets Oldsaksamlings Skrifter, Ny rekke 9, Oslo.

Kolčin, B.A., 1989, *Wooden Artifacts from Medieval Novgorod*, BAR International Series, 495, Oxford.

Krongaard-Kristensen, H., 1987, *Middelalderbyen Viborg*. Projekt Middelalderbyen, 4.

Kurth, G., 1963, Nyare naturvetenskapliga aspekter på människans historia. *Ymer*, 83:1-2, 20-48.

Kyhlberg, O., 1973, 'De arabiska silvermynten, stratigrafi', in Ambrosiani *et al.*, 200-6.

Lebecq, S., 1983, *Marchands et Navigateurs Frisons du Haut Moyen Age*, 1-2, Lille.

Lebedev, G.S., 1982, 'Monety Birki kak istoricheski istochnik', *Skandinavski Sbornik*, XXVII, 149-63.

Lidén, H.E., 1977, 'Urban archaeology in Norway', in Barley (ed.), 83-101.

Linder-Welin, U., 1973, 'Myntbestämningar', in Ambrosiani *et al.*, 197-9.

Lindquist, S.-O. (ed.), 1985, *Society and Trade in the Baltic during the Viking Age*. Acta Visbyensia VII. Visby.

Lund, N. (ed.), 1984, *Two Voyagers at the Court of King Alfred*, York.

Lundström, A. (ed.), 1988, *Thirteen Studies on Helgö*, SHM Studies 7, Stockholm.

Lundström, P., 1974, 'Paviken bei Västergarn – Hafen, Handelsplatz und Werft, in Jankuhn *et al.* (eds), 82-93.

Lundström, P., 1981, *De Kommo Vida . . . Vikingars Hamn vid Paviken på Gotland*, Stockholm.

Lundström, P., 1983, 'Gotlandshamnar', in Jansson (ed.), 99-116.

Lundström, P., 1985, 'Paviken bei Västergarn', in Lindquist (ed.), 265-8.

MacGregor, A., 1978, 'Industry and commerce in Anglo-Scandinavian York', in Hall (ed.), 37-57.

MacGregor, A., 1982, *Anglo-Scandinavian Finds from Lloyds Bank, Pavement, and Other Sites*, Archaeol. of York 17/3.

MacGregor, A., 1985, *Bone, Antler, Ivory and Horn. The Technology of Skeletal Materials Since the Roman Period*, London.

Macphail, R.I., 1981, 'Soil and botanical studies of the dark earth', in M. Jones and G. Dimbleby (eds), *The Environment of Man*, BAR 87, Oxford, 309-31.

Macphail, R.I., 1983, 'The micromorphology of dark earth from Gloucester, London and Norwich: an analysis of urban anthropogenic deposits from the late Roman to early medieval periods in England', in P. Bullock and C. Murphy (eds), *Soil Morphology I*, Oxford, 245-52.

Mahany, C. and Rolfe, D., 1983, 'Stamford. The development of an Anglo-Scandinavian borough', *Anglo-Norman Studies*, 5, 197-219.

Mainman, A.J., 1990, *Anglo-Scandinavian Pottery from Coppergate*, Archaeol. of York 16/5.

Malmer, B., 1966, *Nordiska mynt före år 1000*. Acta Archaeologica Lundensia, Series in 8°, 4, Lund.

Malmer, B., 1989, *The Sigtuna Coinage*, Commentationes de Nummis Saeculorum IX-XI, in Suecia Repertis, Nova Series 4, KVHAA, Stockholm.

Mann, J.E., 1982, *Early Medieval Finds from Flaxengate*, Archaeol. of Lincoln XIV:1.

Mason, D.J.P., 1985, *Excavations at Chester*, Grosvenor Museum Archaeol. Excavation and Survey Reports 3, Chester.

Mayer, T. (ed.), 1958, *Studien zu den Anfängen des Europäischen Städtewesens. Reichenau-Vorträge 1955–1956*, Vorträge und Forschungen, 4, Lindau und Konstanz.

McGrail, S. (ed.), 1982, *Woodworking Techniques before A.D. 1500*, BAR Int. Ser. 129, Oxford.

Miller, U. and Hedin, K., 1988, *The Holocene Development of Landscape and*

Environment in the South-East Mälaren Valley, with Special Reference to Helgö. Excavations at Helgö, XI, KVHAA.

Milne, G., 1989, 'Lundenwic to London Town: from beach-market to merchant port', *Arkeologiske Skrifter fra Historisk Museum Bergen*, 5, 160-5

Milne, G. and Goodburn, D., 1990, 'The early medieval port of London AD 700–1200', *Antiquity*, 64, 620-28.

Milne, G. and Hobley, B. (eds), 1981, *Waterfront Archaeology in Britain and Northern Europe*, CBA Res. Rep., 41, London.

Mitchell, G.F., 1987, *Archaeology and Environment in Early Dublin*, Medieval Dublin Excavations 1962-81, Ser. C., 1, Dublin.

Møller, J.T., 1986, 'Relict spits in Denmark as evidence of old straits', *Boreas*, 16, 381-5.

Morris, R., 1983, *The Church in British Archaeology*, CBA Res. Rep., 47, London.

Moulden, J. and Tweddle, D., 1986, *Anglo-Scandinavian Settlement South-west of the Ouse*, Archaeol. of York 8/1.

Mühle, E., 1989, 'Gnezdovo – das alte Smolensk? Zur Deutung eines Siedlungskomplexes des ausgehenden 9. bis beginnenden 11. Jahrhunderts', in Müller-Wille (ed.), 358-410.

Müller-Wille, M., 1988, 'Hedeby und sein Umland', in Hårdh *et al.* (eds), 271-8.

Müller-Wille, M. (ed.), 1989, *Oldenburg – Wolin – Staraja Ladoga – Norgorod – Kiev. Handel und Handelsvetbindungen im südlichen und östlichen Ostseeraum während des frühen Mittelalters*, Bericht der Römisch-Germanischen Kommission, Band 69, Mainz.

Murray, H., 1983, *Viking and Early Medieval Buildings in Dublin*, BAR 119, Oxford.

Myrvoll, S., 1986, 'Skien og Telemark – naturresurser, produkter og kontakter i sen vikingtid och tidlig middelalder', *Viking*, 1985/86, 161-80.

Mårtensson, A. (ed.), 1976, *Uppgrävt förflutet för PKbanken i Lund*, Archaeologica Lundensia VII, Lund.

Nerman, B., 1958, *Grobin – Seeburg. Ausgrabungen und Funde*, KVHAA, Stockholm.

Noonan, T.S., 1989a, 'The impact of the silver crisis in Islam upon Novgorod's trade with the Baltic', in Müller-Wille (ed.), 411-47.

Noonan, T.S., 1989b, *The Millennium of Russia's first Perestrojka: The Origins of a Kievan Glass Industry under Prince Vladimir*, Kennan Institute for Advanced Russian Studies, Washington DC.

Nordenskiöld, A.E., 1889, *Facsimile-Atlas till Kartografiens Äldsta Historia*, Stockholm.

Nosov, E.N., 1987, 'New data on the Ryurik Gorodishche near Novgorod', *Fennoscandia Archaeologica*, 4, 73-85.

O'Connor, T., 1982, *Animal Bones from Flaxengate, Lincoln, c. 870-1500*, Archaeol. of Lincoln XVIII:1.

Ohlsson, T., 1976, 'The Löddeköpinge Investigations I. The settlement at Vikhögsvägen, *Meddelanden från Lunds Universitets Historiska Museum*, 1975-76, 58-161.

Olaus Magnus, 1555, *Historia de Gentibus Septentrionalibus*, Rome (Sw. translation 1909-1925: *Historia om de nordiska folken*, Stockholm).

Olsen, O. and Crumlin-Pedersen, O., 1978, *Five Viking Ships from Roskilde Fjord*, Copenhagen.

Ó Ríordáin, A.B., 1971, 'Excavations at High Street and Winetavern Street, Dublin', *Med.Archaeol.*, 15, 73-85.

Ó Ríordáin, A.B., 1976, 'The High Street excavations', in B. Almqvist and D. Greene (eds), *Proceedings of the Seventh Viking Congress*, Dublin, 135-40.

Ó Ríordáin, A.B., 1981, 'Aspects of Viking Dublin, in Bekker-Nielsen *et al.* (eds), 43-5.

Östergren, M., 1989, *Mellan stengrund och stenhus*, Theses and Papers in Archaeology, 2, Stockholm.

Ottaway, P., 1984, '*Colonia Eburacensis*: a review of recent work', in Addyman and Black (eds), 28-33.

Palliser, D.M., 1984, 'York's west bank: medieval suburb or urban nucleus?, in Addyman and Black (eds), 101-8.

Perin, P. and Feffer, L.-C., 1985, *La Neustrie*, Paris.

Perring, D., 1981, *Early Medieval Occupation at Flaxengate, Lincoln*, Archaeol. of Lincoln IX:1.

Phillips, D., 1985, *Excavations at York Minster II*, London,

Pirenne, H., 1939, *Mahomet and Charlemagne*, London.

Plummer, C. (ed.), 1896, *Venerabilis Baedae. Historiam Ecclesiasticam Gentis Anglorum*, Oxford.

Qualmann, K., 1986, 'Winchester – Nunnaminster', *Current Archaeology*, 103, 204-7.

Radley, J., 1971, 'Economic aspects of Anglo-Danish York., *Med. Archaeol.*, 15, 37-57.

Rahtz, P.A., 1977, 'The archaeology of west Mercian towns', in A. Dornier (ed.), *Mercian Studies*, Leicester, 107-27.

Rahtz, P.A., 1979, *The Saxon and Medieval Palaces at Cheddar*, BAR 65, Oxford.

Raudonikas, W.J., 1930, *Die Normannen der Wikingerzeit und das Ladogagebiet*, KVHAA Handlingar 40:3, Stockholm.

Reece, R., 1980, 'Town and country: the end of Roman Britain', *World Archaeol.*, 12:1, 77-92.

Resi, H.G., 1979, *Die Specksteinfunde aus Haithabu*. Berichte über die Ausgrabungen in Haithabu, 14, Neumünster.

Resi, H.G., 1987, 'Reflections on Viking Age local trade in stone products', in Knirk (ed.), 95-102.

Resi, H.G., forthcoming, *Die Wetz- und Schleiffsteine aus Haithabu*. Berichte über die Ausgrabungen in Haithabu, Neumünster.

Reynolds, S., 1977, *An Introduction to the History of English Medieval Towns*, Oxford.

Reynolds, S., 1987, 'Towns in Domesday Book', in J.C. Holt (ed.), *Domesday Studies*, Royal Historical Society, London, 295-309.

Richardson, K.M., 1959, 'Excavations in Hungate, York', *Archaeol. Jnl.*, 116, 51-114.

Rimbert 1986, *Vita Ansgarii* (Sw. translation: *Boken om Ansgar*, by Eva Odelman, Stockholm).

Roesdahl, E., 1987, *Vikingernes Verden*, Copenhagen.

Roesdahl, E. *et al.* (eds), 1981, *The Vikings in England*, London.

Rogerson, A. and Dallas, C., 1984, 'Excavations in Thetford 1948-59 and 1973-80', *E. Anglian Archaeol.*, 22.

Rosenberg, B., 1984, *Åhus*, Rapport Medeltidsstaden, 52, Stockholm.

Royal Frankish Annals, in *Carolingian Chronicles*, translated by B.W. Scholz, Michigan 1972.

Rumble, A.R., 1980, 'HAMTUN *alias* HAMWIC (Saxon Southampton): the place-name traditions and their significance', in Holdsworth 1980, 7-20.

Rybakov, B.A., 1982, Die Kultur des mittelalterlichen Nowgorod', in Herrmann (ed.), 239-62.

Rydh, H., 1936, *Förhistoriska undersökningar på Adelsö*, KVHAA Monografier, Stockholm.

Sandred, K.I. and Lindström, B., 1990, *The Place-names of Norwich*, English

Place-Names Society, 61.

Sawyer, P., 1971, *The Age of the Vikings* (2nd ed.), London.

Sawyer, P., 1982, *Kings and Vikings*, London.

Sawyer, P., 1988, *Da Danmark blev Danmark*. Gyldendals og Politikens Danmarkshistorie 3, ed. by Olaf Olsen, Copenhagen.

Schia, E., 1987, 'Reconstructing townyards on the periphery of the European urban culture', *Norwegian Archaeological Review*, 20:2, 81-96.

Schietzel, K., (gen. ed.), 1969-, Berichte über die Ausgrabungen in Haithabu.

Schietzel, K., 1981, *Stand der siedlungsarchäologischen Forschung in Haithubu – Ergebnisse und Probleme*, Berichte über die Ausgrabungen in Haithabu, 16, Neumünster.

Schietzel, K., 1985, Haithabu: a study on the development of early urban settlements in northern Europe', in Clarke and Simms (eds), 147-81.

Schmidt, H., 1977, 'Bebyggelsen', in *Fyrkat, En jysk vikingeborg, I. Borgen och Bebyggelsen*, by Olaf Olsen and Holger Schmidt. Nordiske Fortidsminder Serie B 3, Copenhagen.

Schofield, J. and Leech, R. (eds), 1987, *Urban Archaeology in Britain*, CBA Res. Rep., 61.

Schohknecht, U., 1977, *Menzlin. Ein frühgeschichtlicher Handelsplatz an der Peene*, Berlin.

Schohknecht, U., 1978, 'Handelsbeziehungen der frühmittelalterlichen Siedlung Menzlin bei Anklam', *Zeitschrift für Archäologie*, Berlin, 225-34.

Schück, A., 1926, *Studier rörande det svenska stadsväsendets uppkomst och äldsta utveckling*, Uppsala.

Schulz, E.-L., 1988, 'Varikkoniemi, Muinanen kauppapaikka ja käsityökeskus', *Häämenlinna-Wanaja, Kotiseutujulkaisu*, XXXVIII, 2-4.

Schulz, E.-L. and H.-P., 1989, 'Häämenlinna Varikkoniemi-Myöhäisrautakautinen ja varhaiskeskiaikainen kauppapaikka', in *Häämenlinna – Meidän kaupunkimme*, ed. by A. Pakkannen and I. Lehmusvaara, Häämenlinna, 9-21.

Sedov, V.V., 1982, 'Ostslawen, Balten und Esten', in Herrmann *et al.*, 225-38.

Selling, D., 1955, *Wikingerzeitliche und Frühmittelalterliche Keramik in Schweden*, Stockholm.

Shoesmith, R., 1980, *Excavations at Castle Green. Hereford City Excavations 1*, CBA Res. Rep., 36.

Shoesmith, R., 1982, *Excavations On and Close to the Defences. Hereford City Excavations 2*, CBA Res. Rep., 46.

Smith, A.H., 1937, *The Place-names of the East Riding of Yorkshire and York*, English Place-names Society, 14.

Smyth, A.P., 1977, *Scandinavian Kings in the British Isles 850-880*, Oxford.

Smyth, A.P., 1975-1979, *Scandinavian York and Dublin*, 2 vols, Dublin.

St Wilfrid, *The Life of Bishop Wilfrid by Eddius Stephanus*, edited and translated by B. Colgrave, Cambridge, 1927.

Stalsberg, A., 1989, 'The Scandinavian Viking Age finds in Rus' ', in Müller-Wille (ed.), 448-71.

Stenberger, M., 1947-1958, *Die Schatzfunde Gotlands der Wikingerzeit*, I-II, KVHAA Monografier, Stockholm.

Stenton, F.M., 1971, *Anglo-Saxon England* (3rd ed.), Oxford.

Steuer, H., 1984, 'Zur ethnischen Gliederung der Bevölkerung von Haithabu anhand der Gräberfelder', *Offa*, 41, Kiel, 189-212.

Stolpe, Hj. and Arne, T.J., 1912, *Graffältet vid Vendel*, KVHAA Monografier, Stockholm.

Strömberg, M., 1978, 'En kustby i Ystad – före stadens tillkomst', *Ystads fornminnesförenings årsskrift* XXIII, Ystad.

Struwe, K., 1989, 'Starigard–Oldenburg. Der historische Rahmen', in Müller-Wille (ed.), 20-47.

Sutherland, C.H.B., 1948, *Anglo-Saxon Gold Coinage in the Light of the Crondall Hoard*, Oxford.

Tatton-Brown, T., 1986, 'The topography of Anglo-Saxon London', *Antiquity*, 60, 21-8.

Tatton-Brown, T., 1988, 'The Anglo-Saxon towns of Kent', in Hooke (ed.), 213-32.

Tatton-Brown, T. and Macpherson-Grant, N., 1985, 'Anglo-Saxon Canterbury topography and pottery', *Current Archaeology*, 98, 89-93.

Tesch, S., 1983, *Ystad*, I-II, Rapport Medeltidsstaden, 44-5, Stockholm.

Tesch, S., 1989a, 'Sigtunaforskning – arkeologiskt läge och möjligheter', in Tesch (ed.), 115-35.

Tesch, S. (ed.), 1989b, *Avstamp – för en ny Sigtunaforskning*, Sigtuna.

Thordeman, B., 1920, *Alsnö hus*, Stockholm.

Thorvildsen, E., 1972, 'Dankirke', *Nationalmuseets Arbejdsmark*, Copenhagen, 47-60.

Thorvildsen, K., 1957, *Ladbyskibet*, Nordiske Fortidsminder 6:1, Copenhagen.

Thrane, H., 1987, 'Das Gudme-Problem und die Gudme-Untersuchung', *Frühmittelalterliche Studien*, 21, 1-48.

Toločko, P.P., 1989, 'Kiev und seine überregionalen wirtschaftlichen Verbindungen im 9.-11. Jahrhundert', in Müller-Wille (ed.), 344-57.

Tweddle, D., 1986, *Finds from Parliament Street and Other Sites in the City Centre*, Archaeol. of York 17/4.

Udolph, J., 1987, ' "Handel" und "Verkehr" in slavischen Ortsnamen', in Düwel *et al.*, 570-615.

Ulbricht, I., 1978, *Die Geweihverarbeitung in Haithabu*, Die Ausgrabungen in Haithabu, 7, Neumünster.

van der Walle, A., 1961, 'Excavations in ancient Antwerp', *Med. Archaeol.*, 5, 123-36.

van Es, W.A. and Verwers, W.J.H., 1980, *Excavations at Dorestad 1: The Harbour: Hoogstraat 1*, Nederlandse Oudheden 9.

van Es, W.A. and Verwers, W.J.H., 1985, Karolingisch draaischijfaardwerk uit Deventer, *Van Beek en Land en Mensenhand: Feestbundel voor R. van Beek*, Utrecht, 22-40.

Verhulst, A., 1985, 'Villes et view urbaine', in P. Perin and L.-C. Feffer (eds), *La Neustrie*, Paris, 333-45.

Verhulst, A., 1989, 'The origins of towns in the Low Countries and the Pirenne thesis', *Past and Present*, 122, 3-35.

Verwers, W.J.H., 1988, 'Dorestad: a Carolingian town?', in Hodges and Hobley (eds), 52-6.

Vince, A., 1984, 'The Aldwych: mid-Saxon London discovered?', *Current Archaeology*, 93, 310-13.

Vince, A., 1988, 'The economic basis of Anglo-Saxon London', in Hodges and Hobley (eds), 83-92.

Vince, A., 1989, 'The urban economy in Mercia in the ninth and tenth centuries', *Arkeologiske Skrifter fra Historisk Museum Bergen*, 5, 136-59.

Vince, A., 1990, *Anglo-Saxon London*, London.

Vogel, V., (ed.), 1983- , *Ausgrabungen in Schleswig*, Berichte und Studien 1- , Neumünster.

Wacher, J., 1979, 'Silver Street', in Colyer and Jones, 81-4.

Wade, K., 1978, 'Sampling at Ipswich: the origins and growth of the Anglo-Saxon town', in J.F. Cherry *et al.* (eds), *Sampling in Contemporary British Archaeology*, BAR 50, Oxford, 279-84.

Wade, K., 1988, 'Ipswich', in Hodges and Hobley (eds), 93-100.

Wallace, P., 1985, 'The archeology of Viking Dublin', in Clarke and Simms (eds), 103-46.

Wallace, P., 1987a, 'The economy and commerce of Viking age Dublin', in Düwel *et al.* (eds), 200-45.

Wallace, P., 1987b, 'The layout of Viking Age Dublin: indications of its regulation and problems of continuity', in Knirk (ed.), 271-85.

Wallace, P. (ed.), 1988, *Miscellanea* 1, Medieval Dublin Excavations 1962-81, Ser. B 2, 1-6.

Warnke, D., 1978, 'Funde und Grabsitten des Gräberfeldes in den "Schwarzen Bergen" bei Ralswiek im Rahmen der kulturellen Beziehungen im Ostseegebiet', *Zeitschrift für Archäologie*, 275-82.

Warnke, D., 1985, 'Skandinavische Einflüsse in nordwestslawishen Grabefunden', in Lindquist (ed.), 229-36.

Waterman, D.M., 1959, 'Late Saxon, Viking and early medieval finds from York., *Archaeologia*, 97, 59-105.

Webster, L.E. and Cherry, J., 1972, 'Medieval Britain in 1971', *Med. Archaeol*, 16, 147-212.

Wenham, L.P. *et al.*, 1987, *St Mary Bishophill Junior and St Mary Castlegate*. Archaeol. of York 8/2.

Westholm, G., 1985, 'The settlement at Vi, at the foot of the cliff', in Lindquist (ed.), 293-304.

Westholm, G., 1989, 'Visby Bönders hamn och handelsplats-Visbysamhällets uppkomst och utbredning under förhistorisk tid och äldre medeltid', in Engeström *et al.*, 49-114.

Wihlborg, A., 1984, *Medeltidsstaden Helsingborg och dess förhistoria*, Riksantikvarieämbetet UV-Syd's skriftserie, Lund, 5.

William of Malmesbury, *Willelmi Malmesbiriensis Monachi De Gestis Regum Anglorum* edited by W. Stubbs, London 1887-89.

Williams, J.H., 1979, *St Peter's Street, Northampton*, Northampton.

Williams, J.H., 1984a, 'A review of some aspects of late Saxon urban origins and development', in Faull (ed.), 25-34.

Williams, J.H., 1984b, 'From "palace" to "town": Northampton and urban origins', *Anglo-Saxon England*, 13, 113-36.

Williams J.H. *et al.*, 1985, *Middle Saxon Palaces at Northampton*, Northampton.

Wilson, D.M., 1967, 'The Vikings' relationship with Christianity in northern England', *Journal of the British Archeological Association*, 3rd ser. 30, 37-46.

Wilson, D.M. (ed.), 1976, *The Archaeology of Anglo Saxon England*, London.

Wilson, D.M., 1986, 'England and the Continent in the eighth century – an archaeological viewpoint', *Settimane di studie del centro italiano di studi sull' alto medioevo*, 32, 219-47.

Wiséhn, E., 1989, *Myntfynd från Uppland*, Sveriges Mynthistoria, Landskapsinventeringen, 4, Stockholm.

Yanin, V.L., 1990, 'The archaeology of Novgorod', *Scientific American*, February 1990, 72-9.

Yorke, B., 1982, 'The foundation of the Old Minster and the status of Winchester in the seventh and eighth centuries', *Proc. Hants Field Club*, 38, 75-83.

Youngs, S.M. *et al.*, 1988, 'Medieval Britain and Ireland in 1985', *Med. Archaeol.*, 30, 114-98.

Youngs, S.M. *et al.*, 1986, 'Medieval Britain and Ireland in 1987', *Med. Archaeol.*, 32, 225-314.

Yule, B., 1990, 'The "dark earth" and late Roman London', *Antiquity* 64, 620-28.

Index